Jagdgeschwader 2 Richthofen

Jagdgeschwader 2 Richthofen

A Photo Chronicle

Holger Nauroth

Schiffer Military History
Atglen, PA

Translated from the German by David Johnston
Book Design by Ian Robertson.

Library of Congress Catalog Number: 2004101956

Printed in China.
ISBN: 0-7643-2094-7

This book was originally printed under the title,
Jagdgeschwader 2 Richthofen Eine Bildchronik by Motorbuch Verlag

Published by Schiffer Publishing Ltd.
4880 Lower Valley Road
Atglen, PA 19310
Phone: (610) 593-1777
FAX: (610) 593-2002
E-mail: info@schifferbooks.com.
Visit our web site at: www.schifferbooks.com
Please write for a free catalog.
This book may be purchased from the publisher.
Please include $3.95 postage.
Try your bookstore first.

In Europe, Schiffer books are distributed by:
Bushwood Books
6 Marksbury Avenue
Kew Gardens
Surrey TW9 4JF
England
Phone: 44 (0) 20 8392-8585
FAX: 44 (0) 20 8392-9876
E-mail: info@bushwoodbooks.co.uk.
Free postage in the UK. Europe: air mail at cost.
Try your bookstore first.

Contents

1

Manfred Baron von Richthofen

1 May 1892
Manfred Baron von Richthofen was born on the Schweidnitz estate near Breslau, into a family of noble descent. His ancestors had almost all been farmers and soldiers. The Schweidnitz estate was situated near Kriblowitz on the road from Breslau to Schweidnitz. In the town of Kriblowitz lived *Generalfeldmarschall* Neidhardt von Blücher, Prince of Wahlstatt. Blücher had defeated the French at Wahlstatt.

1911
The young Richthofen joined the cadet corps in Wahlstatt. He subsequently joined the Kaiser Alexander III Uhlan Regiment in Silesia as an officer cadet. He was an outstanding cavalrymen, and in 1913 he was the only one to complete the field portion of the Kaiser Ride with no errors.

August 1914
When war broke out the cavalry regiment in which von Richthofen was serving was moved to the Eastern Front. *Leutnant* Baron von Richthofen was made a patrol leader. One day he and his patrol penetrated 110 km behind enemy lines and returned safely.

Soon afterwards, his regiment was transferred to France. But the days of cavalry patrols were numbered. The young, enthusiastic *Leutnant* had no desire to spend the war in the trenches or serving in some headquarters. This had nothing to do with arrogance, rather it had everything to do with his sense of duty, his courage, and most of all his inner feelings toward his country, something that is difficult to explain today.

Richthofen was supposed to be transferred to a rear-echelon post as a supply officer, but, bypassing the chain of command, he wrote to the commanding general. In his unconventional style, he informed "His dear Excellency", that he had not got into the war to "gather cheese and eggs". He requested a transfer to the air corps.

June 1915
Von Richthofen's transfer request was approved, and he was sent to Grossenhain for observer training. His first reconnaissance mission was over von Mackensen's army on the Eastern Front. His pilot was Count Holck, then a very famous horseman.

Richthofen appreciated the vital importance of aerial reconnaissance to army operations, but he wanted more than to be an observer. He wanted to become a pilot.

21 August 1915
Leutnant von Richthofen had returned to the Western Front as an observer in a large bomber, but there was not much to do in Ostende, where he was stationed. Soon afterwards his reconnaissance unit moved to the Champagne region of France. The machines designed by Anthony Hermann Gerard Fokker (1890-1939), a Dutchman living in Germany, were the best fighter aircraft extant. The first Fokker-designed aircraft entered service in 1914, and these were followed by the D I biplane and the E-series monoplanes (*Eindecker*). The later Fokker Triplane, which entered service in 1917, was with great success by von Richthofen. He praised the Fokker aircraft:

"With the thing it makes no difference whether one is flying inverted, dives vertically or performs any other sort of trick. One flies just like a bird and, unlike the Albatros, which tends to flutter, the whole thing is just a flying engine."

The best German fighter was the Fokker D VII powered by a 185-h.p. BMW engine. This aircraft was flown by all the top German aces in 1917-18 and assured German air superiority until the end of the war.

The first single-seat fighters were introduced by the French at the turn of the year 1914-15. The Nieuport Bébe and Morane Parasol were both equipped with fixed forward-firing machine-guns. The Nieuport's machine-gun was mounted to fire over the propeller arc, while the Morane's fired through it. The Morane's propeller was fitted with metal deflector's to prevent machine-gun bullets from damaging the blades. One such aircraft fell into German hands in 1915. Tests revealed that French copper-jacketed bullets could not penetrate the deflectors, however these could not stand up to German bullets, which were chrome-nickel jacketed. Fokker, then 25 years old, solved the problem by synchronizing the machine-guns with the engine. An engineer by the name of Franz Schneider had patented a synchronizer (Reich Patent No. 276 396) on 15 July

1915, however he had been unable to interest the army in his invention. Fokker now took over the patent, but changed the control mechanism.

With the appearance of the single-seat fighter, the war from the air had become a war in the air. Gone were the days when airmen fired at each others with pistols as they passed. The Fokker single-seaters gave the German *Fliegertruppe* an aircraft that was superior to anything the Allies had.

1 September 1915

Von Richthofen and his pilot Zeumer were aloft in their two-seater. He was not especially happy on this flight, for on a previous mission his bombs had missed the target by a wide margin. Then he spotted a British Farman, and Zeumer flew toward the enemy aircraft. The two machines began circling, and von Richthofen and the enemy observer opened fire. Richthofen had fired just four rounds, when the enemy aircraft got behind them and began firing its machine-gun. Skillful flying by Zeumer enabled him to outmaneuver the enemy. Von Richthofen had fought his first air battle, but without the desired success.

1 October 1915

Leutnant Zeumer, von Richthofen's pilot, had transferred to the fighters and was now flying a Fokker *Eindecker*, much to the displeasure of the young baron. On that day von Richthofen traveled to a new sector. Sitting at a table in the dining car was a *Leutnant*. Although there was nothing to outwardly distinguish the man, he had already been named in the army communiqué and had four victories to his credit. His name was *Leutnant* Oswald Boelcke. When asked how he had done it (meaning the four victories), he replied spontaneously, "By God, its quite simple. I merely fly in close and aim well, then he goes down!" It was a rather cocky answer, but it was true. Many World War Two aces gave similar responses when asked the secret to their success. Soon von Richthofen had frequent opportunities to spend time with Boelcke and came to know and respect him. Manfred von Richthofen was eager to fly one of Fokker's single-seat fighter with a fixed machine-gun. At that time *Leutnant* Oswald Boelcke was flying with *Leutnant* Max Immelmann in a combat aviation unit of the Bavarian 6th Army. These units were the predecessors of the later *Jagdstaffeln* (*Jastas*). In addition to flying missions, Boelcke spent a great deal of time thinking about air combat. He devised a set of rules for air fighting and created the first tactical unit, the *Jagdstaffel*. The logical result was the formation of fighter wings (*Jagdgeschwader*). With them, the young German aviation corps concentrated its forces against the numerically-superior enemy. Boelcke was tireless. He constantly devised and tested new tactics. Part of his new system involved the use of intelligence. Observation posts were set up in the front lines. These provided a steady flow of information on the type and number of enemy aircraft and their movements. The other leading figure of the nascent German fighter arm was *Leutnant* Max Immelmann, the "Eagle of Lille". Immelmann was an outstanding pilot and marksman. It was he who introduced the "Immelmann Turn", a maneuver in which the pilot climbed and then turned left or right about the vertical axis, reversing direction. This extraordinary flier, fighter pilot and tactician fell during an air engagement on 18 June 1916. The exact circumstances of his death have never been fully explained.

Hauptmann Oswald Boelcke supported von Richthofen's efforts to become a pilot. Soon he began flight training and, after 25 hours, he was ready to solo. The flight turned into a fiasco. A botched landing resulted in the aircraft standing on its nose. The machine was a write-off and von Richthofen had failed.

But he did not give up. Fourteen days later von Richthofen was ready for a second attempt. The takeoff, practice maneuvers and even the landing were successful, but still he failed to pass. It looked as if he would have to abandon his dream of becoming a fighter pilot. Then von Richthofen was transferred back to the Eastern Front, where he flew as an observer in one of the fat two-seaters of *Kampfgeschwader 11*. But he never gave up on his dream, and he secured a transfer to Döberitz for flight training. Now, on his third try, von Richthofen succeeded, and his deepest wish was fulfilled. He got to fly a single-seater, the Fokker E III. Then von Richthofen was transferred back to the Eastern Front, but not as a fighter pilot. Even though he was flying a bomber, he was still flying. In Russia von Richthofen carried out bombing missions against Russian troop concentrations, railway stations and airfields.

August 1916

Oswald Boelcke visited von Richthofen's bomber wing in Kovel. He was forming a new *Jagdstaffel* in France. Von Richthofen would dearly have loved to join him, but he dared not ask Boelcke. *Hauptmann* Oswald Boelcke was to return to France the next day. Early in the morning he knocked on von Richthofen's door and asked him directly if he would like to become his student. Von Richthofen could have hugged Boelcke—of course he wanted to go. And so von Richthofen headed back to the Western Front, this time for good.

17 September 1916

Manfred von Richthofen eagerly learned from Oswald Boelcke as the latter brought down more of the enemy.

It was expected that the English would be active, so on this morning *Hauptmann* Boelcke decided to commit the entire *Staffel* against the enemy for the first time. The pilots were all beginners and none had scored even one victory. On reaching the front the Germans spotted a group of enemy aircraft heading in the direction of Cambrai. The five German fighters dove on the seven enemy aircraft, all large two-seaters.

Boelcke was first to close with the enemy, with von Richthofen close behind. He opened fire and the enemy aircraft fired back. After a while the enemy aircraft's propeller stopped and it was forced to land. It came down near a German airfield. Manfred von Richthofen had achieved his first victory in the air. He had a marker placed on the graves of his fallen foes.

30 September 1916
Richthofen downed his third enemy aircraft.

Hauptmann Boelcke had developed the *Jagdstaffel* as a tactical unit. As commander of the unit, he was always in danger, and Boelcke always watched out for the others in the *Staffel*. He had the ability to act with lightning speed when the situation required and was capable of intervening immediately when a fellow pilot was in distress. Manfred von Richthofen would later display the same characteristics. Every member of the *Staffel* knew that Boelcke would never leave them in the lurch.

8 October 1916
Oswald Boelcke scored his 30th victory. Just two days later he collided in midair with his friend Erwin Böehme. He and von Richthofen were the first two pilots Boelcke had brought back from Russia to join his new unit. Boelcke tried to land, but as he glided beneath von Richthofen's machine, a wing was seen to break off and he spun to the ground. Böhme, who had innocently caused the collision, followed his friend down. His aircraft sustained only minor damage. Böhme later wrote to his wife that Boelcke could have survived the crash, which was not excessively violent, if he had been strapped in.

On 11 November an English airman dropped a wreath with a ribbon and letter of condolence over the Boelcke *Staffel*'s airfield. It read: "In memory of *Hauptmann* Boelcke, our brave and chivalrous foe—from the Royal English Flying Corps." It was a chivalrous gesture in a war that was becoming a battle of machines and materiel.

3 November 1916
Leutnant von Richthofen shot down his seventh enemy aircraft.

4 January 1917
After scoring his 16th victory, von Richthofen was awarded the Pour le Mérite and named commander of *Jagdstaffel 11*.

By this time von Richthofen's name was appearing in the army communiqués almost daily. He received early promotion to *Oberleutnant* and soon after to *Rittmeister* (cavalry captain).

2 and 5 April 1917
On both days *Rittmeister* von Richthofen shot down two enemy aircraft. His second victim on 2 April demonstrated an unquenchable fighting spirit. As von Richthofen flew low over the downed enemy machine, the pilot removed the machine-gun from its mount and opened fire, riddling his Albatros.

13 April 1917
Rittmeister von Richthofen shot down three more enemy aircraft.

29 April 1917
von Richthofen downed four enemy machines, raising his victory total to 52.

Kaiser Wilhelm II congratulated von Richthofen on his 25th birthday and invited him to the grand headquarters, where he sat at the Kaiser's table between *Generalfeldmarschall* von Hindenburg and *Generalquartermeister* von Ludendorff.

By now *Rittmeister* Manfred Baron von Richthofen had become famous to friend and foe alike. He had had his aircraft, an Albatros D III, painted red, and the "Red Air Fighter" was born. To the English, von Richthofen was the "Red Baron", to the French "*Le diable rouge*". No matter what he was called, von Richthofen was feared and respected by his enemies.

The Staffel received a visitor from Germany. He had never seen an air combat. *Leutnant* Schäfer said to von Richthofen, "We can have some fun with him." The two men climbed into their flying machines, which is what they called their aircraft at that time, and took off. The other pilots took off and followed after them. The visitor was placed behind a binocular telescope used by the artillery. He did not have long to wait. No sooner did the German aircraft reached 2000 meters when five English aircraft appeared. Things happened quickly now.

The German fighters attacked. In a single pass two of the English aircraft went down in flames, while the other three came down on the German side of the lines. On this day six fighters of the *11. Staffel* shot down thirteen enemy aircraft. Previously only the *Jagdstaffel Boelcke* had recorded such a success. *Leutnant* Wolff brought down four of the enemy, while Richthofen accounted for three. One of the English pilots asked about the red machine, for there was a rumor going round in his squadron that it was flown by a young woman, a sort of Joan of Arc. He was quite surprised when Richthofen assured him that the "maiden" was standing before him.

April 1917
The English formed an anti-Richthofen squadron, whereupon Richthofen directed that all the aircraft in his *Staffel* should be painted red.

14 May 1917
Oberleutnant Lothar Baron von Richthofen, Manfred's younger brother, was also a member of the *Staffel*. After his fortieth victory he was also awarded the Pour le Mérite.

25 June 1917
On this day Manfred von Richthofen shot down his 56th enemy aircraft.

26 June 1917
The commanding general of the air forces, *Generalleutnant* von Hoeppner, issued the following order for the formation of the first *Jagdgeschwader*:

"Grand Headquarters, 26 June 1917. By decree of the Chief of Staff of the Field Army on 23 June 1917, *Jagdgeschwader 1* is to be formed from *Jagdstaffeln 4, 6, 10* and *11*. The *Geschwader* is a homogenous unit. It is to be deployed in vital sectors to achieve and maintain air superiority.

Chief of the General Staff
signed Thomsen."

Placed in command of this first *Jagdgeschwader*, the very first German fighter wing, was the leader of *Jagdstaffel 11*, *Rittmeister* Manfred Baron von Richthofen. The bulk of the new formation was quartered in Marckebeek Castle in Flanders. *Jasta 4* and *Jasta 11*, von Richthofen's old unit, were based nearby at Bisseghem, while *Jasta 10* was stationed at Marcke. The *Geschwader* was equipped with Albatros D V and Pfalz D III fighter aircraft. Both types were braced biplanes of mixed construction, powered by a Mercedes engine producing 160 h.p. The aircraft had a maximum speed of 165 km/h, range of 350 km and a service ceiling of 5000 meters. Both were armed with two Type 08/15 machine-guns.

The *Geschwader*'s *Staffel* commanders were veteran fighter pilots. *Jasta 4* was led by *Oberstleutnant* Dostler, who was killed soon after the formation of the *Geschwader*. *Jasta 10* was commanded by Baron von Altenburg, who had distinguished himself in the skies over Verdun, earning the Pour le Mérite. Richthofen's old *Staffel* was led by *Leutnant* Kurt Wolff, another wearer of the "Blue Max". Wolff was killed in action on 15 September 1917. The staff consisted of *Oberleutnant* Bodenschatz, Richthofen's adjutant, and the Technical Officer, *Leutnant* Krefft. The *Geschwader*, which had 45 pilots and an equal number of aircraft, was completed by a medical officer, a paymaster and 62 non-commissioned officers and enlisted men. Richthofen immediately demanded changes in organization. He was determined to change the practice of mission orders being issued by constantly changing commands. He wanted to decide for himself how to deploy his fighters, based the situation in the air in his sector. Telephone lines were laid to reporting posts in the front lines. These kept him informed of enemy activity. A newly-laid telephone line allowed von Richthofen to issue mission orders directly to all four *Staffeln*.

The situation at that time was threatening. German forces were under constant attack from enemy fighters, bombers and close-support aircraft.

4 July 1917

After the completion of the establishment process and the moves to new airfields, *Jagdgeschwader 1* achieved operational status on this date.

5 July 1917

Oberleutnant Dostler, *Staffelführer* of *Jasta 6*, shot down an enemy balloon, the first victory by the Imperial Air Force's first large formation.

6 July 1917

Engagement with British bombers. Richthofen attacked one of the Vickers two-seat aircraft. The safeties were still on his machine-guns as he moved in close to his prey, the way Boelcke had taught him. The observer in the British bomber opened fire first and the first burst was on target. Manfred von Richthofen was hit in the head, and for a few seconds his entire body was paralyzed. The Albatros aircraft went out of control and entered a spin. Though blinded, von Richthofen recovered from the spin. After reducing power and switching off the ignition, he found himself dangerously low over the shell-torn battlefield. Then his vision returned. He was able to see, but as if through a fog. He began to feel faint, but with the last of his strength he was able to find a level spot to land his aircraft. Von Richthofen crawled from the machine before it began to burn. German infantry arrived at the crash seen and cared for him as best they could until the ambulance arrived to take him to hospital. His Majesty the Kaiser wanted von Richthofen to stop flying and take a position on *General* von Hoeppner's staff, where he could pass on his knowledge and experience to younger pilots. Like Boelcke before him, however, von Richthofen refused, and returned to his *Geschwader* at the front.

Summer 1917

At the front fighting raged in Flanders. *Jagdgeschwader 1* received the first Fokker Dr. I triplane. Until then only the English had flown triplanes. A *Feldwebel* from another unit attacked the triplane and shot it down, killing the pilot. The unfortunate pilot was ordered before a court martial. When von Richthofen learned of this, he intervened with the investigating officers and had the charge dropped. He had argued that the *Feldwebel* was not at fault, rather it was his superiors who were to blame for not informing the other units about JG 1's new triplanes. Finally von Richthofen requested that the *Feldwebel* be transferred to his unit and achieved his aim: the pilot was rehabilitated.

18 March 1918

The German armies had launched a major offensive. The operation has certain parallels to the Ardennes Offensive during the Second World War. The German air force's role was to protect the buildup against enemy reconnaissance aircraft and bombers. As a result, JG 1's first major air battle developed over Le Cateau. It was supported by two fighter groups with a total of 60 aircraft. The thirty aircraft of JG 1 attacked a formation of Sopwith Camels. Richthofen shot down one machine and its Canadian pilot was taken prisoner. A group of Bristol Fighters joined the battle and he shot down one of the two-seat fighters with *Leutnant* Gassmann. Richthofen and his men attacked two more formations of enemy aircraft. He and *Leutnant* Löwenhardt pursued another machine which was brought down by Löwenhardt. Richthofen downed his fourth victim of the day over Mortain, the enemy aircraft making a forced landing.

Spring 1918

Following his 75th victory *Rittmeister* Manfred Baron von Richthofen was awarded the Order of the Red Eagle, Third Class. *General* Ludendorff expressed the opinion to the general staff that von Richthofen deserved the Golden Oak Leaves to the Pour le Mérite. When a member of the general staff replied that the Oak Leaves were only awarded for battles won, Ludendorff declared: "Richthofen has won more than one battle!" Nevertheless, he was not awarded the Oak Leaves.

21 March 1918
Jasta 37, commanded by *Leutnant* Ernst Udet, was stationed beside the road to Le Cateau. It was raining and the tents were just going up. Someone clapped Udet on the shoulder. He turned around and found himself facing von Richthofen. "Good day Udet, lovely weather today!" And then von Richthofen asked, "How many victories do you have?" Udet replied, "Nineteen confirmed, one claimed." "Hmm, twenty then, it's time you joined us. Are you interested?" Of course Udet was interested. There were many good *Jagdstaffeln* in the army, and *Jasta 37* was far from being the worst. But there was only one *Jagdgeschwader Richthofen*, as JG 1 was called unofficially. And so Udet replied, "Yes, *Herr Rittmeister*!" The two men shook hands and that was it. Soon afterwards *Leutnant* Ernst Udet took over *Jasta 4* in Richthofen's *Geschwader*. On 9 April 1918 he was awarded the Pour le Mérite. When the war ended, Ernst Udet had 62 victories, making him the most successful German fighter pilot of the First World War after von Richthofen.

26 March 1918
At 1645 hours von Richthofen shot down a Sopwith south of Contalmaison for his 69th victory. At 1700 he downed an R.E. 2 two kilometers north of Albert, also on the German side of the lines.

27 March 1918
Albrecht Baron von Richthofen received a telegram from the commanding general of the German air forces, *General* von Hoeppner:

"Today your son Manfred shot down his 71st, 72nd and 73rd enemy aircraft. The *Rittmeister*'s 71st victory rounded off the number of air victories by your two sons at 100. With grateful admiration, the air forces and I congratulate the parents of the two brothers, so proud in their accomplishments and so modest in nature. Today the fondest wishes for your sons are glowing in many thousands of German hearts."

30 March 1918
Somewhat later, Manfred von Richthofen also received congratulations from the General of Air Forces:

"We congratulate you on your latest success, dear Richthofen, the most successful bearer of the fighter pilot's victorious spirit.
Your commanding general,
von Hoeppner."

The much honored von Richthofen had by now put his own ideas down on paper in his book, "The Red Air Fighter":

"I am writing it without knowing whether anyone apart from my closest family will ever get to see what I have written. I am contemplating writing a sequel to "The Red Air Fighter", and for a very specific reason. The war that is being fought on all fronts has become quite devilishly serious. There is nothing left of the light-hearted, carefree war, as our activities were described in the beginning. Now we are forced to fight desperately everywhere to prevent the enemy from breaking into our country. I have the dark impression that the people now see a Richthofen much different than the one in "Red Air Fighter"—as I feel myself. When I read the book, I grin to myself conceitedly. I certainly don't feel conceited anymore, not because I imagine what it will be like if death one day finds me, surely not, even though I am reminded often enough that it could happen. Those in high places have had me told that I should give up flying, for one day it will be the end of me. But I would feel wretched if, encumbered with fame and decorations, I was to now live out my life as a pensioner of my worth to preserve my precious life for the nation, while every poor fellow in the trenches, who is doing his duty just like me, sticks it out. I feel wretched after every air battle. This is probably due to the aftereffects of my head wound. As soon as my feet are back on the ground at the airfield, I head straight for my four walls and have no desire to see anyone or hear anything.

I believe that's how it really is. It is not as the people at home imagine it, cheering and shouting, it is all much more serious, more grim..."

20 April 1918
That evening, at 1900 hours, von Richthofen scored his 79th and 80th victories, shooting down two enemy aircraft in two minutes. On the way home he flew low over German columns, and the German troops waved enthusiastically. Everyone at the front recognized the red triplane.

21 April 1918
It was Sunday morning, 1130 hours. Manfred von Richthofen flew west over the German lines at about 1500 meters. With him were four aircraft of *Jagdstaffel 11*, flown by his cousin Wolfram, who had only recently joined the *Staffel*, *Oberleutnant* Wolff, *Oberleutnant* Karjus and *Vizefeldwebel* Scholz. Just beyond the lines they saw seven Sopwith Camels. Seven more appeared at a higher altitude. The German fighters immediately attacked the formation. Richthofen fired at one enemy aircraft, which went down vertically. After a long dive the British aircraft pulled out and von Richthofen went after it. All the while a strong east wind was blowing the aircraft farther to the west. The other pilots lost contact with von Richthofen during the engagement and returned to the airfield. There they waited in vain for the return of *Rittmeister* Manfred Baron von Richthofen. When he failed to return they hoped that their commander had been captured but was still alive. It soon turned out, however, that this hope was false. Manfred von Richthofen's 81st victory had been his last, and he did not survive it for long. The circumstances of death remain unclear to this day, but it is certain that he was not shot down in air combat. At the time it was believed that von Richthofen had been shot down by machine-gun fire from the ground, a view that his successor, *Hauptmann* Wilhelm Reinhard, expressed in a letter to Richthofen's mother on 30 April 1918. Canadian fighter pilot Captain Roy Brown claimed to have shot down a red triplane, but it could not have been von Richthofen's.

He had most likely been shot down by ground fire. This theory was supported by gunners of Section F of the Anti-Aircraft Battery Royal Garrison Artillery, which was then attached to the Australian 11th Infantry Division. They had observed the air combat from their positions and fired at the low-flying triplane with their machine-guns. Von Richthofen also flew over an Australian field artillery battery, which also fired at the red triplane. Exactly who fired the fatal shot will probably never be known with certainty. It would exceed the scope of this work to examine all of the theories that have been put forward. Only several possibilities will be described here: *Leutnant* Hans Joachim Wolff, who was in Richthofen's flight, lost sight of the *Rittmeister* during the engagement. *Vizefeldwebel* Scholtz, another member of the flight, saw von Richthofen's dive to the earth, but no English aircraft in the area. *Leutnant* Wenzel and other members of JG 1 saw a red machine sitting on the ground. *Leutnant* Hippel saw Richthofen land. He wrote in his diary: "10 July, 1100 hours, 81st combat mission DVe 5630. *Rittmeister* von Richthofen smooth landing on the other side of the lines." The state of the triplane suggested that it had made a rather hard landing. The fact that he was flying so low over the front may have been due to engine trouble. This idea is supported by the fact that he was the only one to head east in the direction of his airfield before the engagement was over. He was then fired on from the rise northwest of Corbie and was fatally struck.

Two doctors of the Australian Flying Corps, Colonel G.W. Barber and Major L.C. Chapman, examined von Richthofen's body and came to the conclusion that the fatal bullet had not come from the machine-guns of Captain A.R. Brown but from a machine-gun on the ground. The path of the bullet suggested that von Richthofen had been hit at low altitude as he climbed and turned in the direction of the German lines.

22 April 1918
Rittmeister Baron von Richthofen was buried with full military honors in a small church graveyard not far from where he came down by members of an Australian artillery regiment.

23 April 1918
The news agency Reuters reported the von Richthofen's death.

24 April 1918
Army Communiqué

Rittmeister Baron von Richthofen has not returned after pursuing an enemy aircraft over the battlefield on the Somme. According to English reports he was killed.

British airmen dropped a wreath with an attached report over the German lines.

On 10 March 1918 Manfred Baron von Richthofen left instructions that *Oberleutnant* Reinhard, commander of *Jasta 11*, should assume command of the *Geschwader* in the event that he should fail to return, and this has taken place.

27 April 1918
Hauptmann Reinhard assumed command of JG 1.

2 May 1918
Manfred von Richthofen would have been 26 years old on this day. A memorial service was held in the Berlin Garrison Church.

20 May 1918
On this day the first *Jagdgeschwader* was given the name *Jagdgeschwader* Baron von Richthofen. The awarding of this name began a proud tradition which has continued through three generations to the present day.

3 July 1918
Hauptmann Reinhard was killed at Berlin-Adlershof while testing a prototype Dornier aircraft. The *Geschwader* lost its second commander in a few weeks.

His successor and last commander of the Richthofen *Geschwader* was *Oberleutnant* Hermann Göring.

5 November 1918
This day marked the last time that a member of the von Richthofen family was to shoot down an enemy aircraft. Wolfram Baron von Richthofen, cousin of Manfred and Lothar, scored his eighth victory. In the Second World War he would play a major role in the formation of the close-support units. Under his command the *VIII. Fliegerkorps* achieved great success. On 1 February 1942 von Richthofen was promoted to *Generaloberst* and on 16 February 1943 to *Generalfeldmarschall* and Commander-in-Chief of *Luftflotte 2*. Together, Manfred, Lothar and Wolfram von Richthofen shot down 128 enemy aircraft over the Western Front.

6 November 1918
Jagdgeschwader 1 Baron von Richthofen fought its last air battle, shooting down three SPADs at approximately 1130 hours.

11 November 1918
The *Geschwader* received orders to cease hostilities. By that time JG 1 had shot down 644 enemy aircraft while losing 64 pilots.

12 November 1918
Early that morning the Richthofen *Geschwader* flew back to Germany. One *Staffel* lost its way and landed in Mannheim instead of Darmstadt. To their surprise, the pilots were disarmed by the soldiers there. Only then were they allowed to fly on to Darmstadt to join the rest of the *Geschwader*. When Göring learned of this he ordered the entire *Geschwader* to take off again and fly to Mannheim. The officers that had been disarmed landed, while the rest of the *Geschwader* circled overhead. They delivered an ultimatum from Göring to the soldiers' council: "The airfield will be flattened unless the weapons are returned immediately." The weap-

ons were immediately handed back and the *Geschwader* flew back to Darmstadt.

16 November 1918

The cease-fire came into effect—the First World War was over.

19 November 1918

In Aschaffenburg the first *Jagdgeschwader* of the German Air Force was disbanded. The First World War was over. Unlike all previous wars it had been dominated by materiel and technology, both in terms of quality and quantity. The use of artillery at Verdun and Ypres far surpassed anything seen before. The war of materiel, the era of the dominance of technology had begun. The First World War was also the first conflict to see the use of aircraft.

The first large-scale use of the fighter aircraft occurred over Verdun on 21 February 1916. The aircraft involved had a maximum speed of 120 km/h and a ceiling of about 4000 meters. Soon after the war these figures were raised to more than 200 km/h and 7000 meters. During the Second World War the pace of development would be even more breathtaking.

Manfred Baron von Richthofen in the uniform of an imperial cadet. With him are his bother Lothar, stroking their beloved dog, and Bolko, the youngest, sitting on the sled wearing a sailor hat.

Manfred at the tender age of seven.

Von Richthofen photographed while training to be an observer. He does not look particularly happy.

Left: Boelcke in conversation with *Leutnant* Haene, the latter sitting in the cockpit of a captured D.H. 2. On the right is Manfred Baron von Richthofen.

Below: A Fokker E. II circa 1915. It was powered by a 100-h.p. engine. Armament consisted of one MG 14 machine-gun synchronized to fire through the propeller disc.

Above: Richthofen's Albatros biplane on approach to land. The aircraft was painted red overall. Because of his red aircraft, the English soon began calling him the "Red Baron", while the French dubbed von Richthofen "*Le diable rouge*". Below left: *Jagdstaffel 11* (*Jasta 11*), von Richthofen's unit. His red-painted Albatros is second in line.

***Rittmeister* von Richthofen in the cockpit of his Albatros.**

Hauptmann Oswald Boelcke was the first to develop tactical concepts for the German air service's nascent fighter arm. He created the *Jagdstaffel* as a tactical unit.

Oberleutnant Max Immelmann was the practician. First alone, later in conjunction with Boelcke, he developed the aerial maneuvers required for air combat. The "Immelmann Turn" is still used by fighter pilots today. In the Second World War many pilots used this maneuver to escape dangerous situations and regain the initiative.

Rittmeister Manfred Baron von Richthofen combined courage, piloting skill, marksmanship and above all the ability to see what was happening around him. Even in the fiercest dogfight he was able to tell when a member of his unit was in a dangerous situation and go to his aid. In most cases von Richthofen moved in close before opening fire and dispatched the enemy with a few bursts. His study "Lessons in Air Combat" has been studied by jet pilots and unit commanders. It is a surprising fact is that most of von Richthofen's points are still valid today.

Von Richthofen in 1917 with pilots of Jasta 11. From left to right: *Leutnant* Gassmann, *Leutnant* Schubert, *Leutnant* van der Osten, *Leutnant* Steinhäusser, *Rittmeister* Baron von Richthofen, *Leutnant* Esser, *Leutnant* Lubbert, *Oberleutnant* Boddien, *Leutnant* von Linsingen, *Leutnant* Möhricke and *Feldwebel* Scholtz.

Baron von Richthofen in conversation with *Leutnant* Voss. Voss was a very successful fighter pilot who led the Boelcke Jasta after Boelcke's death. On 8 April 1917 he was awarded the Pour le Mérite after 48 victories. *Leutnant* Voss was shot down and killed on 23 September 1917; he was just twenty and a half years old.

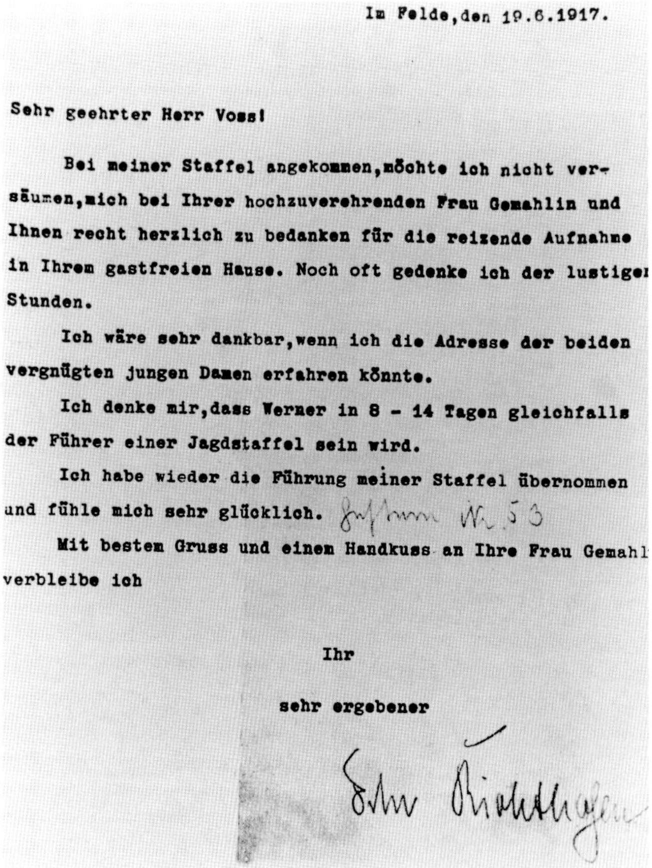

Im Felde, den 19.6.1917.

Sehr geehrter Herr Voss!

Bei meiner Staffel angekommen, möchte ich nicht versäumen, mich bei Ihrer hochzuverehrenden Frau Gemahlin und Ihnen recht herzlich zu bedanken für die reizende Aufnahme in Ihrem gastfreien Hause. Noch oft gedenke ich der lustigen Stunden.

Ich wäre sehr dankbar, wenn ich die Adresse der beiden vergnügten jungen Damen erfahren könnte.

Ich denke mir, dass Werner in 8 - 14 Tagen gleichfalls der Führer einer Jagdstaffel sein wird.

Ich habe wieder die Führung meiner Staffel übernommen und fühle mich sehr glücklich.

Mit bestem Gruss und einen Handkuss an Ihre Frau Gemahl[in]
verbleibe ich

Ihr

sehr ergebener

A letter from von Richthofen to Voss' father. In it he thanks Voss' parents for their hospitality and asks for the addresses of two young women he met at their home. He then goes on to say that he thinks that their son will be placed in command of a *Jagdstaffel* in 6 to 14 days.

Half frozen, a pilot leaves the cockpit of his aircraft with the help of his aircraft mechanic.

Oberleutnant Robert Ritter von Greim of the Bavarian *Jagdstaffel* 34 in front of his Albatros. On 8 October 1918 von Greim was awarded the Pour le Mérite after 25 victories. When the Second World War ended he was a *Generalfeldmarschall* and commander of the *Luftwaffe*. Von Greim committed suicide on 24 May 1945.

Below: A Fokker D VII performing aerobatics over Flanders.

Leutnant Zahler heads toward a reported formation of English aircraft in his Albatros fighter.

Rittmeister von Richthofen with several of his pilots. On the far left is *Leutnant* Kurt Wolff, commander of von Richthofen's old *Staffel*. He was awarded the Pour le Mérite on 4 May 1917 after 33 victories. Wolff was killed on 15 September of the same year.

Manfred von Richthofen in the cockpit of a Roland D II fighter. The photograph was taken in autumn 1917.

Manfred von Richthofen after another successful combat. On 3 September 1917 he recorded his 61st victory. The pilot of the enemy aircraft was Lieutenant Bird of the Royal Flying Corps, seen here with von Richthofen. On this day the enemy lost 19 aircraft and two tethered balloons.

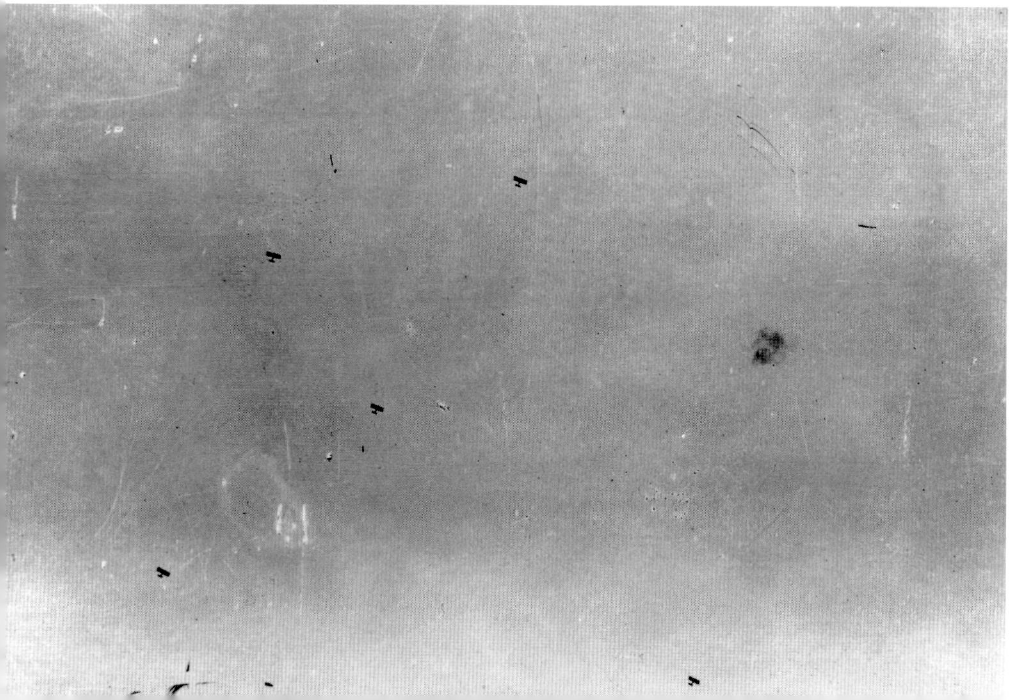

An English squadron overflies the front. A German anti-aircraft shell explodes too low.

Aviation was not the only field still in its infancy. Here field guns are being used as improvised anti-aircraft guns. Specialized anti-aircraft guns were a recent innovation and few were in actual service.

The *Geschwader* was frequently called upon to move from one airfield to another, resulting in major problems. Trucks were in short supply.

Rittmeister **Baron von Richthofen sustained a head wound while attacking an English two-seater. Here he is seen on the steps of Hospital No. 76, St. Nicolas Hospital in Courtrai, with visiting pilots from his** ***Geschwader*****.**

The ***Geschwader*** **has received news that** ***Oberleutnant*** **Ritter von Dostler was awarded the Pour le Mérite on 6 August 1917. At a small party given by** ***Jasta 6*****, von Richthofen hung his own decoration around the neck of the proud victor in 26 air combats. On 21 August 1917 von Dostler failed to return from a mission.**

Above: Courtrai, Flanders, August 1917. Kaiser Wilhelm II visits *Jagdgeschwader 1. Rittmeister* Baron von Richthofen and the assembled members of his *Geschwader* salute His Majesty.

Left: The Kaiser congratulates Richthofen on his success and that of his *Geschwader*.

The Kaiser and his staff inspect JG 1's aircraft.

Approaching French fighter.

Baron von Richthofen takes off in his Albatros D III. Note the Iron Cross hastily painted on the fuselage. The Albatros company emblem is visible on the machine's rudder.

Summer 1917—the *Geschwader* receives the first Fokker Dr I triplanes. They have more powerful engines than previous machines and are more maneuverable. Richthofen's machine, again painted red overall, stands ready for the next sortie.

***Rittmeister* Baron von Richthofen's Fokker Dr I flies low over the airfield.**

Fokker Triplane with tail raised in preparation for boresighting of the machine-guns.

Rittmeister von Richthofen crashed his Fokker Triplane but escaped injury.

The German air service was the first to provide its pilots with parachutes. Here personnel are trained in the use of the parachute. The British flew without parachutes, which limited their chances of survival if shot down.

Richthofen in the cockpit of a Pfalz triplane. The Alzeyer Aircraft Construction Company made the aircraft available to the famous ace for test purposes.

Fokker Dr I triplanes lined up in front of the maintenance tents.

Above: Another family reunion at the front. Manfred tries out a bicycle while his father, *Major* Baron von Richthofen, watches in amusement. Not the Albatros D III in the background.

Left: Brothers Lothar and Manfred von Richthofen in front of Manfred's aircraft. Lothar was also a successful fighter pilot and was awarded the Pour le Mérite on 14 May 1917 after 40 victories. He survived the war but died on 4 July 1922.

March 1918 – The commanding general of the air service, *Generalleutnant* von Hoeppner, visits the *Geschwader* to congratulate von Richthofen on his 71st, 72nd and 73rd victories, scored on 27 March.

In spite of von Richthofen's successes, it was impossible to deny that the situation was becoming serious. The Allies were slowly gaining air superiority. This German two-seater was damaged in combat with enemy fighters and crash-landed on its airfield.

Left: *Leutnant* Ernst Udet, seen here while still with *Jasta 37*, in front of his Albatros D V. On 20 March 1918 he joined JG 1 at von Richthofen's request. At that time he had 20 victories and by the end of the war he would raise his total to 62. He was thus the most successful German fighter pilot of the First World War after von Richthofen.

Rittmeister von Richthofen visits Jasta 10. From left to right: Löwenhardt, Bodenschatz, Kühn, von Richthofen, Heldmann, Schäfer, Aue and Graßmann.

Richthofen in conversation with *Leutnant* Klein, commander of *Jasta 10*, who had 22 victories to his credit when this photograph was taken. Soon afterwards, Klein was wounded in action for the second time.

Fokker Dr I.

Generalleutnant Ernst von Hoeppner speaks with *Leutnant* Kurt Wolff (sitting in cockpit). On the right is *Rittmeister* von Richthofen.

In spite of the war's growing harshness, there was still room for humanity. Here von Richthofen is seen with an English pilot whom he had just shot down. The pair are sitting on the crash-landed machine.

Cappy airfield. Not long before, it had been home to the SE. 5A fighters of No. 24 Squadron of the Royal Flying Corps. JG 1 moved in on 16 April 1918. It was to be the last airfield von Richthofen would know.

Cappy, April 1918. Air battle over the airfield. Hannemann, Uetersen and von Richthofen observe the action using binocular telescopes, a ranging telescope and ordinary binoculars.

Rittmeister von Richthofen with his beloved dog Max, which he bought from a Belgian for five Reichsmark. This would be the last time he played with his dog.

April 1918, Cappy airfield. The last photograph of Manfred von Richthofen while he was alive. The pilots are waiting for a report on the strength and course of an approaching enemy formation. Tensely they wait for the telephone to ring. From left to right: Wolfram von Richthofen, Karjus, Joachim Wolff, Lübbert, Manfred von Richthofen, Löwenhardt, Just and Weiß.

Manfred Baron von Richthofen is dead. The remains of Richthofen's triplane.

Officers of the Australian Flying Corps examine the machine-guns from von Richthofen's aircraft. Canadian Captain Roy Brown was credited with having brought down von Richthofen, however, from the very beginning there were doubts that he had been shot down from the air. The latest research tends to support the theory that he was killed by ground fire.

Monday, 23 April 1918. *Rittmeister* Manfred Baron von Richthofen is taken to a small church cemetery for burial. Twelve Australian soldiers provide the honor guard, leading the wagon bearing von Richthofen's coffin. Behind the wagon are six captains of the Royal Flying Corps, all highly-decorated unit commanders, plus 50 officers, NCOs and men of No. 3 Squadron.

In a gesture of respect for a fallen foe, a British aircraft dropped a wreath over the German lines. The attached message read: "To the German Flying Corps. *Rittmeister* Baron Manfred von Richthofen was killed in aerial combat on April 21st, 1918. He was buried with full military honors—from the British Royal Air Force."

Rittmeister von Richthofen was buried with full military honors. Australian soldiers fire a salute from their Lee Enfield rifles.

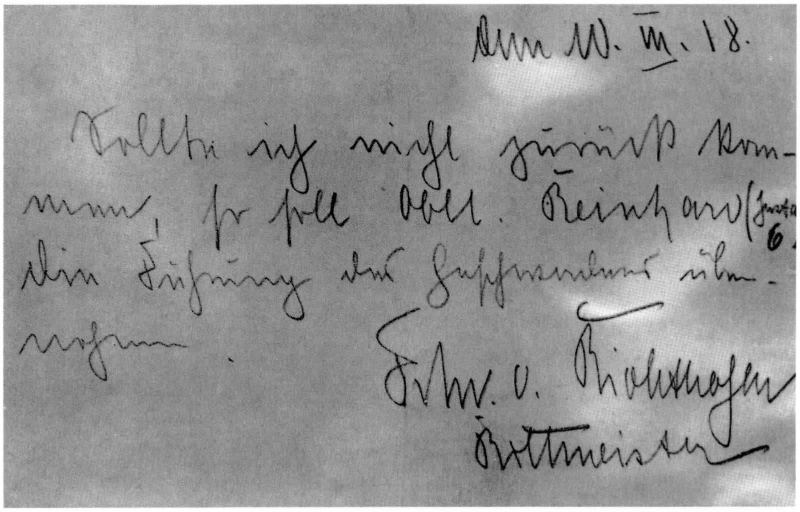

Den 10. III. 18.

Sollte ich nicht zurück kommen, so soll Oblt. Reinhard (Jasta 6) die Führung des Geschwaders übernehmen.

Frhr. v. Richthofen
Rittmeister

Just seven weeks before his death, *Rittmeister* von Richthofen wrote this note, designating his successor as commander of JG 1.

Oberleutnant Wilhelm Reinhard took over *Jagdgeschwader 1*. He was killed on 3 July 1918 while testing a new machine.

His gravestone has survived and today holds a place of honor on the grounds of the modern *Jagdgeschwader Richthofen* in Wittmundhafen.

Oberleutnant **Hermann Göring, here in the cockpit of his fighter, assumed command of the** ***Geschwader*** **after Reinhard's death. Note the bulged cover over the ammunition feed, not unlike the bulges over the ammunition feeds of the Bf 109 G-6 fighter of World War Two. Göring was still commander of JG 1 when the war ended.**

Leutnant **Friedrich returned from combat with a severely-damaged wing and crashed his Fokker D VII among the tents and parked aircraft at Cappy-Bray airfield on the Somme. On the right, wearing the light-colored jacket, is** ***Oberleutnant*** **Schäfer, and next to him the aircraft designer Antony Fokker. The machines parked in the foreground are also Fokker D VIIs.**

Losses mounted in the face of the enemy's growing superiority in men and materiel. Here an honor guard fires a salute over the grave of ***Leutnant*** **Rolff at Bernes airfield in August 1918.**

2

Creation of the New *Luftwaffe*

22 March 1922
Representatives from various political circles and the *Reichswehr* meet for secret talks concerning the creation of an air force.

1924
The first steps are taken to train aircrew, technicians and other personnel. This is done in the strictest secrecy. Later, pilots are trained outside the country, in Lipetsk, Russia for example.

In Germany, pilot training is carried out by the DVS (*Deutsche Verkehrsflieger Schule*, or German Commercial Pilots School) and the DLS (*Deutsche Luftsport-Verband für Motorflieger*, or German Aviation Sport Union for Powered Flight).

January 1931
By this time the first three fighter squadrons (*Jagdstaffeln*) have been formed. They are based at Fürth, Staaken and Königsberg. These so-called "Advertising Squadrons" were the first, albeit secret, aviation units in postwar Germany. They were attached to the army.

1931
Secret efforts begin to create a German Air Force by 1932-33. These plans have to be abandoned for political, but mainly technical and organizational reasons. 1934 is declared "A Year".

20 February 1934
Hermann Göring, the State Minister of Aviation, orders the secret formation of a new air force.

1 April 1934
The headquarters squadron Fl.St. 132 is formed.

20 April 1934
Decree L.A. Nr. 1090/34 is issued. Subparagraph 3 declares that "*Jagdgeschwader 132* is to be formed at Döberitz on 1 July 1934".

1 June 1934
The *Jagdstaffeln* 1./132, 2./132 and 3./132 are formed in rapid succession. *Major* Ritter von Greim is named to command the *I. Gruppe*. For reasons of secrecy the unit is given the cover title of "Central German Advertising Squadron of the German Aviation Sport Union". Its base is Döberitz, near Berlin, however the actual flying is done at Staaken, as the airfield at Döberitz is not yet complete. The members of the unit are "sent on leave" from the *Reichswehr*. Instead of wearing the uniforms and rank badges of the 100,000-man army, they wear those of the German Aviation Sport Union.

1 October 1934
The *Geschwader* has reached its interim authorized strength, however expansion is far from over.

Beginning of 1935
The State Ministry of Aviation issues a directive calling for the procurement of 4,021 aircraft for all branches of the new air force by 30 September 1935. These include bombers, fighters, reconnaissance aircraft, transports, liaison and training machines. By years end the German aviation industry delivers 50% of the aircraft needed to equip the future *Luftwaffe*.

Eighty of these aircraft, Arado Ar 65 fighters, are delivered to *Jagdgeschwader 132*.

These are later joined by the Ar 68, which is already behind the state of the art. The first fully operational German fighter aircraft was the Heinkel He 51.

26 February 1935
On this day the *Reichsluftwaffe* is made an independent service effective 1 March 1935. The title *Reichsluftwaffe*, chosen by Hitler, does not meet with acceptance and is soon replaced by the title *Luftwaffe*. The still secret units are gradually revealed to the German public and the world.

1 March 1935
One of the first units to be unveiled is the "Central German Advertising Squadron". It is officially placed in service as *Jagdgeschwader 132*. The same day the members of the *Geschwader* are issued the uniforms of the new *Luftwaffe*, along with correct insignia and rank badges.

13 March 1935
Hitler restores Germany's military sovereignty on land, at sea and in the air.

14 March 1935
Jagdgeschwader 132 based at Döberitz receives the honorary title "*Jagdgeschwader Richthofen*". As a visible symbol of their identity and in keeping with tradition, the members of the *Geschwader* are issued cuff bands bearing the name Richthofen.

16 March 1935
The "Law for the Establishment of the Armed Services" proclaims Germany's freedom to defend itself, or defense sovereignty for the German Reich. The *Staffeln* of *Jagdgeschwader 132* fly their Heinkel biplanes over the city of Berlin as the announcement is made. This is meant to demonstrate to the world that Germany has a strong air force capable of defending further expansion of the armed services, which begins with the proclamation of compulsory military service.

28 March 1935
The *Stab* and *I. Gruppe* of *Jagdgeschwader Richthofen* are based at Döberitz.

1 April 1935
As part of the continued expansion of the *Luftwaffe*, the *II./132* of the "*Jagdgeschwader Richthofen*" is formed at Jüterbog/Damm. The new *Gruppe* is commanded by *Major* Dipl.Ing. Dr. Raithel. The *Geschwader* is reorganized and enlarged. The commander of the *I. Gruppe*, von Greim, leaves. He is succeeded by *Major* von Doering. Three *Staffelkapitäne* plus non-commissioned officers and enlisted men also leave, taking their experience to newly-formed units and assisting the buildup of the *Luftwaffe*. Both *Gruppen* of the *Geschwader* are designated "*Jagdgeschwader Richthofen*" *Nr. 132*, however they are independent units under the overall command of *Oberst* Sperrle.

This was the first air unit to supplement the formations that had existed since 1930, the so-called "Advertising Squadrons", *Deutsche Lufthansa*'s provisional bomber wing in Berlin with its Ju 52 bombers, the navy's seaplane squadron, and several factory units.

Both *Gruppen* of the "*Jagdgeschwader Richthofen*" flew the Ar 65 and later the Ar 68.

3 April 1935
The dive-bomber *Gruppe* I./162, based at Schwerin and formed from the "*Jagdgeschwader Richthofen*", receives the honorary title of "*Immelmann Geschwader*".

Summer 1935
"*Jagdgeschwader Richthofen*" is reequipped with the Heinkel He 51.

1 March 1936
Major von Schoenebeck, a member of the *Richthofen Geschwader* from the First World War, becomes commander of the *II./JG 132*.

Later, the *II. Gruppe* will be commanded in turn by *Major* Meyer, *Major* Laumann and *Major* Huth.

1 April 1936
Oberstleutnant von Doering is appointed commander of the newly-formed *Jagdgeschwader "Horst Wessel"*. *Major* Dr.Ing. Raithel, commander of the *II. Gruppe*, becomes *Kommodore* of the "*Jagdgeschwader Richthofen*". *Major* Viek, formerly chief instructor at the fighter training school at Schleissheim, is named *Kommandeur* of *I./JG 132*.

Spring 1936
The *Luftwaffe* creates new units using the so-called "Cell Division" method. The *I.* and *II. Gruppe* of *JG 132* provide a core of personnel for the *III.* and *II./JG 134* at Lippstadt and Werl. Other personnel are detached to assist in the formation of *JG 234*, which becomes *JG 26 "Schlageter"* in 1939.

9 June 1936
JG 132 receives another new *Kommodore*, *Oberst* Gerd von Massow. The "*Jagdgeschwader Richthofen*" was the primordial cell of the new fighter arm and other elements of the *Luftwaffe*. Through rapid "cell division" the trained units provided personnel for a series of units formed in rapid succession. Of course, this mainly affected the commanders of *Staffeln*, *Gruppen* and even *Geschwader*.

1937
This year the fighter units began converting to the Messerschmitt Bf 109. In 1938 the abbreviation Bf for the Bäyerische Flugzeugwerke was changed to Me for Messerschmitt, after the Bäyerische Flugzeugwerke became the Messerschmitt AG and Professor Willy Messerschmitt became director of the company. The Me designation was used for all later aircraft designs, such as the Me 210, Me 163 and Me 262.

In March the "*Jagdgeschwader Richthofen*" *Nr. 132* became the first to equip with the Bf 109.

This year also saw the first night flights carried out, in preparation for a planned night-fighter force.

Autumn 1937
In Spain, civil war had been raging for more than six months. Germany entered the war on the side of General Franco against the Republican government which was supported by the Soviet Union. Germany sent forces to Spain as the *Legion Condor*, which consisted almost exclusively of air force units.

Members of JG 132 were among the first to volunteer for service in Spain.

12 March 1938
The *I. Gruppe* is ordered to provide air cover over Vienna. The "*Anschluss*", which saw Austria become part of the Reich, took place on 13 March. It returned to Döberitz on 17 March.

The purpose of the mission may have been to protect Hitler, who on 15 March gave his famous speech in Heroes' Square in Vienna concerning the joining of Austria to the German Reich.

?? March 1938
On this day the *I. Gruppe* of the "*Jagdgeschwader Richthofen*" flew to Munich and then to Vienna-Aspern. By this time it was equipped with the Bf 109 E-1. Meanwhile the *II. Gruppe* was retraining on the Bf 110, the new twin-engined fighter with a crew of two. The *Gruppe* thus became the core of the first *Zerstörergeschwader*. A *Staffel* formed at Döberitz was already undertaking night fighting trials. It later left JG 132.

21 April 1938
On the twentieth anniversary of Richthofen's death, a memorial stone was unveiled at the Döberitz air base. To the right and left of the stone were placed a red Fokker Dr I and a Bf 109. They symbolized the transition from the air forces of the First World War to the new *Luftwaffe* in the tradition of the unforgettable Red Baron.

1 July 1938
The *IV./JG 132* is formed at Werneuchen under the command of *Major* Theo Osterkamp, a wearer of the Pour le Mérite.

1 July 1938
On this day the *10./JG 132 "Richthofen"* is formed from units of the *Jagdfliegerschule Werneuchen. Hauptmann* Fritz Ultsch is named the unit's first commander. The *Staffel*'s list of flying personnel includes *Leutnante* Bauer and Schnell, *Oberfeldwebel* Beek, *Feldwebel* Pelzer, *Leutnant* Knauth, *Oberfähnrich* Führing and pilots Falting, Eggers, Hecht and Bürschgens. The unit is equipped with Bf 109 D fighters in dark green camouflage and wearing the Richthofen emblem beneath the windscreen.

1 August 1938
On this date *JG 132* is organized as follows:

Kommodore of *JG 132 "R"* at Döberitz: *Oberstleutnant* von Massow
Kommandeur of the *I. Gruppe* at Döberitz: *Major* Viek
Kommandeur of the *II. Gruppe* at Damm: *Major* Huth
Kommandeur of the *III. Gruppe* at Damm: *Major* Dr.Ing. Bormann
Kommandeur of the *IV. Gruppe* at Werneuchen: *Oberstleutnant* Osterkamp

On the same day *Oberstleutnant* Osterkamp is replaced as *Kommandeur* of the *IV. Gruppe*. His successor is *Hauptmann* Janke.

On 12 August the *III. Gruppe* is reformed at Damm and equipped with the Bf 110 *Zerstörer*. It will later be renamed *II./JG 141*.

1 September 1938
The *IV./JG 132* moves to Oschatz. From there it flies one mission during the occupation of the Sudetenland.

1-10 October 1938
Case Green, the entry of German forces into the Sudetenland, is put into effect. Almost 500 aircraft take part in this operation. An air fleet of 400 fighter aircraft, 600 bombers, and 200 dive-bombers and close-support aircraft stands ready to intervene if there is resistance. The *IV. Gruppe* makes a demonstration flight over Eger and Karlsbad.

6 October 1938
The *IV. Gruppe* transfers to Karlsbad.

29 October 1938
The *IV. Gruppe* moves again, to Mährisch-Trübau.

1 November 1938
With the continued rapid expansion of the *Luftwaffe*, the *IV. Gruppe* leaves the "*Jagdgeschwader Richthofen*" and is renamed 1./JG 331. This later becomes the *I. Gruppe* of the new JG 77. The *II. Gruppe* also leaves, after its pilots have been retrained on the Bf 110 twin-engined fighter. As previously mentioned, the *III. Gruppe* becomes *JG 141*, the later *I./ZG 1*, the first unit of the *Zerstörer* arm. The *II. Gruppe* becomes the I./ZG 76. On this eventful day *Jagdgeschwader 132 "Richthofen"* is renamed *Jagdgeschwader "Richthofen" Nr. 131*. The *Geschwader* consists solely of the *Stab* and the *I. Gruppe*.

For the *Geschwader*, the carousel of formation and reorganization has reached its climax.

13 January 1939
The formation of the *10./JG 131* as a night-fighter *Staffel* is ordered. It is attached to the *I. Gruppe*.

1 May 1939
With a further reorganization of the *Luftwaffe* the *Geschwader* is redesignated "*Jagdgeschwader Richthofen" Nr. 2*. On the same day the *10. Staffel* is renamed *10.(N)/JG 2*.

Spring 1939
The state of the air forces of Europe:

	Total	Fighters
England	5,500	?
France	4,650 (+ 2,400 1 April 1940)	1,100
Soviet Union	6,000	1,400
Poland	900	270
Italy	3,800	?
Germany	4,333	771

15 July 1939
The *1./JG 20* is attached to the *Geschwader* until November of this year.

Summer 1939
More and more *Geschwader* of the *Luftwaffe* leave their peacetime bases and move to operational airfields in the east. Several are moved to the west of the Reich to guard the border.

25 August 1939
An attack on Poland is now imminent. Part of JG 2 moves to Straussberg, east of Berlin.

Located near Berlin, Döberitz air base was established in 1934. It had been used as a military airfield during the time of the Kaiser. The photograph shows the main guardhouse. Even now people use the term "Döberitzer" when speaking of the first members of the new *Luftwaffe*. Döberitz was the cradle of JG 2. The *Stab* and I/JG 132 were initially based there.

Above: Another airfield was opened at Jüterbog/Damm, not far from Döberitz. Seen here is the main gate. The *Geschwader*'s *II. Gruppe* was based there from 1 April 1935.

Left: A familiar sight to all "Döberitzer" was "Icarus", located near the mess in the pine forest.

An interesting photograph taken in 1934 during the secret buildup of the *Luftwaffe*. Here Ernst Udet is seen during a visit to the *Geschwader*. He is wearing the uniform of the German Aviation Sport Union with the rank badges of a Flieger-Vizekommodore. Beside him wearing the white summer cap is Fliegerkommodore Bodenschatz. When the *Luftwaffe* was created, the uniform as worn by the Flugkapitän on the right was retained, but the rank badges were changed. Above the breast pocket is the pilot's emblem of the DLV.

Group photo of the "command team" taken after the existence of the *Luftwaffe* was revealed. In the center of the front row is *Major* Ritter von Greim, the first *Kommodore* of JG 132. On von Greim's right is *Major* Dr.Ing. Raithel, who later succeeded him as *Kommodore*. Between them in the second row is *Oberleutnant* von Below; he later became Hitler's *Luftwaffe* adjutant.

The Arado Ar 65 biplane was JG 132's first fighter aircraft. Powered by a BMW 12-cylinder inline engine, the type first appeared in 1931.

After the "unmasking" of the *Luftwaffe* the Arado Ar 68 E and Heinkel He 51 became the standard fighter types. The Ar 68 was powered by a Junkers Jumo 210 engine producing 640 h.p. and was armed with two 7.9-mm MG 17 machine-guns in the forward fuselage.

Above: A *Staffel* of Ar 68 E fighters lined up on the airfield. Note the name "Heine" on the wooden two-blade propeller.

Right: As the new *Luftwaffe* expanded, units were formed quickly. Flight incidents were common. This aircraft wears the markings of a flight school in Luftkreiskommando 2 in Berlin.

The He 51 was Heinkel's first single-seat fighter. Here a number of these aircraft are seen in formation. They still carry the combined registration for civilian and military aircraft that was used from 6 July 1933 until April 1934. The national marking consists of black, white and red stripes on the fin and rudder.

A Heinkel He 51 on takeoff. It wears the national symbol, the Swastika in a white field on a red background. The first *Staffeln* of JG 132 "Richthofen" were equipped with this biplane fighter in 1935. The BMW engine produced 750 h.p. The He 51 was also armed with two 7.9-mm machine-guns.

Above: On 14 March 1935 the Luftwaffe's first flying unit, whose camouflage designation was the "Central German Advertising Squadron", was given the honorary title "Jagdgeschwader Richthofen". From that day on, the members of the Geschwader wore a cuff band bearing the title "Jagdgeschwader Richthofen". Hitler attended the ceremony and here is seen reviewing the I. Gruppe of Jagdgeschwader 132 "Richthofen" accompanied by the Geschwaderkommodore, Oberstleutnant von Doering, left, and General Göring, the Commander-in-Chief of the Luftwaffe.

Dienstag, 19. März 1935
№ 66

Berliner illustrierte

2. Ausgabe

Nachtausgabe

10 Pf.
auswärts 15 Pf.

Das erste Geschwader der neuen deutschen Luftwaffe über Berlin

Der Führer verlieh ihm den Namen „Richthofen"

Zahlreiche Verletzte

Expreßzug tötet sieben Arbeiter

Schweres Zugunglück in Belgien

Drahtbericht unseres Berichterstatters

Brüssel, 19. März. Auf der Strecke Brüssel—Antwerpen fuhr heute morgen bei Mecheln der Expreßzug 206, aus Antwerpen kommend, in eine auf dem Bahnkörper arbeitende Kolonne von 10 Mann. Sieben Arbeiter wurden sofort getötet und mehrere andere verletzt.

Zur Zeit des Unglücks herrschte ziemlich dichter Morgennebel. Von der Arbeitsleitung waren die üblichen Vorsichtsmaßnahmen getroffen und Wachtposten aufgestellt. Es wird vermutet, daß durch das Geräusch eines vorbeifahrenden Güterzuges die Rufe der Posten, die das Nahen des Expreßzuges ankündigen wollen, übertönt wurden.

Zum Gedenken an das ruhmreiche Jagdgeschwader

Hermann Göring an die Mutter des Helden / „Ich löse hiermit ein heiliges Vermächtnis ein!"

Im Zusammenhang mit der Berliner Luftschutzübung erschienen Jagdflieger aus Döberitz über der Stadt. Wie wir dazu von zuständiger Stelle erfahren, gehörten sie dem Jagdgeschwader an, dem der Führer und Reichskanzler auf Vorschlag des letzten Kommandeurs des ruhmreichen Richthofen-Geschwaders, des Reichsministers der Luftfahrt General der Flieger Göring den Namen „Jagdgeschwader Richthofen" verliehen hat.

Dazu wird uns von unserem Breslauer Berichterstatter gedrahtet:

st Breslau, 19. März. Die in der schlesischen Stadt Schweidnitz lebende Mutter des deutschen Fliegerhelden Manfred v. Richthofen hat von dem Reichsminister der Luftfahrt, Ministerpräsident Göring ein Schreiben erhalten, in dem ihr eine Ehrung ihres Sohnes mitgeteilt wird. Das erste deutsche Nachkriegsfliegergeschwader soll den Namen ihres Sohnes tragen.

Das Schreiben hat folgenden Wortlaut:

„Hochverehrte gnädige Frau! Unser Führer [...] fohlen, daß das erste Fliegergeschwader, das wieder über ein freies Deutschland schützend seine Schwingen breitet, den Namen Richthofen trägt. Es ist mir als Kamerad Ihres Sohnes eine herzliche Freude, als Reichsminister der Luftfahrt ein Stolz, Ihnen von diesem Erlaß, dessen Abschrift ich beifüge, Kenntnis geben zu können. Ich löse hiermit ein heiliges Vermächtnis ein, wenn die stolze Ueberlieferung des ruhmreichen Jagdgeschwaders Richthofen, dessen letzter Kommandeur ich war, auf die neue Einheit übertragen wird. Das Beispiel Ihres unvergeßlichen Heldensohnes wird wie damals alle Offiziere und Soldaten der wiedererstandenen deutschen Luftwaffe zur höchsten Kühnheit und Opferbereitschaft erziehen. Mit dem Ausdruck meiner gleichbleibenden Verehrung und Heil Hitler!

Ihr sehr ergebener
Hermann Göring."

*

Manfred Freiherr v. Richthofen, dessen Namen das erste deutsche Nachkriegsfliegergeschwader trägt, wurde am 2. Mai 1892 in Breslau geboren. 1912 wurde er Leutnant im Ulanenregiment 1. im Weltkriege trat er zur Fliegertruppe über und wurde sehr bald der er[...]er Kommandeur des Jagdgeschwaders 1, das b[...] Gegner besonders gefürchtet war. 80 Fluge[...] des Feindes fielen dem schneidigen Richtho[...] dessen Maschine der Gegner genau kannte, [...] Opfer. Am 21. April 1918 aber starb der tap[...] Recke der Lüfte an der Westfront den Helden[...]

Manfred Frhr. v. Richthofen
Scherl-Bilderdienst

Left: The bestowing of the Richthofen name was front page news. The headline reads: "The first wing of the new German air force over Berlin. The *Führer* bestowed upon it the name `Richthofen'."

An Arado Ar 68 in flight near the Döberitz airfield.

The technical personnel of the 1. Staffel pose for a group photo.

Motor mechanics at work. The man on the left is holding the starter crank.

There was plenty of work for the "Black Men" to do. This name was given to the technical personnel on account of their black overalls.

Parade formation by the 3. Staffel of the III. Gruppe. The discs indicate the Staffel number, the wavy line marking indicates the III. Gruppe.

The "*Jagdgeschwader Richthofen*" was the *Luftwaffe*'s show unit. In 1937 Charles Lindberg visited the 1/JG 132 "Richthofen".

An Air Marshal of the Royal Air Force accompanied by *General* Milch and the *Kommodore* during an inspection of the 2 Staffel.

Aligning the guns of a He 51. Once they had been aligned, a plywood disc mounted on the propeller hub was used to moderate their rate of fire.

Raised onto the firing trestle. The aircraft's guns are being fired at a target seen in the background.

The Staffelkapitän, *Oberleutnant* von Seile (right), checks the results. The close grouping indicates that the guns have been properly aligned.

Aircraft maintenance under the open sky during maneuvers. The Heinkel's engine has been removed with the aid of a block and tackle and makeshift tripod.

The engine has been removed from the engine mount and the mechanics set to work.

With the overhaul of the BMW VI liquid-cooled engine complete, it was returned to the aircraft and reinstalled.

On maneuvers. On the left is the *Kommodore* of JG 132 "R", *Major* Raithel, in front of his mobile command post.

Hungry visitors during maneuvers. Young boys are always hungry, especially when there is pea soup with bacon to be eaten out of doors. They have lost interest in the He 51 in the background. The pilot has laid his parachute on the lower wing.

Many residents of Berlin turned out when, in 1925, the remains of Manfred Baron von Richthofen were taken to the Invaliden Cemetery for burial. The elderly Reich President, Paul von Hindenburg, walks behind the coffin at the head of a lengthy procession. On the coffin is a shako, as worn by an Uhlan regiment.

Guard of honor at the grave of Manfred Baron von Richthofen.

Jagdgeschwader Richthofen

Jagdgruppe II/132 Jüterbog-Damm.

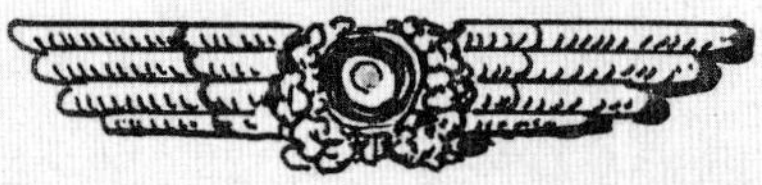

4. Staffel 1. Januar 1937 - 31. Mai 1938.

An dieser Stelle sei gesagt wer sich mit der Staffel plagt:

des Führers Jagdflieger im Geiste voran Richthofen Boelcke und Immelmann!

Hptm. Graf Schönborn
Hptm. Reinecke

Commodore: Oberstltn. v Massow
Adjutant: Obltn. Falk

Gruppenkommandeur:		II/132	Major Huth
Stabskompanie:		Hptm.	Albrecht
4. Staffel:	Staffelkapitän	Hptm.	Reinecke
	Hauptfw. (Spieß)	Hfw.	Patzeck
	Werkmstr.	Fw.	Bott.

Flugzeugführer: 4. Staffel:

Ltn. Prinz Hubertus v. Preussen
Ltn. Resch
Ltn. Lutz
Ltn Blume
Ltn. Wien
Ltn. Köhler

Ogfr. Löhde
Ofw. Sigmund, Braunschweiger
mein Jagdlehrer.
Ogfr. Tismer
Gfr. Gerstmann
Gfr. Hollitzki

April 1936 at the Jüterbog/Damm air base: the Heinkel He 51s of JG 132 are prepared for flight.

A pilot of 3 Staffel II Gruppe sits in the cockpit of his aircraft as ground crew start the engine using a hand crank.

Three flights of three He 51s in vee formation. This type of formation was also used by the bomber units. The fighter units later switched to a four finger formation.

Officers of the Gruppenstab around a map, planning an exercise. The fighters will fly the selected route to the target and then engage ground targets.

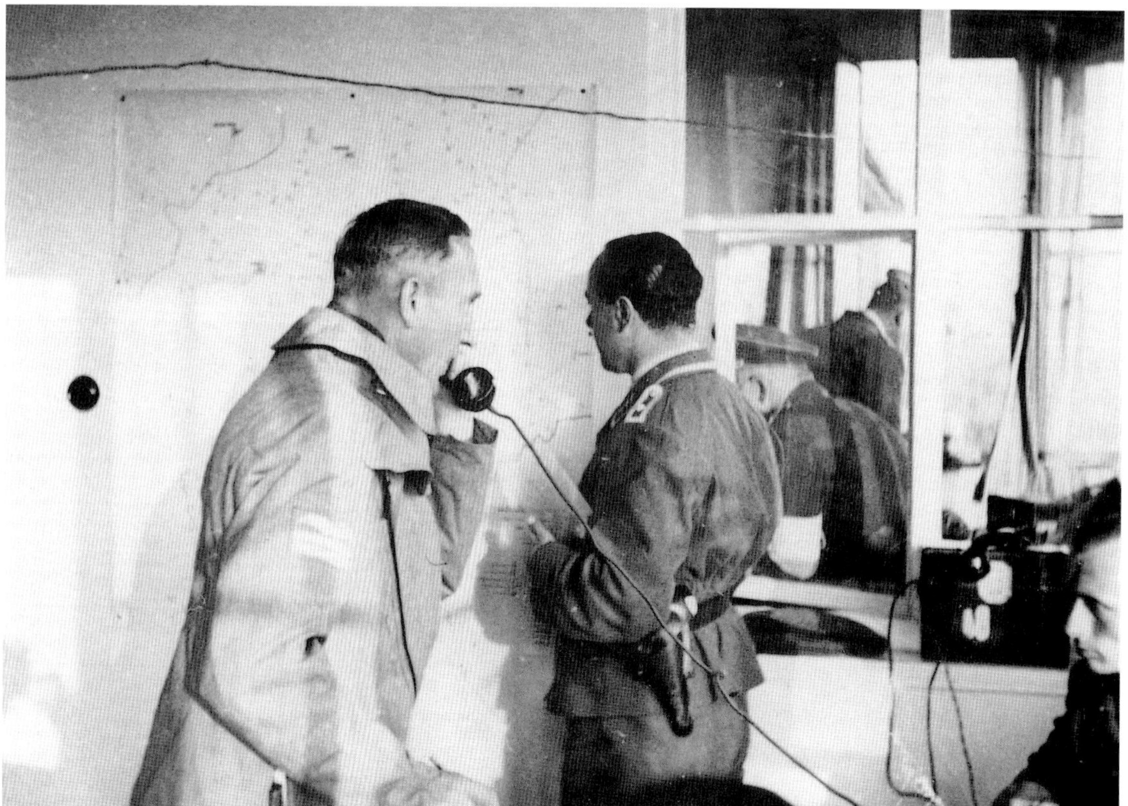

The commander of II Gruppe issues his final instructions by telephone.

Above left: The *Kommandeur*, already wearing his helmet, goggles and flight suit, makes final preparations. Perhaps he is having a second breakfast before taking off. Above right: This Heinkel He 51 bears the *Kommandeur*'s chevron followed by a horizontal bar, the symbol of II Gruppe. It is the aircraft of the *Gruppenkommandeur*, *Major* Meyer.

Left: Döberitz airfield seen from the air: visible are the hangars plus administration and technical buildings.

A low-flying He 51 approaches a gunnery target on the ground. Observers in a bunker (below the aircraft on the right) watch each firing pass and assess the results.

In 1937 a large gravestone bearing the family name was erected at the gravesite of Manfred von Richthofen. In the foreground is the slab bearing the von Richthofen coat of arms and the name of Manfred von Richthofen.

By this time the person of Manfred Baron von Richthofen had become more than a war hero in the minds of many people. He was a symbol of chivalry and fairness. As a result, memorials and monuments were built in his memory. The memorial seen here was erected at von Richthofen's birthplace in Schweidnitz. The Baron's fame also extended beyond Germany's borders. In the English-speaking world he became famous as the "Red Baron".

JG "Richthofen" was the first fighter unit of the *Luftwaffe* to receive the new fighter aircraft produced by the Bayerische Flugzeugwerke. The Bf 109 B-1 was powered by a 635-h.p. Jumo 210 D and was armed with two MG 17 rifle-caliber machine-guns.

From Jüterbog/Damm the Bf 109 Bs moved to Straussberg. Practice transfers were commonplace. Here the aircraft are seen being serviced in the open. Note the "Maintenance Tent". It provided sufficient room for the mechanics' lifting equipment, a tripod with block and tackle. Waterproof covers were placed over the engine compartment during necessary work.

Final instructions by the Staffelkapitän. The pilots check the assigned route on their maps. The Staffel's Bf 109s may be seen in the background.

The pilot of this aircraft was compelled to make a forced landing, probably by engine failure. The wing-mounted machine-guns identify the machine as a Bf 109 D.

The rapid creation and expansion of the Luftwaffe was not without cost. Funeral for a pilot killed when his Bf 109 B crashed at Döberitz on 3 March 1938.

Mechanical trouble or human failure? Accidents were also often caused by bad weather. In this case the aircraft struck a hole and flipped over.

The pilots and their ground crews, the "Black Men", assembled before their Staffelkapitän, *Oberleutnant* Bock. The cheerful faces suggest that nothing unpleasant was happening.

***Oberleutnant* Bock has gathered the pilots of his 2 Staffel around him for a short tactical briefing.**

“R” for Richthofen, a binding symbol not only of courage and fulfillment of duty, but also of willingness to sacrifice and loyalty.

Bf 109 B-2s lined up on the airfield.

On 21 April 1938 a military parade was held to mark the twentieth anniversary of the death of *Rittmeister* Manfred Baron von Richthofen.

Watched by von Richthofen's mother, sister and youngest brother Bolko, *General* Hermann Göring, Commander-in-Chief of the *Luftwaffe*, dedicates a memorial in front of the headquarters building in Döberitz.

On 13 March 1938 the Bf 109 B-2s of I/JG 132 provided air cover for the entry of German forces into Austria.

In September 1938, during the Sudeten crisis, the aircraft of JG 132 gave a demonstration of German airpower. One of them was this Heinkel He 112 B-0, which flew to Mährisch-Trübau. After the occupation the twelve Heinkel fighters went to Japan, to whom they had been sold earlier.

On 13 January 1939 orders were issued for the formation of a night-fighter Staffel. It was designated 10/JG 131, but attached to the unit's I Gruppe. When the *Geschwader* was renamed, it officially became 10(N)/JG 2. The IV Gruppe, of which the Staffel was now apart, left JG 2 and was attached to JG 77. This photograph was taken in Norway in 1940 during "Operation Weserübung", in which II/JG 77 took part. Seen here on Varnes airfield are the Bf 109 Ds of the former 10/JG 2, now 10(N)/JG 77. All of the unit's aircraft are marked with an "N" on the fuselage to indicate their night fighting role. By this time the *Luftwaffe*'s day fighter units had converted to the Bf 109 E.

In September 1938 the "*Jagdgeschwader Richthofen*" began receiving the new Bf 109 E-1. This latest version of Messerschmitt's fighter was powered by a Daimler Benz DB 601 engine producing 1,150 h.p. Armament consisted of two MG/FF 20-mm cannon in the wings and two 7.9-mm MG 17 machine-guns in the upper fuselage.

Shielded against prying eyes, Bf 109 E-1 fighters parked in the grass at Döberitz air base.

Most Staffeln were still flying the B and C versions of the Messerschmitt fighter, and conversion would continue through the winter of 1938-39.

A trio of Bf 109 B-2s takes off on a winter training sortie.

Civil war had broken out in Spain in 1936. Germany threw its support behind the Nationalist side against the Republicans, forming an expeditionary force dubbed the "Legion Condor". Made up of air force units for the most part, it remained in Spain until March 1939.

Right: In 1937 Bf 109 B-2 fighters replaced the He 51 in Spain. Seen here are aircraft of 2/J 88. This was the designation assigned to the second Staffel of the fighter Gruppe of the "Legion Condor".

A Bf 109 E near Saragossa in 1939. The war in Spain gave the *Luftwaffe* an opportunity to test its aircraft, weapons and equipment under actual combat conditions. German pilots gained valuable operational experience in Spain.

The pilot of this Messerschmitt was forced to crash-land his damaged machine. Against the black disc on the fuselage is the emblem of the Falange, General Franco's nationalist movement.

The civil war in Spain is over. In a large tent camp outside the gates of Berlin, pilots, including those of the Richthofen *Geschwader*, wait for the start of the victory parade. In the center of the group is Werner Mölders.

The last commander of the "Legion Condor", *Generalmajor* Wolfram Baron von Richthofen, leading his men in the victory parade in Berlin.

MERKBLATT

FÜR DEN 6. JUNI 1939

1. Antreten und Meldung in der Marmorgallerie.
   Mütze aufbehalten. Koppel umgeschnallt lassen.
   Aufstellung in Linie zu 2 Gliedern.
   Am rechten Flügel die 3 Befehlshaber der Legion Condor, Admiral Carls, Admiral Boehm Oberst d. G. Warlimont und die Offiziere des Sonderstabs W.
   Dann nebeneinander
   die spanischen Offiziere
   die italienischen Offiziere
   Sonderstab W
   die Kommandeure und Kommandanten
   die Offiziere mit Spanienkreuz in Gold mit Brillanten
   die Offiziere mit Spanienkreuz in Gold
   die Unteroffiziere mit Spanienkreuz in Gold.
   Innerhalb der einzelnen Blocks nach den Wehrmachtteilen antreten.
   Reihenfolge: Luftwaffe, Heer, Kriegsmarine.
   Innerhalb der Wehrmachtteile dem Dienstalter nach aufstellen.
2. Der Führer betritt die Gallerie von der Mitte der Nordseite der Gallerie.
3. General der Flieger Sperrle meldet dem Führer. Dabei grüßen alle Generale und Admirale, während alle anderen Offiziere und Unteroffiziere in Grundstellung bleiben und Augen rechts bzw. links nehmen.
4. Der Führer geht die Front vom rechten Flügel aus ab. Er wird begleitet von den Oberbefehlshabern der 3 Wehrmachtteile, Generaloberst Keitel und Generaloberst Milch. Die Befehlshaber der Legion Condor und Oberst d. G. Warlimont schließen sich an.
5. Nachdem der Führer die Front abgeschritten hat, begibt er sich in sein Arbeitszimmer. Es folgen ihm alle deutschen und ausländischen Generale und Admirale. Die anderen angetretenen Offiziere und Unteroffiziere begeben sich sofort in den Mosaiksaal und Speisesaal und verteilen sich dort auf die Tische. Die auf der Rückseite namentlich aufgeführten Offiziere und Unteroffiziere nehmen an den numerierten Tischen Platz. Es bleiben alle Herren an ihren Stühlen stehen bis der Führer den Marmorsaal betreten und sich gesetzt hat.
6. Der Führer wird zuerst an einem Tisch in dem Mosaiksaal, dann an einem Tisch im Speisesaal Platz nehmen. Wenn er den Speisesaal betritt, haben sich alle Herren von ihren Plätzen zu erheben.
7. Nach dem Essen kann zwanglos herumgegangen werden.
8. Das Rauchen ist in sämtlichen Räumen der Reichskanzlei nicht gestattet, auch nicht im Ehrenhof und Garten.

Strict rules of behavior were laid down for those attending the banquet in the Reich Chancellery that followed the parade.

S P E I S E S A A L

TISCH 11:

General **Don Juan Yague**
Generalmajor **Battisti**
General d. Fl. z. D. **Wilberg**
Generalmajor Frhr. **von Richthofen**
Konteradmiral **Fanger**
Oberst Ritter **von Thoma**
Oberstleutnant **von Donat**
Major **Neudörffer**
Major **Harlinghausen**
Major **Wolff**
Hauptmann **Schellmann**
Hauptmann **Harder**
Oberleutnant Graf **Hoyos**
Oberleutnant **Bertram**
Oberleutnant **Oesau**
Oberleutnant **Enzlen**
Oberfeldwebel **Hofmann**
Oberfeldwebel **West**
Feldwebel **Huth**

TISCH 12:

Generalfeldmarschall **Göring**
General **Don Rafael Garcia Valino**
Oberst Prinz **Alfonso de Orleans y Borbon**
General d. Fl. **Schweikhard**
Oberst **Kressmann**
Oberstleutnant **Seidemann**
Oberstleutnant **Holle**
Major **Handrick**
Hauptmann **Aldinger**
Feldwebel **Rochel**
Feldwebel **Brohammer**
Unteroffizier **Betz**

TISCH 13:

Generaloberst **Keitel**
General **Don Camilo Alonso Vega**
Oberst **Aurelia**
Oberstleutnant **Siber**
Major **Grabmann**
Major **Kuprian**
Major **Wäntig**
Hauptmann **Schröter**
Hauptmann **Knüppel**
Oberfeldwebel **Fischer**
Oberfeldwebel **Franz**
Unteroffizier **Bellharz**

The seating arrangement. Seated at Table 11 were three future members of the Richthofen *Geschwader*: *Hauptmann* Schellmann, *Oberleutnant* Bertram, and *Oberleutnant* Oesau.

Watched by *General* Sperrle, the first commander of the "Legion Condor", Hitler welcomes *Hauptmann* Wolfgang Schellmann. With 12 victories, he was second only to Werner Mölders as the most successful German fighter pilot in Spain. On 3 September 1940 he assumed command of JG 2 "Richthofen".

3

Jagdgeschwader 2 "Richthofen" in Action in Poland and France

31 August 1939
This is a day of hectic activity. Recent events have made war seem inevitable. On 23 August Russia and Germany signed a non-aggression pact in Moscow, and two days later Great Britain and Poland formed a military alliance. At the same time, Germany and Poland negotiated over a link between Germany and East Prussia, the so-called "Corridor". These talks broke down after Britain's promise of assistance to Poland. In the afternoon an order is issued restricting all members of the *Geschwader* to their bases. At approximately 2100 hours a telex is received: mission orders for the attack on Poland!

1 September 1939
Hitler speaks on German radio: "We have been returning fire since 0545 hours." "Case White" has begun. Germany is at war with Poland. At the time no one can know that it is also the start of the Second World War, although many suspect it. JG 2's mission is to guard the Reich capital against air attack.

1 September 1939
When war comes JG 2's units are situated at the following airfields:

Luftgaukommando III Berlin

	Stab/JG 2 "R"
	Oberst Gerd von Massow
	Straussberg
	Bf 109 E
Authorized strength	3
Actual strength	3
	I. Gruppe
	Major Carl Viek
	Straussberg
	Bf 109 E
Authorized strength	41
Actual strength	40
	10. (N)/Staffel
	Hptm. Albert Blumensaat
	Straussberg
	Bf 109 D
Authorized strength	9
Actual strength	9

The *Geschwader* remains idle on this and the following days. One *Staffel* is sent to Lyck in East Prussia, but it too has no contact with the enemy.

The *Gruppe* is scrambled, but it turns out to be a false alarm. The reported enemy bombers are in fact He 111s returning from an operation over Poland.

2 September 1939
I Gruppe returns to Döberitz. The *10. (N)/JG 2* flies to its new base at Brandenburg.

9 September 1939
The *1. Staffel* is moved to Rostken in East Prussia. All remains quiet, no enemy aircraft are seen.

12 September 1939
Missions are flown into the Grajuro—Augustow—Bialystok area. The intended targets are troop and vehicle columns and railway installations. The first attacks are against columns of horse-drawn vehicles, then trucks and buses bringing troops to the front. Locomotives and a munitions train follow. No enemy aircraft are seen.

15 September 1939
The *1. Staffel* returns to Döberitz. Otherwise JG 2 "Richthofen" is untouched by the war in Poland. Conversion to new equipment and other preparations continue, so that the unit will be ready to support the rapidly advancing units of the army and air force.

19 September 1939
After the conclusion of operations in Poland, JG 2 continues to guard the capital until November.

Early November 1939
I./JG 20, which has been attached to *JG 2*, leaves the *Geschwader* and becomes *III./JG 51*. In its place, *I./JG 7* is attached to the *Richthofen Geschwader*. At the same time, *I./JG 2* releases elements to assist in the formation of *JG 3*. *Oberstleutnant* Viek becomes the new *Kommodore*. His place as *Kommandeur* of *I./JG 2* is taken by *Hauptmann* Roth.

1 November 1939
The *Stab* and *I. Gruppe* move to Frankfurt-Rebstock. In the months to come it will defend the airspace over the frontier between Schneeifel and Saarbrücken and provide escort for reconnaissance aircraft.

November 1939
The *II. Gruppe* if formed at Zerbst. *I./JG 2*, *I./JG 3* and the Schleissheim Fighter Training School provide assets to the new *Gruppe*. The formation process is directed by *Hauptmann* Schellmann, who then assumes command of the unit.

22 November 1939
The first engagement with French fighters. *Leutnant* Wick and *Oberfeldwebel* Klein each shoot down a Curtiss fighter.

15 December 1939
The new *II. Gruppe* commanded by *Hauptmann* Schellmann becomes operational. It is not placed under the direct command of the *Geschwader*, however. Instead it is assigned a defensive role in central Germany.

1939 – 10 May 1940
All quiet on the Western Front – the calm before the storm. The French dub this period "Drôle de Guerre", the happy war. For seven months action on the ground and in the air is restricted to minor skirmishes and patrols.

January 1940
10. (N)/JG 2 operates from the island of Langeoog and other airfields on the East Friesian Islands. The N stands for night. The *Staffel* has Bf 109 D fighters equipped for the night-fighter role and its pilots have been trained in night flying. The *Staffel* emblem, an owl, appears on the cowlings of its Messerschmitts. The unit flies night patrol and intercept missions over northern Germany. It continues to fly the Dora until the end of 1940, although the day fighter units have long since received newer machines.

1 February 1940
At Jever *10.(N)/JG 2* and night-fighter *Staffeln* from other *Geschwader* are combined to from the *IV. Gruppe*. It is the first true night-fighter *Gruppe* and will later become *III./NJG 1*.

9 March 1940
Oberfeldwebel Jaenisch scores the *Geschwader*'s third victory during a patrol by *3. Staffel*. The unit's seven Bf 109s engaged 14 French fighters. Four more victories will be scored before the start of the French Campaign for the loss of one of the *Geschwader*'s fighters.

15 March 1940
The *II. Gruppe* under *Major* Schellmann moves to Nordholz to protect the airspace over the German Bight, the Kaiser-Wilhelm Canal and Hamburg.

15 March – 10 April 1940
The *III. Gruppe* is formed at Magdeburg. *Major* Dr. Erich Mix becomes the first commander of the new unit. The *Gruppe* is transferred to Frankfurt am Main, joining the *Geschwaderstab*.

1 April 1940
Oberstleutnant Harry von Bülow-Bothkamp, who commanded the *Jagdstaffel Boelcke* in World War One and scored six victories, replaces *Oberst* von Massow as *Geschwaderkommodore*. *Oberst* von Massow has been appointed *Jagdfliegerführer* (Commander of Fighters). When the war started *Oberstleutnant* von Bülow was *Kommandeur* of *JG 77*'s *II. Gruppe*.

Early April 1940
The *II. Gruppe* transfers to Frankfurt-Rebstock.

7 April 1940
Shortly before the *II. Gruppe*'s arrival in Frankfurt, the *Geschwaderstab* moves to Wengerohr near Trier and the *I. Gruppe* to Bassenheim near Coblenz.

Spring 1940
I./JG 76, commanded by *Oberstleutnant* Kraut, is attached to JG 2.

Spring 1940
The *Geschwader*'s dispositions at the beginning of the French Campaign:

- *Geschwaderstab* at Wengerohr near Trier
  I. Gruppe transferred from Bassenheim to Kirchberg and Dockendorf
- *II. Gruppe* Münster in Westphalia
- *III. Gruppe* transferred from Frankfurt-Rebstock to Ferschweiler

Areas of operation:
- *Geschwaderstab*, *I. Gruppe* and *III. Gruppe*
  Metz – Verdun
- *II. Gruppe*
  Holland – Rotterdam

10 May 1940
0500 hours local time. The campaign in the west begins: 0635 is X hour. The Bf 109 Es taxi through the thinning morning mist. The Stabsschwarm takes off on a dawn patrol.

Jagdführer (Jafü) Deutsche Bucht Jever
(Fighter Commander German Bight)

II. Gruppe
Hptm. Wolfgang Schellmann
Nordholz

Authorized strength	47
Actual strength	35

IV. (N) Gruppe
Maj. Albert Blumensaat
Hopsten

Authorized strength	31
Actual strength	30

Luftwaffenkommando 3
Southern Sector Bad Orb
Jafü 3 Wiesbaden

Stab JG 2
Oberst Harry von Bülow-Bothkamp
Frankfurt Rebstock

Authorized strength	4
Actual strength	4

I. Gruppe
Hptm. Roth
Frankfurt-Rebstock

Authorized strength	45
Actual strength	33

III. Gruppe
Hptm. Dr. Erich Mix
Frankfurt-Rebstock

Authorized strength	42
Actual strength	11

10 – 13 May 1940
The *Stab* plus the I. and *III. Gruppe* of JG 2 "Richthofen" are deployed in Army Group A's attack sector between Maubeuge and Metz. Operating from Münster, *II. Gruppe* provides fighter cover for bomber units operating against Holland.

In mid-May the *Stab* and the two *Gruppen* move to the Belgian airfield near Bastogne. One week later they transfer to Signey-le-Pétit in France.

11 May 1940
II./JG 2 transfers to Hamminkeln. From there it takes part in the air fighting over Rotterdam.

13 May – 4 June 1940
The *II. Gruppe* operates from Peer, Attenrode and Grandglise in Belgium.

14 May 1940
Oberfeldwebel Machold of the *1. Staffel* scores JG 2's first victory in the western campaign, shooting down a Morane fighter. This is to be a very significant day for the German fighters on the Western Front.

14 May 1940
This is the "Day of the Fighters". German tanks breach the Maginot Line at Sedan. In response the Allies mobilize 145 British and French bombers and 100 fighters. Fierce air battles erupt on a front of 80 kilometers and last most of the day. The *Luftwaffe*'s superiority is overwhelming. Panzer Group Kleist is able to expand the breakthrough, which marks the beginning of the end for France.

German fighters fly 814 sorties and shoot down 89 British and French aircraft.

Most successful is *I./JG 53* with 39 victories. *I. Gruppe* under *Hauptmann* Roth and *III. Gruppe* under *Major* Dr. Mix also take part.

The war diary of the *II. Fliegerkorps* calls 14 May the "Day of the Fighters".

18 May 1940
From the start of the French Campaign the units of *JG 2 "Richthofen"* fly mainly "free chase" missions, keeping the airspace above the rapidly-advancing German divisions clear of enemy bombers. Its area of operations covers St. Quentin, Laon, Beauvais, Cambrai, Arras-Douai, Calais and Dunkirk, almost the entire northern front.

19 May 1940
JG 2 provides fighter escort for St.G. 1 to La Neuville. The difficult mission is a success. JG 2 receives praise from the army group for providing effective fighter cover.

20 May 1940
After ten days of combat in the French Campaign, *JG 2 "Richthofen"* is able to report:

"*Oberfeldwebel* Machold has scored his 5th and the *Geschwader*'s 100th victory."

21 May 1940
Major Dr. Mix, *Kommandeur* of the *III. Gruppe*, shoots down a French Morane fighter. As he does so, he is attacked by another enemy fighter, which shoots him down in flames. Wounded, *Major* Mix bales out of his spinning machine. The 42-year-old *Major* hides during the day and walks in the direction of the German front by night. On 23 May he meets a forward unit of the German Army and soon afterward is returned to his unit. Three days later he receives the 1939 Clasp to the Iron Cross, First Class.

21 May – 18 June 1940
JG 2 "Richthofen" has enjoyed much success in the "free chase" role. Now it is assigned to protect bombers, dive-bombers, reconnaissance aircraft and close-support machines against enemy fighters. In carrying out this mission the fighters prime responsibility is to get their charges safely through to the target and home again. They are under orders not to allow themselves to be diverted from their mission by engaging enemy aircraft. This mission was surely not to the liking of the fighter pilots, however they performed extremely well in the unaccustomed role. *JG 2 "Richthofen"* provided fighter cover for *II.(S)/LG 2* (commanded by Knight's Cross wearer *Hauptmann* Otto Weiss) from 13 to 20 May. That unit's war diary record praises the job done by the *Geschwader*'s fighter pilots.

28 May – 4 June 1940
The events of these days, what the English call the "Miracle of Dunkirk", will have a fateful impact on the subsequent German prosecution of the war.

The *II. Gruppe* of *JG 2* transfers from Münster to the Western Front. There it provides fighter escort for bomber units attacking the port of Dunkirk, from where the British have begun evacuating 400,000 French and British troops. Hitler surprised both the British and his generals when he ordered the army units advancing on the pocket to stop. One can only speculate as to the reason behind this inexplicable decision. In any case, it could not have been for the reasons offered officially and unofficially at the time, that the terrain was unsuitable for tanks, that the army units urgently needed rest, etc. It is more likely that the halt was a gesture to Great Britain by Hitler aimed at securing a peace in the west. Hitler had never wanted war with England. He viewed the people of the island kingdom as a sort of brother Germanic race and was surprised by England's declaration of war, believing to the end that it would not happen. Another factor that may have influenced Hitler's decision was Göring's claim that his air force alone could halt the evacuation of the Allied forces.

Over Dunkirk the German air force meets large numbers of British Spitfire fighter aircraft for the first time.

Determined to save their expeditionary corps, the RAF commits the fighter squadrons it has been holding in reserve. For the first time the Messerschmitt pilots encounter aircraft that is, in many respects, equal or superior to theirs. For the first time in the war the *Luftwaffe* suffers significant losses.

Generalfeldmarschall Kesselring, Commander-in-Chief of *Luftflotte 2*, later declares that the massive commitment of RAF fighters made possible the evacuation of Dunkirk. For an entire week the German army sits idly by and watches the evacuation.

338,000 men, mostly British, are saved. The German army is not prepared for an invasion of England, saving Great Britain when it is most vulnerable.

The British Isles remain an unsinkable aircraft carrier from which Britain and its allies can launch air raids on Germany.

1 and 2 June 1940
The *Stab* and both *Gruppen* of *JG 2* arrive at Couvron near Laon. *JG 2* leaves *II. Fliegerkorps* and comes under the command of *VIII. Fliegerkorps*.

3 June 1940
Large numbers of German bombers with an equally strong fighter escort launch "Operation Paula". Airfields and armaments factories near Paris are attacked and heavily damaged.

The *Gruppe* shoots down 12 French fighters.

Oberst von Massow, former *Kommodore* of *JG 2*, is shot down by anti-aircraft fire 20 km north of Paris. He successfully bales out of his Bf 109 and manages to reach the German lines.

4 June 1940
Dunkirk falls to German forces.

5 June 1940
I./JG 76, which with 60 victories has made a major contribution to *JG 2*'s success, leaves the *Geschwader*. It is replaced by II./JG 2, which arrived at Monceau-le-Vast the day before. All three *Gruppen* are now under the *Geschwader*'s direct command.

5 June 1940
0400 hours. The German armies launch a new offensive. It begins with a massive artillery barrage and heavy bombing attacks by Stukas and conventional bombers. *JG 2* escorts bombers attacking targets in Paris. In the days that follow, it switches to attacks against ground targets: infantry and vehicle columns, horse-drawn artillery and limbered machine-guns, tanks, and infantry, anti-aircraft and artillery positions. Every military movement on the ground is paralyzed or hindered.

6 June 1940
JG 2 reports its 200th victory.

7 June 1940
German troops breach the Weygand Line on the Somme along its entire length. It is the last line of defense before the French capital.

10 June 1940
Railway stations, railway installations and trains, especially locomotives, are now added to the list of targets. French supply traffic is paralyzed. Attacks on airfields are intensified and many enemy aircraft are destroyed on the ground.

During the course of the French campaign the *Armée de l'Air*, the French air force, is largely destroyed on the ground. In addition to attacks against ground targets, *JG 2* is frequently called upon to provide fighter escort for formations of bombers. Although the pilots are more used to free chase missions, the successfully carry out this assignment as well.

4 – 15 June 1940
The war diary of *St.G. 2 "Immelmann"*, which operated with the fighters of JG 2 in these days, is full of praise for the effectiveness of the fighter escort provided by the *Richthofen Geschwader*. Ignoring enemy fire, the fighters stay with the Stukas through their diving attacks.

6 – 15 June 1940
Fighters of *JG 2* fly escort for reconnaissance aircraft of *2. (F)/123*. The reconnaissance unit acknowledges the vital role of the fighter escort in the successful completion of its missions.

Fighters of the *Richthofen Geschwader* also fly escort for the close-support aircraft of *Hauptmann* Weiß' *Gruppe*.

The following is a breakdown of the *Geschwader*'s missions:

Type	Sorties	Victories
Free chase	209	177
Stuka escort	237	8
Bomber escort	84	7
Reconnaissance escort	43	3
Close-support escort	78	8
Total	651	203

The operational descriptions and statistics are from a report by *JG 2* to the commanding general of *V. Fliegerkorps*, *Generalleutnant Ritter* von Greim, dated 16 July 1940.

The following is a breakdown by percentages:

Type	Percentage	Percentage of Victories
Free chase	32%	87%
Escort	68%	13%

Conclusions:
Until now the success achieved by the fighters has been measured only by the number of victories and not their overall success. Escort missions have made up 68% of all missions flown and almost no credit has been given to the discipline shown by the pilots in carrying out these missions, which surely denied them further victories. As well, the ground-attack missions flown after resistance in the air diminished have received little recognition. In some cases the results have had much more military value than one or two victories. Since these ground-attack missions sometimes face heavy defensive fire, they must be considered equal to the successful participation in an air battle.

End of report to the air corps.

12 – 13 June 1940
The *II. Gruppe* is now operating from Oulchy-le-Château, not far from where the *Richthofen Geschwader* was based during the First World War. Four days later it moves to Marigny, where the *Gruppe* remains until the end of the campaign in France.

13 June 1940
The German divisions are at the gates of Paris. Low-level attacks near Château-Thierry. Eight enemy aircraft are destroyed on the ground in an attack on the Troyes airfield.

14 June 1940
German troops enter Paris. The capital of France has fallen.

17 June 1940
France's government requests a cease-fire.

22 June 1940
JG 2 "Richthofen" has moved into the Evreux area and is attached to the *V. Fliegerkorps*. *Hauptmann* Strümpell, former *Kapitän* of the *3. Staffel*, assumed command of *I. Gruppe* after *Hauptmann* Roth, who is ill, is transferred to the air ministry.

For the months to come the *Richthofen Geschwader* will operate from the airfield at Beaumont-le-Roger. Quarters and hangars must be built before operations can commence.

25 June 1940
The guns fall silent at 0035 hours, the cease-fire takes effect at 0200. The *Wehrmacht*'s campaign against France is over.

During the fighting in the west *JG 2* has recorded 245 victories over aircraft of the French and British air forces.

I. Gruppe	123 victories
II. Gruppe	44 victories
III. Gruppe	18 victories
IV. Gruppe	60 victories

The *Geschwader*'s operations in France were summed up in a report written by *Kommodore* von Bülow for *Generalleutnant Ritter* von Greim:

"Several days ago I reported that the fighter pilots have gained the impression that the fighters' performance and accomplishments are not valued as highly as those of the other branches of the air force. Concerning this question I wish to submit the following:

In the past the fighters' performance and accomplishments were rated mainly by the number of victories achieved. This seems quite obvious at first, for the original role of the fighter was to engage and destroy the enemy wherever he was met. This was best achieved by 'free chasing' in a specified area in which the goal was absolute air superiority.

After the start of operations in the west at the beginning of May, the fighters were employed according to these principles and with great success. Soon, however, a new type of operation became increasingly common, fighter escort for bomber and Stuka formations and reconnaissance aircraft. During escort missions, the original purpose of the fighter, to shoot down the enemy wherever he was found, was moved completely into the background. Their sole purpose was to protect the formation or reconnaissance aircraft being escorted against attack by enemy fighters, at all costs. This protection could only be assured by giving up many absolutely certain victories. On countless occasions the escorting fighter unit reported that it had sighted enemy aircraft but had been unable to attack because this would have meant abandoning the formation it was escorting. Even when repulsing enemy attacks, the fighters could not allow themselves to engage in lengthy battles and be drawn away from the unit being escorted.

The vast majority of the 210 victories achieved by the Jagdgeschwader Richthofen came during 'free chases'. Toward the end, when escort missions were flown almost exclusively, there was a clear decline in the number of victories.

Fighter pilots want to and must shoot down enemy aircraft. Only by shooting down the enemy do they see their efforts crowned, and in the past victories brought the only outward recognition. The escorted units and aircraft have often expressed their thanks for the effective fighter escort that made it possible for them to achieve their missions. Only yesterday, when I congratulated Major Dinort on his Knight's Cross, he told me that he felt obliged to thank the Geschwader for the decoration, for he and his Gruppen would never have achieved the success they did without effective fighter protection. This gratitude is not enough to satisfy the fighter pilots, however, for it cost them what they desire most, victories.

As well as inner satisfaction over missions accomplished, outward recognition of successes achieved is an important moment for the spirit of the unit. Under the prevailing conditions, however, the fighter pilots see ever fewer opportunities to distinguish themselves, for in the end the individual is still judged by the number of his victories. While the bombers and reconnaissance aircraft receive recognition and decorations based on 'missions accomplished' and the number of sorties flown, the abandonment of the 'free chase' and the restrictions associated with escort missions have significantly reduced the opportunities for fighter pilots to achieve recognition by shooting down enemy aircraft. It is extremely noticeable that the number of Iron Crosses, First Class awarded to bomber and Stuka units is significantly greater than that of even very successful fighter units. The question 'How many victories do you have?', which is still being asked to every fighter pilot and every fighter unit, should actually not be asked in that form any more, for it in no way covers the question, 'Have you always accomplished your mission?' The danger also exists that the healthy desire for victories that exists in the heart of every fighter pilot may cause him to neglect his escort mission to achieve victories, as this is the only way to achieve 'success' and 'decorations'. The result of this would be that the bomber and Stuka units and reconnaissance aircraft would no longer be able to carry out their missions so successfully and relatively loss-free. I will soon be submitting a list of successful escort missions based on the war diaries of the Stuka units and a list of successful low-level attack missions. In future I request that participation in successful escort missions and low-level attacks also be considered when evaluating submissions for decorations, not just the number of victories."

The rapid advance by the German armies made it necessary for the *Geschwader* to move frequently to keep pace.

Stab, I. and *III. Gruppe*
17 May – 19 May Bastogne, Belgium
20 May – 30 May Signy-le-Petit
1 June – 13 June Couvron near Laon
II. Gruppe
11 May Hamminkeln and Rotterdam
13 May – 17 May Peer
17 May – 25 May Attenrode
25 May – 4 June Grandglise
13 June – 15 June
Ouchy-le-Château, *Stab* and all three *Gruppen*
16 June – 22 June
Marigny-le-Grand, end of the French Campaign
27 June 1940
Transfer to Evreux-East and West airfields

The string of short-notice movements required a high degree of precision, planning and prudent action by all areas of the *Geschwader*.

These virtues continued to be in demand in the subsequent fighting in the west.

26 July 1940

Almost simultaneously, the *Stab* and the three *Gruppen* arrive at Beaumont-le-Roger in northern France. This airfield will be the *Geschwader*'s base of operations for a long time to come.

During the Polish Campaign a number of *Staffeln* were moved to East Prussia to defend the Reich's border.

A Bf 109 takes off on a patrol.

No enemy aircraft were encountered during patrols along the border and into Polish airspace.

This aircraft made a forced-landing near Olmütz. With the help of a tripod crane the aircraft was raised and its wings removed.

A truck was driven under the Bf 109, which was then lowered onto the bed for transport back to the airfield.

The war in Poland nears its end. JG 2 did not meet any enemy aircraft in the air during this period.

***Generalfeldmarschall* Hermann Göring, Commander-in-Chief of the *Luftwaffe*, visits JG 2.**

A Bf 109 E-1 of the *IV. Gruppe* of JG 132 in Poland, 1939. In the foreground is the aircraft of *Hauptmann* Hannes Trautloft, commander of the *2. Staffel*. Trautloft would later command JG 54 "Grunherz".
In the background are the aircraft of the *Gruppen* and *Geschwader* adjutants.

Leutnant Erich Dolmasch, Technical Officer of II./JG 2, climbs into the cockpit of his Bf 109 E. At the end of 1939 the *Gruppe* was based in northern Germany. On the fuselage is the black chevron and disc, the symbol of the *Gruppe* technical officer.

Winter 1939-40. The "Drôle de Guerre", or Merry War, as the French called it, saw little action in the air. For the pilots of *JG 2* it meant patrols along the German-French border.

Above: A Messerschmitt fighter takes off on a patrol over the Saarbrücken—Trier area.

Left: *Hauptmann* Wolfgang Schellmann, *Kommandeur* of the *II. Gruppe*, prepares for a flight. His crew chief helps put on his parachute. On his Bf 109 E is the Top Hat emblem used by 2./J 88 during the Spanish Civil War.

A Bf 109 E at Zerbst in the winter of 1939-40. Beneath the nose of the aircraft is a portable heater which fed warm air into the engine compartment. The tarpaulins draped over the cowling were supposed to prevent the heat from dissipating too quickly.

The pilots had to deal with the cold in other ways. Here "Assi" Hahn is seen wearing a woolen scarf. This type of headwear surely did not come from *Luftwaffe* clothing stores. Note the seat-type parachute.

Oberstleutnant Gerd von Massow. He commanded JG 2 "Richthofen" from 1 September 1939 to 7 March 1940.

The *Kommodore*'s Bf 109 E-1 in front of a hangar at Frankfurt-Rebstock in January 1940. The numeral "1" above the *Geschwaderkommodore* marking is unusual.

The "Merry War" is over. On the morning of 10 May 1940 two air fleets of the *Luftwaffe* and five armies of the German Army stood ready to attack. After eight months of waiting, the invasion of France was about to begin. England and France had declared war on Germany on 3 September 1939.

Right: The Bf 109 Es of *II. Gruppe*, parked beneath trees. The fighters are fueled and armed and ready for takeoff. The pilots are at mission briefing.

Noon on 10 May 1940. All morning the *Staffeln* and *Gruppen* of the *Richthofen Geschwader* have flown escort missions in support of bombers and Stukas. While several pilots and members of the ground crew enjoy a break in operations, the *8. Staffel* of the *III. Gruppe* takes off on another mission.

The Messerschmitts of *I. Gruppe* are already in the air at altitude. They have been ordered to conduct a free chase, however no British or French aircraft are sighted.

An aircraft of the *1. Staffel* ready for the next mission. Just visible on the engine cowling is the unit's "Bonzo" emblem, named after the *Staffel*'s dog. The engine will soon be started.

A Bf 109 E of the *3. Staffel* en route to attack a French airfield.

The Bf 109 E of *Oberleutnant* Otto Bertram, commander of the 1. Staffel. Bertram was obliged to make a forced landing near Cambrai, shearing off the starboard undercarriage leg and tailwheel. It was Bertram who introduced the "Bonzo" *Staffel* emblem.

The intervals between sorties were busy times for the ground crews, or "Black Men". Working quickly, but with their usual precision, they rearmed, refueled, serviced and, when necessary, repaired the machines just back from a mission. An aircraft of the *3. Staffel* is seen here. These men played an essential role in the success of the fighter units.

Unteroffizier Hans Tilly of 3./JG 2 poses for a photograph with his Emil. Lying on the wing are his parachute and radio-telegraphy helmet, or FT-Haube in *Luftwaffe* parlance.

Making life at the front bearable—a parcel from home, good music, a glass of excellent Bordeaux and a cigar. The pilot is wearing his life jacket and the Bf 109 in the background has been rolled out of its blast pen, indications that the next mission is imminent.

This Bf 109 developed engine trouble during takeoff. The aircraft failed to get off the ground and collided with a DF shack.

III. Gruppe was based at Signy-le-Petiti during this period. The pilots of *8. Staffel* are on standby and wait for the next mission. On the right is *Feldwebel* Willinger. Six months later he would score JG 2's 500th victory over England.

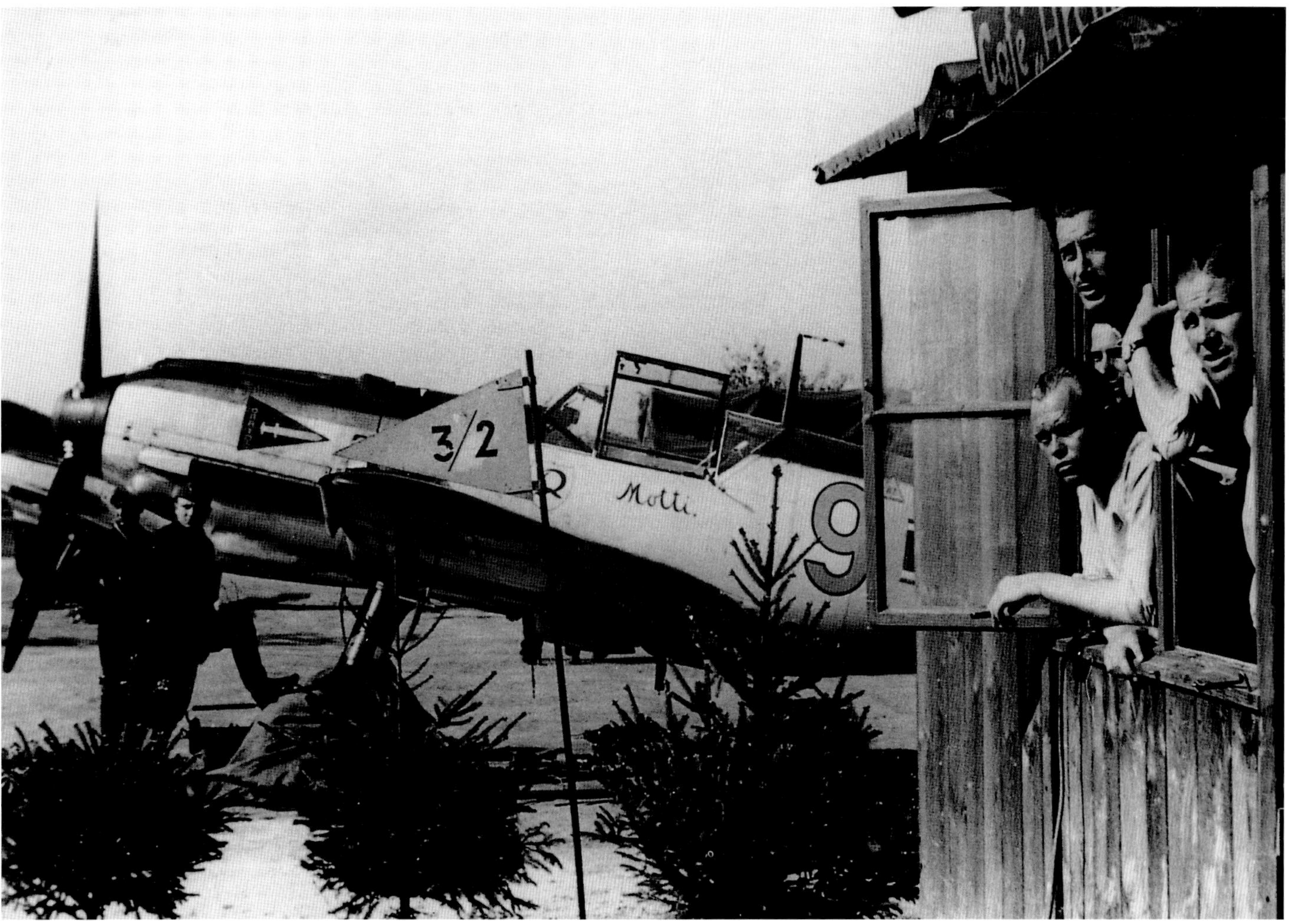

Summer interlude in the "Café Archambault", 3./JG 2's quarters and ready room. In the window are *Unteroffizier* von Moller (top), *Leutnant* Rudi Pflanz (right) and *Unteroffizier* Franz Jaenisch (bottom).

The French Campaign is nearing its end. Army units roll past a Bf 109 E.

Members of the ground crew congratulate *Oberfeldwebel* Siegfried Schnell after another successful mission.

The British Expeditionary Corps was evacuated from France in an operation without precedent in modern warfare, leaving vast quantities of materiel on the beaches of Dunkirk.

New machines were delivered to the units in France after the cessation of hostilities. The machine illustrated here is having its guns aligned. The photograph provides an excellent view of the aircraft's DB 601 A engine.

A Ju 52 transport aircraft of KGzbV 1 delivers ammunition and spare parts.

All of the *Geschwader*'s aircraft received a thorough overhaul. This Bf 109 has just been rearmed. New and difficult missions lie ahead.

JG 2 "Richthofen" suffered only minor losses during the fighting in France. Early in the campaign this machine of the *1. Staffel* collided with a fruit tree in full bloom after a forced landing. The aircraft was torn apart by the impact.

An extremely difficult mission lies ahead. The German fighter arm prepares to meet a much tougher opponent. The aerial campaign against Britain will decide the outcome of the war in the west, but for now there is quiet. The aircraft wait in their blast pens. It is the calm before the storm.

The great regrouping of forces has begun. JG 2 moves to airfields on the English Channel. This tent has already been emptied. The equipment housed in this and other shelters waits to be loaded aboard transports.

4

The Battle of Britain

2 July 1940
Hitler orders planning to begin for an invasion of Great Britain.

Beginning of July 1940
Royal Air Force Fighter Command has 22 squadrons of Hawker Hurricanes and 20 squadrons of Supermarine Spitfires. Each of these 42 squadrons has a front-line strength of 16 fighters, for a theoretical strength of 672 aircraft. Of these, approximately 500 are serviceable at any time. Nineteen squadrons with 200 aircraft are based around London and in the southeast of England. Six of these are equipped with Spitfires and 13 with Hurricanes. The duel between opposing fighter forces is set to begin.

Hitler, who has never seriously considered attacking England, is unprepared. After the lightning victory over France, neither the army, navy nor air force is ready or capable of mounting an invasion.

3 July 1940
Luftwaffe bombers drop mines into the river mouths. Ports and shipping are bombed. Bombers with fighter escort attack convoys in the Channel. For the first time in recent history, England has become a war zone. But the German attacks are not part of a unified strategy and are therefore sporadic and ineffective. Subsequent operations are directed against armaments factories, airfields, transportation targets and known military installations, but they are uncoordinated pinpricks rather than a serious aerial campaign. Meanwhile the *Luftwaffe* has massed approximately 700 Bf 109s and 200 Bf 110 *Zerstörer* close to the Channel. The fighters are under the command of *Luftflotten 2* and *3*.

Jagdgeschwader 2 is part of *Luftflotte 3*. Together with *JG 53* and *ZG 2*, it is under the command of fighter commander *Generalmajor* Junck.

6 July 1940
The *Luftwaffe* intensifies its attacks and continues them in the days that follow. They still cannot be called major operations that reveal a strategic concept.

10 July – 18 August 1940
The first phase of the Battle of Britain begins. The mission of the *Luftwaffe* is to block the Channel to enemy shipping. At first the RAF's fighters hold back and do not engage in combat. Air Marshal Sir Hugh Dowding, leader of RAF Fighter Command, has issued strict orders to hold his fighters back; in fact he even refuses to provide fighter cover for coastal convoys. German bombers begin attacking armaments factories, airfields, rail installations and coastal fortifications. This is only a foretaste of what is to come, nevertheless in England 10 July 1940 is regarded as the start of the Battle of Britain.

16 July 1940
Hitler orders preparations to begin for "Operation Sea Lion", the invasion of England. It had never been his intention to attack England. This is reflected in the *Wehrmacht*'s total lack of preparation. The *Kriegsmarine* is far too weak to cover a crossing of the Channel or provide the necessary transport capacity and landing craft. Work begins to convert vessels used on the Rhine into landing craft with which to transport the first wave to England.

The army units selected for the landings are equally unprepared. They begin embarkation and landing exercises, however they are small in scale and their only value is for propaganda. If the operation is to have any chance of success, the *Luftwaffe* must first win unconditional air superiority over the Channel and the areas of coastline chosen for the landings.

19 July 1940
Hitler gives his famous "appeal to reason " speech to the German Reichstag in which he makes a peace offer to Great Britain. Even now it is difficult to say whether or not he was serious. There is some reason to think that he was, for Hitler viewed the British as a Germanic "brother race". But this "brother race" rejected peace with Hitler. England was suspicious of a strong Germany. On the one hand it had been disappointed by the events of the past, on the other Germany had become too strong in Europe for the British. It had always been English policy to oppose the strongest power on the Continent and in the past it had made alliances based on this concept. Now the *Luftwaffe* would have to force the decision.

30 July 1940
The *Wehrmacht* communiqué reported an increase in German air operations over the Channel. Escorted by fighters of *JG 2 "Richthofen"*, dive-bombers attack the port city of Dover. Fifteen British fighters are shot down.

Losses mount rapidly on both sides. For the first time, the Germans are dealing with an enemy who cannot be overrun in the first assault, for its territory is an island and this foe fights back. The decisive battle with the British fighters does not materialize. RAF Fighter Command does not accept battle the way the German side has hoped and planned. When the British fighters do accept combat, there are German losses. The combination of the Spitfire fighter, which is equal to anything the Germans have, and the skill and determination of the British pilots prevent the *Luftwaffe* from achieving a quick success.

2 August 1940

Hermann Göring, Commander-in-Chief of the *Luftwaffe*, issues orders for the decisive phase of the air assault on England to begin on 13 August. It is code-named *"Adlertag"* (Eagle Day).

In the period since the German victory over France, Lord Dowding has formed new units and trained more pilots. The new Minister of Armaments, the Canadian Lord Beaverbrook, spurs production of fighter aircraft. While it is approximately 20 km/h slower than the Bf 109 E, the Supermarine Spitfire is able to outturn its German opponent. It also has a better climb rate, although the lack of a fuel injected engine proves to be a disadvantage. The British fighters are not armed with cannon, instead they have a battery of rifle-caliber machine-guns. When Göring asked Galland what he could do for the German fighter arm, he replied, "Give me Spitfires".

4 August 1940

The *III. Gruppe* of *JG 2* moves from Evreux-West to Le Havre. From 2 July to 4 August the *Gruppe* had been in Frankfurt while its aircraft were overhauled in Wiesbaden.

8 August 1940

The air war against Great Britain enters a new and decisive phase. The *Luftwaffe* increases its pressure against enemy shipping in the Channel. Stukas attack a convoy between Dover and the Isle of Wight. Both sides suffer heavy losses, although the figures published by the two sides differ sharply.

The British Air Ministry reported the following figures: 24 bombers and 36 fighters of the *Luftwaffe* had been shot down. The *Luftwaffe* High Command reported that German fighters had shot down 49 British aircraft, including 33 Spitfires, for the loss of 10 of its own aircraft. This inflated claims were not made for purposes of propaganda. Several pilots who attacked the same enemy aircraft might both claim its destruction, for example. The German side had a rigid confirmation process, however in whirling dogfight involving more than 100 aircraft it was not always possible to determine whether an aircraft that had been fired on was actually destroyed or only damaged. In August alone the OKW reported more than 1,200 enemy aircraft destroyed. According to British records, the RAF's actual losses were 390 Spitfires and Hurricanes destroyed and 197 seriously damaged. The *Luftwaffe* Quartermaster-General's records show that 231 Bf 109s were lost in the same month, while another 80 sustained varying degrees of damage. As a result, both sides developed an inaccurate picture of the other's losses, a problem that was never solved. Had the RAF's claims been true, the *Luftwaffe* would very quickly have been forced to cease operations. The German side's claims for enemy aircraft destroyed were equally optimistic, a fatal error. One other factor significantly affected the enemy's combat strength. German aircrew shot down over England became prisoners of war, while those of the RAF climbed into another Hurricane or Spitfire and rejoined the battle. British fighters damaged in combat could be quickly repaired and returned to action, while German machines with even minor damage were lost. Another disadvantage faced by the Germans was the short range of Messerschmitt's Bf 109 E. After taking off, forming up and joining the bombers, they were left with a maximum of just 20 minutes of combat time over England. Many failed to get back, coming down in the Channel or landing on the French coast after running out of fuel.

The problems facing the pilots of the Bf 109s were made worse when they were ordered to fly close escort for the much slower bombers. This cost maximum concentration, fuel and nerves, but most importantly time. Hitler's bias in favor of the bomber war did not allow an increase in production of fighters, which would have been entirely possible in 1940. Adolf Galland described this at length in his book *The First and the Last*. In it he details the reasons why Germany failed to win the Battle of Britain. These were confirmed by Galland and others in conversations with the author.

11 August 1940

The aerial offensive against Great Britain is stepped up. At 0900 hours the *Luftwaffe* units assemble at Cherbourg/Théville. III./JG 2 had taken off from Le Havre at 0845 hours and flown to Cherbourg, where it landed at about 0845. At 1055 hours it takes off for England. Over Portland and the Isle of Wight large numbers of enemy fighters intercept the German bombers. JG 2 returns at 1203 hours. It claims 22 enemy aircraft shot down for the loss of three of its own. Other sources place the *Gruppe*'s losses at eight aircraft and five pilots.

The *Geschwader* is now based near the coast at Le Havre, Calais and Cherbourg. Paul Temme, a young *Leutnant* in the *Stabsschwarm* of *JG 2 "Richthofen"*, wrote in his diary: "We had orders to pin down the British fighters for 35 minutes at any cost. Returning before that was out of the question." *Leutnant* Wick claims three victories on this day. The *Wehrmacht* High Command reports 90 enemy aircraft shot down on the entire Channel front for the loss of 26 German machines. The Commander-in-Chief of *Luftflotte 3*, *Generalfeldmarschall* Sperrle, expresses his appreciation to the fighter pilots.

12 August 1940

On this day the Stukas make one of their last attacks against British radar stations. Radar is a decisive advantage, for it provides early warning of a German attack. On 15 August Göring orders attacks on the radar stations halted, as none has yet been put out of action.

13 August 1940

On this day *JG 2* is stationed at the following airfields:

Luftflottenkommando 3 Headquarters Paris
VIII. Fliegerkorps Deauville
Jagdflieger 3 Deauville

Stab JG 2 "R"
Oberstleutnant Harry von Bülow-Bothkamp
Beaumont-le-Roger

Authorized strength	3
Actual strength	3

I. Gruppe
Hauptmann Henning Strümpel
Beaumont-le-Roger

Authorized strength	34
Actual strength	32

II. Gruppe
Hauptmann Wolfgang Schellmann
Beaumont-le-Roger

Authorized strength	36
Actual strength	28

III. Gruppe
Major Dr. Erich Mix
Le Havre

Authorized strength	32
Actual strength	28

13 August 1940

This day goes into the history of the Second World War as "*Adlertag*". England is to be brought to its knees with nonstop attacks. *Gefreiter* "Jupp" Bigge, a pilot in the *8. Staffel*, wrote: "The strong fighter and flak defenses (the latter especially around London and Portsmouth) have made these weeks much tougher for the fighter pilots than the days of the buildup. Almost every mission results in fierce fights with formations of Hurricanes or Spitfires. On this day the fighting reached a new height. We were ordered to attack the war port of Portsmouth and airfields to the south and southeast of London in bad weather. 'Eagle Day', as it was codenamed in Göring's order for the action issued eleven days before, was to decide the battle."

2,000 German aircraft—Stukas, bombers, destroyers and fighters—are supposed to strike a decisive blow against RAF Fighter Command and achieve air superiority over the British Isles, but it does not work out that way. Bad weather grounds the *Luftwaffe* until afternoon. On this and the following days, the *Luftwaffe*'s plans are frustrated by continued bad weather and other factors. Both sides suffer heavy losses, but the *Luftwaffe* fails to achieve the desired success. In spite of all setbacks, the German fighter pilots remain confident that they can achieve their goal, namely to protect the bombers, engage the British fighters and achieve air superiority. On many days the *Luftwaffe* commits 500 aircraft. Attacks on airfields in the southeast and around London are especially successful. But possible success is denied by a shift in targeting by Hitler. The *Luftwaffe* enjoys a number of advantages in its attacks on airfields in the southeast of England. The bombers cross the Channel so quickly that the RAF fighters are often caught on the ground. Nevertheless, the *Luftwaffe* fails to achieve its main objective of engaging and destroying the British fighters.

On 13 August the *Luftwaffe* flies 1,485 sorties and many thousands more in the days that follow, but it fails to achieve air superiority. There are many reasons for this. One is the cessation of raids on British radar stations on 12 August. Had these attacks continued, RAF Fighter Command might have faced a serious crisis. More advanced than its German counterpart, the British radar system allowed them to direct their fighters onto incoming German aircraft. The British had other aircraft reporting systems, but without radar there would have been no early warning. Another reason was the bad weather, which frequently granted a respite to the hard-pressed British fighters. Most of the young pilots on both sides were nearing the point of exhaustion. The high pace of operations wore down men and machines. Germany's attempt to achieve air superiority over Great Britain, a vital condition for a possible invasion, had failed.

18 August 1940

This day, which English historian describes in detail in his book *The Hardest Day*, ends the first phase of the Battle of Britain. The German objective on 18 August is to smash the RAF's fighter airfields, however it ends as a black day for the *Luftwaffe*. The Stuka units suffer such heavy losses in men and machines that they are gradually withdrawn from the fighting over England. The bomber units also suffer heavily; losses in experienced crews can no longer be made good. The Bf 110 "destroyers", which Göring once called his "Ironsides", suffer further heavy losses. From this day forth they require their own escort of single-engine fighters. Though heavily armed, the *Zerstörer* are too slow and are far less maneuverable than the British fighters. The British fighter units lose 183 pilots in the period from 8 to 18 August and are forced to commit inexperienced personnel just out of flying school. The bloodletting continues on both sides.

22 August 1940

Oberstleutnant von Bülow-Bothkamp, *Kommodore* of *JG 2*, is awarded the Knight's Cross. He is the first member of the *Geschwader* to receive the coveted decoration.

26 August 1940

JG 2 receives special mention in the *Wehrmacht* High Command's communiqué: "On 25 August German aircraft attacked the Warmwell airfield northwest of Portland. The enemy lost 72 aircraft in the raid. During the fighting *JG 2* passed the 250 victory mark. *Oberleutnant* Wick scored his 19th and 20th victories."

27 August 1940

Helmut Wick is awarded the Knight's Cross after his 20th victory. He is the second officer of *JG 2* to receive the decoration. His role model is *Hauptmann* Werner Mölders. Wick began his career as a fighter pilot with *I./JG 53*, then commanded by Mölders. The

Gruppenkommandeur gave him a chance to show what he could do, and when Wick left *I./JG 53* he took with him one of Mölders principles that he taken to heart:

"A fighter pilot who is not also a unit leader is of no use to me, no matter how many victories he has!"

End of August 1940

It appears that the *Luftwaffe* command's belief that air attacks are the only way to force the English to seek peace is being proved right. With each day the British defenses are weakening. One-quarter of Fighter Command's pilots have been put out of action and the situation has become extremely serious.

A central problem for both sides is the steadily increasing losses among experienced pilots. The British fought the war against Germany in a pragmatic and uncompromising way, which led to some very harsh measures. German pilots were fired at in their parachutes, for example. The British war cabinet also issued an order for German air-sea rescue aircraft to be forced down or destroyed, in order to prevent downed German crews from returning to action. It should be mentioned that the majority of British pilots disregarded the order. In many cases they, like their German foes, circled over downed airmen drifting in the Channel until rescued.

28 August – 25 September 1940

During this time the *Stab* of *JG 2* plus the *I.* and *II. Gruppe* moved to Mardyk, while the *III. Gruppe* transferred to Oye Plage southeast of Calais. These moves significantly improved the fighter escort for the bombers.

The most successful *Jagdgruppe* in the *Luftwaffe* at this time is *I./JG 2 "Richthofen"*.

3 September 1940

Hitler's growing realization that the air superiority necessary for the invasion of England cannot be achieved has caused him to postpone "Operation Sea Lion" several times. On this day he names 21 September as the date of the attack.

3 September 1940

As part of the injection of younger blood into command positions of the *Luftwaffe*, *Oberstleutnant* von Bülow-Bothkamp, now 42 years old, is transferred to the staff of *Jagdfliegerführer 5*. *Major* Wolfgang Schellmann, *Kommandeur* of *II./JG 2*, is promoted to *Geschwaderkommodore*.

The *Luftwaffe* changes its strategy. Instead of attacking Great Britain with large formations of bombers, it switches to smaller formations with powerful fighter escort. Faced with simultaneous attacks on different targets, the British no longer able to avoid direct confrontations with German fighters to concentrate on the bombers. The Germans are now concentrating their fighters.

Jagdgeschwader 2 "Richthofen", which had previously operated from the Le Havre—Cherbourg area, now flies its missions over England from the Calais area. This change in tactics by the *Luftwaffe* causes a serious crisis in the headquarters of the RAF. But then an unintentional attack on London by several German bombers provokes a cold-blooded and shrewd response. Hitler's ban on attacking London is still in effect. Shortly before this accidental attack, Hitler had reproached one of his generals because a unit attacked London's Croydon airport after mistaking it for the fighter base at Kenley further to the south. In response to the accidental bombing of London, Churchill ordered six raids against Berlin. Hitler reacted as Churchill expected. The attacks on British airfields ceased. The new target ordered by Hitler was London.

In his memoirs, Churchill wrote: " XXXXXXXX"

7 September 1940

The third phase of the Battle of Britain begins with a major raid on England's capital city by more than 1,000 aircraft. Göring himself comes to the Channel to witness the great event. The attack begins in the afternoon. The *Luftwaffe* has assembled 625 bombers and 648 fighters and destroyers. The first of 38 major raids begins, and its targets are port installations and oil storage facilities on the Thames. Wave after wave of German bombers cross the Channel to London. On the same day *Hauptmann* Helmut Wick assumes command of I./JG 2. His predecessor, *Major* Strümpell, has been transferred to the fighter school in Fürth.

15 September 1940

In three months the *Luftwaffe* carries out 60 raids against London, however the outcome is decided within a week of their beginning on 7 September. On 15 September the German formations encounter unexpectedly strong opposition. At about noon the German fighters and bombers are engaged by more than 250 Spitfires and Hurricanes. The RAF pays a heavy price for this show of strength, but at the end of the day one quarter of the German bomber force is no longer serviceable. German losses total 56 machines, 34 of them bombers. The British lose 25 fighters and 12 pilots. After this day, the *Luftwaffe* increasingly turns to night raids.

13 – 26 September 1940

This week marks the climax of the air fighting over England. The *Luftwaffe* has been unable to eliminate the British air defenses, a vital condition for invasion.

19 September 1940

Hitler orders the disbandment of the invasion fleet assembled on the coasts of Holland, Belgium and France. This is made up of hundreds of converted river barges and other ships of every size and type, although many have been destroyed by RAF bombing. Most would not have survived the trip across the Channel in any event.

23 September 1940

Oberleutnant Bertram assumes command of the *III. Gruppe*, replacing *Major* Dr, Mix.

27 September 1940

The *Luftwaffe*'s attacks on targets in Great Britain abate. Germany's air force has failed to achieve its objective of winning air superiority over England.

5 October 1940
Hauptmann Wick's *Jagdgruppe* engages and destroys an entire British fighter squadron. On returning to his airfield, *Hauptmann* Wick is summoned to the telephone. It is *Reichsmarschall* Göring, calling to congratulate Wick and his entire *Gruppe*. The day's second mission is also over the English coast. Once again British fighters appear, far below the German fighters. *Hauptmann* Wick attacks. He shoots down two enemy aircraft to go with the five he shot down in the morning. This raises his victory total to 41. The *I. Gruppe* records 14 victories on this day.

6 October 1940
On this day Helmut Wick becomes the fourth member of the German military to receive the Knight's Cross of the Iron Cross with Oak Leaves. He is also promoted to *Major*.

12 October 1940
Hitler orders the cancellation of "Operation Sea Lion", the planned invasion of Great Britain by the *Wehrmacht*.

20 October 1940
JG 2 moves to Mont de Marsan by way of Tours and Bordeaux-Merignac. The purpose of the move is to provide air cover for a meeting in Hendaye between the dictators Hitler and Franco on 23 October.

26 October 1940
The *III. Gruppe* transfers to Bernay, where it remains until 23 April 1941.

October 1940
The *Ergänzungsstaffel* (replacement training *Staffel*) is established under the command of *Hauptmann* Krock in Le Havre (April 1941?).

28 October 1940
Reichsmarschall Hermann Göring visits *JG 2* and its new *Kommodore* Helmut Wick. Soon afterwards Wick scores his 48th to 53rd victories. Bertram is recalled to Germany. His place as *Kommandeur* of *III. Gruppe* is taken by Knight's Cross wearer *Oberleutnant* Hahn. Hahn will lead the *Gruppe* with great success until November 1942. He later takes over the *II. Gruppe* of *JG 54*, which is stationed on the Eastern Front.

10 November 1940
Orders are received for the formation of a fighter-bomber squadron, or *Jagdbomberstaffel. Oberleutnant* Frank Liesendahl, who has already flown a significant number of fighter-bomber missions, is the first *Staffelkapitän* of *10.(Jabo)/JG 2*.

16 November 1940
Stabsfeldwebel Willinger of the *8. Staffel* scores the *Geschwader*'s 500th victory. *Major* Wick has contributed 54 of these.

28 November 1940
While on another mission against England, *Major* Wick and his formation encounter the Spitfires of No. 609 Squadron at a height of 9000 meters south of the Isle of Wight. In the ensuing combat *Major* Wick shoots down his 55th and 56th enemy aircraft. No one notices that Wick is no longer in the dogfight. Lieutenant Dundas of the RAF reports to his controller that he has shot down a Bf 109. *Oberfeldwebel* Pflanz is already on the Englishman's tail and sees a Bf 109 go down. He then shoots down the young British pilot. Pflanz also notices a parachute drifting toward the ice-cold waters of the Channel. It must have been *Major* Wick. The air-sea rescue service is notified immediately. It dispatches a He 59 seaplane, however there is no sign of the downed German pilot.

All day long the *Richthofen Geschwader* waits for some sign that its beloved *Kommodore* might still be alive. But there is none. *Major* Wick has fallen. He had just turned 25 on 5 August. At the time of his death *Major* Wick was the leading German fighter pilot with 56 victories. Behind him were Mölders with 54 and Galland with 52. Wick had probably had one of the most astonishing careers of anyone in the German fighter arm:

He graduated in December 1935. Four months later he joined the *Fliegertruppe* as a *Fahnenjunker* (officer candidate) and four months later was promoted to *Leutnant*.

He received his education as a fighter pilot in *I./JG 53* under *Hauptmann* Werner Mölders. There he received the tools that would later make him Germany's most successful fighter pilot.

Wick scored his first victory on 22 November 1939. In July 1940 he was made *Staffelkapitän* of *3./JG 2*, and in July he received the Knight's Cross after his twentieth victory. On 7 September 1940 he was named *Gruppenkommandeur* of *I./JG 2* and on 6 October he became the fourth German soldier to receive the Knight's Cross with Oak Leaves. On 20 October Wick was named *Kommodore* of *JG 2 "Richthofen"*.

Born in Mannheim on 5 August 1915, he was killed in action over the Isle of Wight on 28 November 1940.

4 December 1940
"From the *Wehrmacht* High Command: *Major* Wick, commanding officer of the *"Jagdgeschwader Richthofen"*, failed to return from a combat mission after recording his 56th victory. The *Luftwaffe* has lost one of its most skilled and successful fighter pilots.

Major Helmut Wick will live on in the German people and German youth as a shining example!"

29 November 1940
Hauptmann Karl-Heinz Greisert is placed in temporary command of the *Geschwader*.

30 November 1940
JG 2 flies its last mission of the year over England. The unit is stood down due to weather conditions, training requirements and the need to rest exhausted personnel and overhaul equipment.

October – November 1940: Look Back

The hot phase of the Battle of Britain is over. *JG 2* had scored a total of 281 victories. From August to November eight of its members have received the Knight's Cross: *Oberstleutnant* von Bülow-Bothkamp, *Major* Schellmann, *Major* Wick, *Hauptmann* Bertram, *Oberleutnant* Hahn, *Oberleutnant* Krahl, *Oberfeldwebel* Machold and *Oberfeldwebel* Schell. The *Geschwader* has also suffered painful losses, however, including its young *Kommodore* Helmut Wick. The *Kommandeur* of *II. Gruppe*, *Hauptmann* Greisert, was place din temporary command of the *Geschwader*. Under Greisert's command, the *Geschwader* moves several of its units to new airfields in the winter months of 1940-41. The *III. Gruppe* moves to Théville. From there the *7.* and *8. Staffel* are better able to defend the airspace over Brittany. At Christmas the *Stab* and *II. Gruppe* move to Brest, where their mission is to defend the port, where the German battleships *Scharnhorst* and *Gneisenau* are anchored. During the winter *JG 2* is reequipped with the new Bf 109 F fighter. It has a more powerful engine but reduced armament compared to the "*Emil*".

The New Year 1941

The *I. Gruppe* is based at Beaumont-le-Roger, *II. Gruppe* at Brest and the *III. Gruppe* at Bernay. As part of new tactical considerations, the *2.*, *6.* and *7. Staffel* receive fighter-bomber training from the replacement training *Gruppe* in Dinain.

9 January 1941

In the first month of the new year the *Luftwaffe* resumes offensive activities against England. To the extent that the winter weather permits, attacks against armaments centers in the north and the Channel ports are intensified.

5 February 1941

The British begin attacking targets in occupied Europe and the Reich. In the early afternoon there is a raid by several waves of bombers with fighter escort. The combined German defense inflicts heavy losses on the British. Seventeen bombers are shot down, 3 by flak and 14 by fighters. But the British do not give up. They continue their attacks, using twin-engined bombers for the most part. The *Luftwaffe* switches its attacks to the airfields from which the enemy bombers are operating.

16 February 1941

Hauptmann Wilhelm Balthasar, a successful fighter pilot who fought in Spain, arrives to become the new *Kommodore* of JG 2. He had previously served as *Kommandeur* of III./JG 3, but was seriously wounded on 4 September 1940. Balthasar was the second German fighter pilot to be awarded the Knight's Cross, on 14 June 1940. Under his command the *Geschwader* is forced to reequip additional *Staffeln* for the fighter-bomber role. The idea comes from *Oberleutnant* Liesendahl. The pilots receive intensive training, however they are less than enthusiastic about becoming deliverers of bombs, preferring the pure fighter role.

The Messerschmitts are fitted with bomb racks. When carrying a bomb, usually a 250-kg weapon, the fighters are slower and less maneuverable and require a fighter escort.

February – June 1941

At first the Jabos enjoy the element of surprise and achieve a degree of success. The *6. Staffel* sinks or damages several freighters. The *2. Staffel* also enjoys success and sinks a submarine. The fighter-bombers attack British airfields and harbors. *Leutnant* Erich Rudorffer, *Kapitän* of the *6. Staffel*, distinguishes himself in fighter-bomber attacks. He joined *JG 2* in 1940 as an *Oberfeldwebel*. On 1 May he is awarded the Knight's Cross after 19 victories and successful fighter-bomber missions.

In the first six months of the year the *6. Staffel* sinks two freighters of 5,000 and 3,000 tons, a tanker of 2,500 tons and damages an auxiliary cruiser of 1,000 tons and a freighter of 3,000 tons. The *2. Staffel* sinks a submarine.

29 March – 7 April 1941

The *II. Gruppe* moves to Brest to provide air defense for the heavy cruisers and battle ships anchored there. The *Gruppe* is subsequently relieved by a unit of JG 26 "Schlageter". Meanwhile the *I. Gruppe* moves to Théville near Cherbourg and the *III. Gruppe* to Roquancourt near Caen.

Spring 1941 – airfields used by *JG 2*:

I. Gruppe	Théville
II. Gruppe	Brest
III. Gruppe	Caen-Roquancourt

April 1941
The replacement training *Staffel* leaves *JG 2 "Richthofen"*. It and the replacement training *Staffel* of JG 26 are combined to form *Ergänzungsjagdgruppe 2*, which is later renamed *Ergänzungsgruppe West*.

May 1941
With the war expanding into the Balkans and North Africa, the *Luftwaffe* is forced to scale back its operations against England. The deployment of additional units to the east to participate in the coming invasion of the Soviet Union, together with the airborne invasion of Crete at the end of May, draw more fighter and bomber units away from the campaign against Great Britain. Germany is unable to force England out of the war, and the British Isles remain a base from which to prosecute the air war against Germany.

10-11 May 1941
After a less successful major raid, the *Luftwaffe* halts its attacks on England. The Battle of Britain is over.

Looking back on this chapter of the war, Churchill declares: "Never in the field of human conflict has so much been owed by so many to so few." The few were the fighter pilots of the RAF.

Many historians claim that the defeat of the *Luftwaffe* began during the Battle of Britain, not in 1943-44. The fighter arm never recovered from the bloodletting of those months. For the German armed forces, the lost Battle of Britain was the beginning of the end.

Rare photograph of German ground personnel. It is the calm before the storm. Note the camouflaged aircraft in the background.

Unteroffizier Georg Hippel, one of the veteran pilots. His Bf 109 wears a much-modified camouflage scheme. Hippel was a member of the 8. Staffel.

"Black 9", the aircraft of Gefreiter Josef "Jupp" Bigge. On the machine's engine cowling is the unit emblem of the 8. Staffel, which was based on the family coat of arms of the Staffelkapitän, Hauptmann Alex von Winterfeldt.

Unteroffizier Günther Seeger of 3./JG 2 leaves the cockpit of his aircraft following a combat mission over England. On 26 March 1944, while serving with 7./JG 53, Seeger was awarded the Knight's Cross after 46 victories.

The pilot of this Bf 109 apparently misjudged the length of the runway and rolled down an embankment. Here members of the ground crew struggle to push the aircraft back up the slope.

Above: The Staffeln of JG 2 have arrived at their new airfields on the Channel Coast. Accommodations were the most part rather spartan.

Right: Rearming "White 7", a Bf 109 E-3 of 1./JG 2. The armorers have removed the cover over the fuselage machine-guns. Just visible on the engine cowling is the Staffel's "Bonzo" emblem, partially hidden behind the supercharger air intake fairing on the cover panel. This style of camouflage was worn by the Geschwader's aircraft during the Battle of Britain. It was introduced by Oberstleutnant von Bülow-Bothkamp, the Geschwaderkommodore.

The branches used to conceal these Bf 109 fighters have been removed in preparation for a mission. Here the ground personnel receive final instructions.

The order to take off has been received and the Bf 109 E-3s taxi out for takeoff. The aircraft in the center of the photo is just taxiing out from beneath the trees, while the on the far left, probably unserviceable, remains under cover.

The aircraft of the 3. Staffel photographed during a free chase over southern England. Staffelkapitän Oberleutnant Helmut Wick leads the formation in his aircraft "White 1".

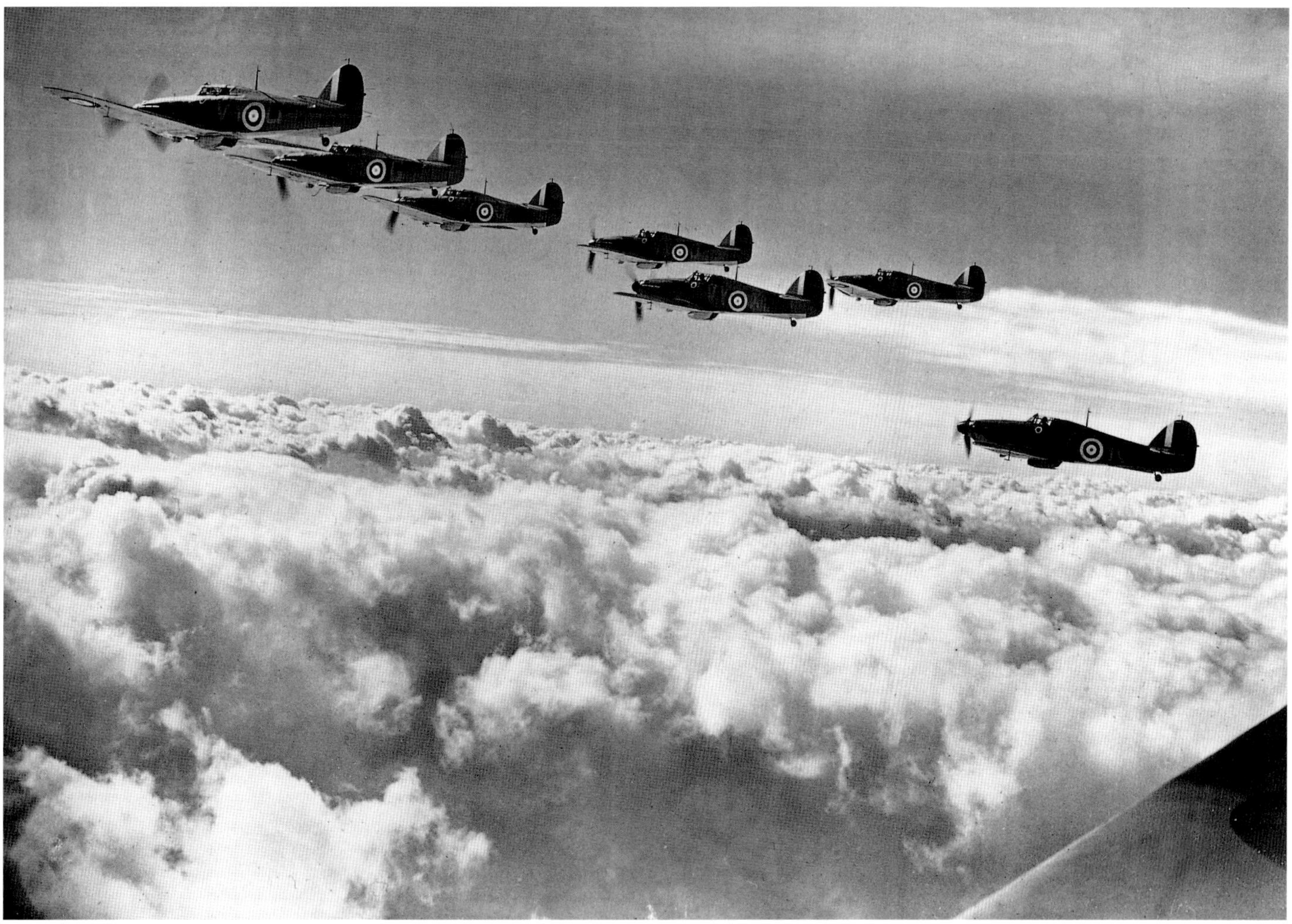

The Hawker Hurricanes of No. 85 Squadron. German aircraft faced the Hurricane Mk I during the Battle of Britain.

A Heinkel He 111 swoops low over a parked Bf 109 of JG 2. Interesting details are the rearview mirror on the canopy, similar to those used by the RAF, and the armor-glass sunglasses in the cockpit.

Above: Oberfeldwebel Werner Machold paints the ninth victory bar on the rudder of his Bf 109. The bars represent 6 French aircraft and 3 British.

Left: Interesting perspective of the engine section of a Bf 109, providing an excellent view of the oil cooler fairing and shutter.

Left: Leutnant Helmut Wick, Staffelkapitän of 3./JG 2. Wick's personal emblem, a pennant bearing the word "Horridoh" and a sword, is clearly visible on the Bf 109's cowling. It later became the official emblem of the 3. Staffel. "Horridoh", the battle cry of the German fighter pilots, has ancient origins. Centuries earlier hunters had used packs of dogs to bring game to bay, urging them on with the cry "Hoh Rüd Hoh". This later became the "Horridoh" of the fighter pilots. Below: Helmut Wick's "Yellow 2" photographed at Beaumont-le-Roger. Note the head armor in the folding hood. The fuselage cross appears larger than usual, the black outline wider. On the rudder are 22 victory bars.

Surrounded by members of his Staffel, Wick admires the 22 victory bars on the rudder of his aircraft. He had been awarded the Knight's Cross on 27 August 1940 after 20 victories, but the intensity of the fighting had prevented him from receiving it by the time this photograph was taken.

Oberleutnant Helmut Wick after receiving the Knight's Cross. The photo shows him with Major Henning Strümpel, Gruppenkommandeur of I./JG 2.

Helmut Wick's career was probably one of the most astonishing of the war:

At the beginning of the war Leutnant Wick is a pilot in 1./JG 53. His commanding officer is Hauptmann Werner Mölders. Wick often said that he owed everything that he became as a man and a fighter pilot to Mölders.

July 1940: Staffelkapitän of 3./JG 2 "Richthofen"

August 1940: Oberleutnant Wick is awarded the Knight's Cross after twenty victories.

7 September 1940: Oberleutnant Wick becomes Kommandeur of I./JG 2.

6 October 1940: After his 42nd victory, Major Helmut Wick becomes the fourth member of the German armed services to receive the Knight's Cross with Oak Leaves.

20 October 1940: At the age of 25, Major Wick becomes the new Kommodore of the Richthofen Geschwader.

28 November 1940: On this day the young Kommodore raises his victory total to 56, however he is shot down south of the Isle of Wight. Posted missing, he is never found.

Wie sie das Ritterkreuz erwarben

Oberstleutnant Schalk — Oberstleutnant Rowehl

Neben Major Mölders ist Major Galland der erfolgreichste Kampfflieger unserer siegreichen Luftwaffe. Nach seinem 40. Luftsieg erhielt er vom Führer das Eichenlaub zum Ritterkreuz verliehen. Generaloberst Udet besuchte den erfolgreichen Jagdflieger und sprach ihm persönlich seine Glückwünsche aus

Oberstleutnant Schalk führt eine Gruppe in dem Zerstörergeschwader des Oberstleutnants Huth. Mit beispielhafter Einsatzfreudigkeit und Tapferkeit hat er seine Gruppe gegen den Feind geführt und zu Leistungen angespornt, die für die Erringung der Luftherrschaft im Westen und damit für den Verlauf der gesamten Operationen von wesentlicher Bedeutung gewesen sind.

Oberstleutnant Rowehl hat die Durchführung der Großraum-Bilderkundung auf sämtlichen Kriegsschauplätzen in unermüdlichem Schaffen, mit höchstem organisatorischem Geschick vorbereitet und geleitet. Er hat durch seine vorbildliche Arbeit die Grundlagen für das Gelingen aller bisherigen Operationen gegeben und sich damit Verdienste von entscheidender Bedeutung um die Gesamtkriegführung erworben.

Major Schellmann hat zehn Luftsiege errungen und dank seiner mitreißenden Führung und seines persönlichen Einsatzes das von ihm geführte Geschwader zu großen Erfolgen in zahlreichen Luftkämpfen angespornt. Er wurde am 19. Juli 1940 außer der Reihe zum Major befördert und führt als Kommodore ein Jagdgeschwader.

Major Lützow hat vierzehn Gegner in der Luft abgeschossen und ist seinen Besatzungen stets ein leuchtendes Vorbild eines tapferen Geschwaderkommodores, der seinen Verband in allen Luftschlachten hervorragend führt. Er nahm als Freiwilliger der Legion Condor am spanischen Befreiungskrieg teil. Aus Spanien kehrte er mit dem Spanienkreuz in Gold mit Brillanten und zahlreichen anderen Auszeichnungen nach Deutschland zurück.

Oberleutnant Joppien, der am 19. Juli 1912 als Sohn eines Arbeiters in Bochum geboren wurde und nach seiner Beförderung zum Leutnant im Dezember 1938 bald Verwendung als Staffeloffizier in einem Jagdgeschwader fand, konnte sich gleichfalls bei zahlreichen Feindflügen durch großen Schneid und überragende Tapferkeit wiederholt auszeichnen.

Oberleutnant Schwarzmann, der bekannte Olympiasieger im Geräteturnen, wurde als Fallschirmabspringer im Einsatz bei Rotterdam schwer verwundet, ist aber jetzt bereits so weit hergestellt, daß er sich schon wieder an seinen geliebten Turngeräten betätigen kann. Vor dem Feind hat er sich durch besonderen Schneid ausgezeichnet.

Oberleutnant Brandenburg hat sich in zahlreichen Einsätzen sowohl in Polen als auch im Westen als Stuka-Flugzeugführer und als Staffelführer hervorgetan. Einen Kreuzer, drei Zerstörer, zwei Transporter und zwei Frachter konnte die von ihm geführte Staffel versenken, außerdem zahlreiche Landziele wirksam mit Bomben belegen.

Oberleutnant Jabs wurde am 14. November 1917 als Sohn eines Oberinspektors geboren. Er trat als Fahnenjunker bei der Luftwaffe ein und wurde als Leutnant in ein Zerstörergeschwader versetzt. Seit dem 1. August 1940 ist er Oberleutnant und hat bereits seinen 17. Luftsieg errungen.

Leutnant Sprick wurde am 29. November 1917 zu Biesen, Kreis Lemgo, Lippe, als Sohn eines Bauern geboren. Nach seiner fliegerischen Au[s]bildung wurde er zum Fähnrich und im November 19[..] zum Leutnant befördert. Er hat sich als Flugzeugführ[er] in einem Jagdgeschwader hervorgetan und ausgezeichn[et].

Feldwebel Eichloff ist einer der besten und zähest[en] Flugzeugführer in seinem Geschwader. Bei zahlreich[en] Feindflügen erzielte er durch seine Tapferkeit, Einsa[tz]freudigkeit und sein Draufgängertum große Erfolge.

Major Schellmann — Major Lützow

Oberleutnant Joppien — Oberleutnant Schwarzmann

Oberleutnant Brandenburg — Oberleutnant Jabs — Leutnant Sprick — Feldwebel Eichloff

Zum Bilde links: Als viertem Offizier der deutschen Wehrmacht überreichte der Führer Hauptmann Wi[ck] nach seinem 40. Luftsieg das Eichenlaub zum Ritterkreuz

Aufn. Scherl-Bilderdienst (8), PK Spieck-Scherl (1), Presse-Hoffmann (1), Jost (1), Rohr

Right: The Luftwaffe magazine "Der Adler" published this report on the Luftwaffe's latest Knight's Cross recipients, among them Major Schellmann and Oberleutnant Wick.

Impressive photo of the nose section of a Bf 109 E of the 9. Staffel. The Staffel's mosquito emblem is clearly visible.

Bf 109 E fighters of 9./JG 2, the "Mosquito Staffel", in close formation. The Staffel was commanded by Oberleutnant Rödgers. In the foreground is aircraft "Yellow 8". Note the non-standard wavy line symbol aft of the fuselage cross, indicating the III. Gruppe. According to the directive issued on 14 December 1937, this should have been a vertical bar.

Bf 109 E "Yellow 7" of the 9. Staffel. The aircraft's badly damaged left wing is about to be replaced. The replacement wing may be seen in front of the Messerschmitt.

Unteroffizier Günther Seeger of 3./JG 2 in the cockpit of his Bf 109 E waiting for the order to take off.

Above: A Bf 109 E of 3./JG 2, probably flown by Leutnant Franz Fiby, flies escort for Heinkel He 111s. Visible on the engine cowling is Helmut Wick's personal emblem, a pennant with sword and the word "Horridoh".

Left: Frontal attack by an enemy fighter. This dramatic photograph of an attacking Spitfire was taken by a member of the propaganda unit who went along on a mission in a He 111.

Heinkel He 111 bombers in close formation. The German bombers were the prime targets of the RAF's Spitfires and Hurricanes.

Air battle in the skies over England. The condensation trails left by the twisting and turning aircraft create a ghostly picture.

?Diesseits oder jenseits

Zeichnungen: H. von Medvey

Eine dunkle Rauchfahne kann auf Austreten von Öl sowie auf Fressen des Motors zurückzuführen sein und zu kurzfristiger Notlandung zwingen. Sie kann auch im Entstehen begriffenen Brand bedeuten. Schwarze oder weiße Fahne lassen also nicht ohne weiteres auf die Vernichtung des feindlichen Flugzeuges schließen

Dieses Bild stellt eine weitere Art der Vernichtung von Flugzeugen dar, die Zerstörung am Boden. Flugzeuge, die dem Angriff Rauch- oder Feuererscheinungen aufweisen, gelten als verbrannt. In unserer Zeichnung wären d beiden auf dem Rollfeld in Brand geschossenen Flugzeuge und die in der Halle brennende Maschine. Die beiden Jag zeuge rechts auf dem Rollfeld scheinen unbeschädigt und können nicht Gegenstand einer Meldung sein

Schwieriger wird die Frage der Anerkennung eines Abschusses, wenn die Besatzung des bekämpften feindlichen Flugzeugs mit dem Fallschirm aussteigt. In diesem Falle gilt der Begriff des Abschusses nur dann als erfüllt, wenn die gesamte feindliche Besatzung ihr Flugzeug verläßt. Für die Beurteilung dieser Sachlage ist eine genaue Kenntnis der Besatzungsstärken der feindlichen Flugzeuge vonnöten. In dem hier dargestellten Falle kann noch kein Abschuß gemeldet werden, denn der Vickers „Wellington" hat fünf bis sechs Mann Besatzung, während nur vier ausgestiegen sind

Das untere Bild zeigt eine weitere Möglichkeit der Vernichtung am Boden: Flugzeuge, an denen das Wegbrechen lebenswichtiger Teile (Rumpfende, Fläche) erkennbar wird, gelten als zerstört

Weisse oder dunkle Fahn

Vorschriften für die Anerkennung von Abschüssen

Es entspricht nur den allgemeinen Anschauungen deutschen Soldatentums, wenn unsere Luftwaffe in der Anerkennung von Abschüssen, Zerstörungen und Schiffsvernichtungen so verantwortungsvoll und sorgfältig vorgeht, daß die in den OKW-Berichten gemeldeten Ergebnisse den äußersten Ansprüchen auf Zuverlässigkeit und Genauigkeit genügen. Nach den reichhaltigen Kriegserfahrungen sind Bestimmungen für die Zählung bzw. Anerkennung der nachweislich festgestellten Feindverluste erlassen worden, deren strengste Einhaltung den Angehörigen der deutschen Luftwaffe zur unbedingten Pflicht gemacht wird. Wie darüber hinaus ein gut durchdachtes Kontrollsystem für die Gültigkeit der deutschen Erfolgsmeldungen sorgt, versucht der ADLER hier in sinnfälliger Weise unter Zugrundelegung der wichtigsten Bedingungen für die Anerkennung von Abschüssen bzw. Zerstörungen zeichnerisch darzustellen

Die beiden wichtigsten und wohl auch häufigsten Fälle des einwandfreien Abschusses, den Aufschlag auf dem Boden und den brennenden Absturz, zeigen die Zeichnungen links oben und Mitte. — Darunter: Lösen sich infolge Beschusses oder durch Überbeanspruchung bei Kampfhandlungen von dem feindlichen Flugzeug lebenswichtige Teile, so daß es flugunfähig wird oder auseinanderplatzt, so gilt dies als „Abmontieren" und damit als Abschuß

Rechts: Zeigt ein Flugzeug die „weiße Fahne", so ist sie meist auf das Austreten von Kühl- oder Betriebsstoff auf Grund von Beschußverletzungen oder Störungen am Flugzeug zurückzuführen, hat aber nicht unbedingt einen Absturz zur Folge

Unten: Wird ein feindliches Flugzeug jenseits der Front zur glatten Notlandung gezwungen, so wird das nicht als Abschuß gezählt. Diesseits der Front, d. h. im eigenen Gebiet, wird es als Abschuß gewertet (1). Gelingt es nachträglich, das jenseits der Front gelandete Flugzeug durch Artillerie oder Bomben gänzlich zu vernichten, so gilt das als Abschuß (2). Das Flugzeug zu (3) ist außerhalb des angenommenen Artilleriebereiches gelandet, kann also nicht zerstört werden und zählt nicht als Abschuß

While on patrol, a flight of Bf 109 Es passes the chalk cliffs of the English coast.

A fighter aircraft goes down in flames.

His aircraft damaged in combat, Oberleutnant Paul Temme, Gruppenadjutant of I./JG 2, was obliged to make a forced landing near Shoreham airport. The airport, which is just on the other side of the railway embankment seen in the photograph, is located on the south coast of the county of Sussex between Brighton and Worthing. Temme was probably shot down by Sergeant J.P. Mills of No. 43 Squadron (Hurricane). He survived the crash and was taken prisoner. The Bf 109's rudder bears three victory bars. Members of the RAF and the police examine the aircraft while members of the Home Guard look on.

This Bf 109 E failed to reach its base, probably after running out of fuel. The aircraft wears an unusual camouflage finish. Just visible beneath the cockpit is the Richthofen Geschwader's "R" emblem.

The Bf 109's greatest shortcomings during the Battle of Britain were its vulnerable cooling system and its limited range. Takeoff, forming up with the bombers, flying close escort for the slower bombers, and combat with enemy fighters often left insufficient fuel to return to base. The German fighters could only stay over England for 20 minutes before they were forced to head for home.

Many aircraft, like this Bf 109 E, ended up on a French beach after running out of fuel.

Pilots who came down in the English Channel faced much greater dangers. Force-landing in the water or coming down by parachute were both risky propositions. Rescue had to come quickly, otherwise the pilot soon succumbed to hypothermia in the cold waters of the Channel.

Combat over the airfield. The men on the ground tensely watch the bitter dogfight between their comrades and the British. The pilot in the white flight jacket is holding a bouquet of flowers, probably to congratulate one of his successful comrades.

Kommodore Major Schellmann has once again emerged the victor in aerial combat. The congratulations begin. In the background is a Focke-Wulf Fw 58 Weihe used by the Geschwader as a communications and transport aircraft.

July 1940: British bombers attack Brest and the battle cruisers anchored there. The submarine base at Lorient is also bombed. Leutnant "Jule" Meimberg succeeds in bringing down three of the bombers, however his Bf 109 E is damaged by one of the escorting fighters and he is compelled to make a forced landing. The landing is a rough one and Meimberg sustains serious head injuries and a broken leg. Here he is seen receiving first aid at the crash scene. A medic can be seen holding an umbrella to shield the injured pilot from the rays of the sun.

The Battle of Britain reached its high point in August 1940. The fighting grows in intensity, increasing the strain on men and machines. The technicians work day and night to keep the Staffeln at or near authorized strength.

Here two armorers are seen servicing the two MG 17 machine-guns mounted above the engine. The opening in the propeller spinner was originally intended to accommodate the blast tube for an engine-mounted cannon, however this not fitted to E-series aircraft.

This Bf 109 E-3 of III./JG 2 is seen undergoing an engine change. The new Daimler-Benz DB 601 engine waits in the foreground.

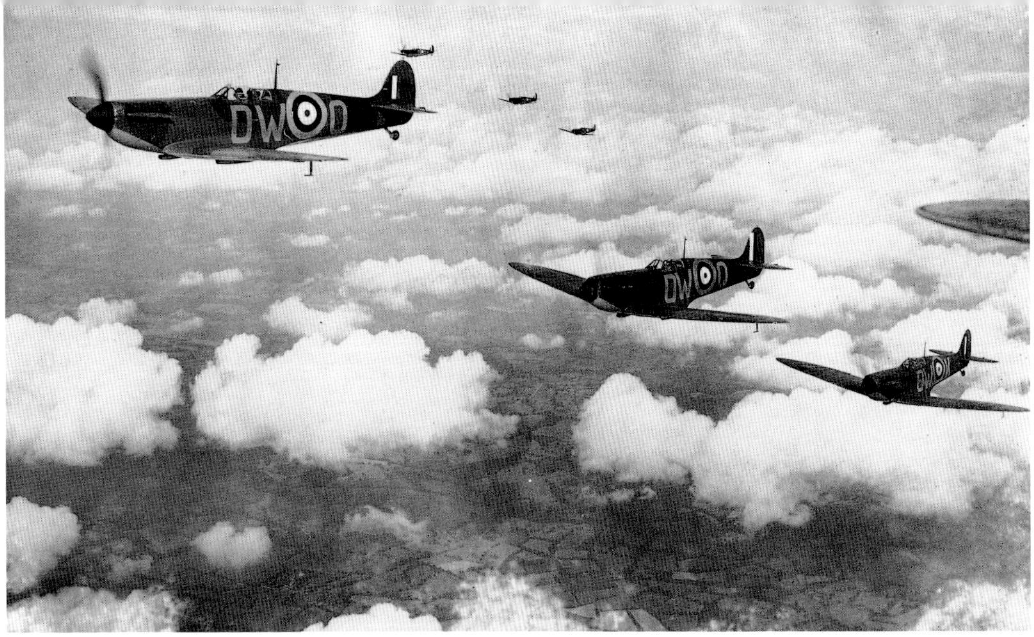

Using radar, the RAF's fighter controllers were able to position the British fighters to intercept incoming raids. Seen here are Spitfires of No. 610 Squadron, based at Biggin Hill in the summer of 1940.

Bf 109s of the Richthofen Geschwader's 9. Staffel over the Channel en route to England.

Dogfight—a Bf 109 E turns to attack a Spitfire.

The first fighters have returned. Mechanics and airfield personnel meet the Staffelkapitän to congratulate him on his latest victory.

The first cigarette—the stress of the difficult mission over the island is still visible in the pilots' faces.

Another aircraft that failed to make it back to base. "Yellow 7" came down on the beach. Here it is seen being loaded onto a truck for transport back to the airfield.

Several aircraft have not returned. Pilots and ground crew wait for news. Have they survived, perhaps as prisoners, or have they been killed?

These rescue floats, so-called "Udet Buoys", were anchored in the English Channel and the North Sea. Inside were medicines, bandages, clothing, food and a small radio. They were intended to help save aircrew who bailed out over or crash-landed in the Channel. One participant of the Battle of Britain wrote, "Well-intended, but the pilots usually came down in the water where there were no buoys."

The airfield at Cherbourg-Querqueville, III./JG 2's base during the first high point of the Battle of Britain in mid-August 1940.

Issuing of rations to the pilots in Querqueville. In the foreground wearing the pilot's scarf is Oberleutnant Bruno Stolle. On the right wearing the life vest is Oberfeldwebel Werner Machold. Machold became the third member of the Geschwader to receive the Knight's Cross after his 21st victory. In September he became the eighth German fighter pilot to reach twenty victories.

Machold's Bf 109. On the rudder are 26 victory bars. By the time this photo was taken, Machold had been promoted to the rank of Leutnant. Here is seen being helped into his parachute by his crew chief. On 6 June 1941 the radiator of Machold's Messerschmitt was holed by gunfire as he flew low over an enemy convoy. He subsequently made a forced landing near Swanage and was taken prisoner. Machold recorded a total of 32 victories in 250 missions.

The RAF also played an offensive role during the Battle of Britain. Small groups of bombers, mainly Bristol Blenheims like the one seen here, attacked transportation targets, airfields and other military facilities.

The remains of an English bomber shot down by a fighter of JG 2 "Richthofen".

A Bf 109 E of the III. Gruppe returns to Cherbourg-Querqueville after a sortie.

The aerial campaign against Britain devised by German planners had two main objectives: to weaken the British armament industry and to eliminate RAF Fighter Command as a prelude to invasion. It is now accepted that Hitler had neither planned for nor wanted an invasion. This position is supported by the facts that Hitler allowed the British Expeditionary Corps to escape from Dunkirk and that neither the army nor navy had done any preparatory planning for an invasion. The following photographs, taken by the author's father, then an NCO in Inf.Rgt. 483 of the 263. Inf.Div., further illustrate the lack of preparations for an invasion.

A standard Rhine barge with the bows cut off and a makeshift landing ramp installed. Such converted barges were to have transported heavy equipment like tanks, trucks and artillery across the Channel.

Simulating a landing: a halftrack (Sd.Kfz. 6/15) tows a light field howitzer over the dunes.

Anti-aircraft defense: an MG 34 machine-gun on a tripod mount.

If one compares these photographs with those of the Allied landings in Normandy in 1944, it becomes apparent how half-hearted and improvised was the German approach to an invasion of England in 1940. "Operation Sea Lion" was finally cancelled on 19 September 1940.

Major Schellmann was appointed Geschwaderkommodore on 3 September 1940. Here he and Major Dr. Mix, Kommandeur of the III. Gruppe, are seen visiting the 8. Staffel in Oye-Plage for the awarding of the Iron Cross, First Class to Oberfeldwebel Willinger. Staffelkapitän Oberleutnant Stolle (left) reports to the Kommodore. From left to right: Stolle, Goltzsch, Ebert (in sailor's garb), Bigge, Zingerle, Willinger (hidden), Schellmann and Dr. Mix.

Le Havre airfield. On the left in the deck chair is Oberleutnant Metz, one of Stolle's predecessors, in conversation with the senior NCO, Feldwebel Rothkirch. On the right are Ebert and Hippel.

A well-camouflaged Bf 109 E in the trees at the edge of the Oye-Plage airfield. Changes in the RAF's focus of operations made it necessary for the Geschwader's units to move frequently.

Hauptmann Helmut Wick, who was appointed Gruppenkommandeur of I./JG 2 on 7 September 1940.

Oberleutnant Hans "Assi" Hahn was awarded the Knight's Cross on 24 September 1940 after his 20th victory. He was made Kommandeur of the III. Gruppe in October 1940 and led the unit with great success until November 1942.

The former Kommodore of JG 2 "Richthofen", now Jagdfliegerführer 2, Generalmajor Kurt-Bertram von Doering (center). On the left is Generalmajor Theo Osterkamp, who would succeed von Doering as Jafü 2. Osterkamp was a successful navy fighter pilot in the First World War and was awarded the Pour le Mérite for his success in air combat.

Unteroffizier Joseph "Jupp" Bigge wearing his life-saving equipment: a kapok life vest, yellow flying helmet cover, yellow scarf, and pouch containing yellow dye markers. In addition to escorting bombers over England, German fighters were increasingly called upon to protect air-sea rescue aircraft during searches for pilots down in the Channel.

Pilots play a quick game of cards to relieve the tension while waiting for the next mission. In addition to planned escort missions, the pilots were now flying more unplanned scrambles to intercept incoming RAF bombers and fighters. On the left is Feldwebel Willinger, on the right Feldwebel Seeger.

Aircraft of the 8. Staffel over the English Channel.

Hauptmann Helmut Wick's Bf 109 E-4 bearing the double chevron of a Gruppenkommandeur and 42 victory bars on the rudder. Visible on the engine cowling is the emblem of the I. Gruppe.

Beaumont-le-Roger, 7 October 1940. Hauptmann Helmut Wick before departing for Berlin to receive the Oak Leaves. Bidding him farewell are Leutnant Erich Leie and Oberleutnant Rudolf Pflanz, both members of Hauptmann Wick's Stabsschwarm. On the right is an officer of the staff.

With the awarding of the Oak Leaves, Helmut Wick was also promoted to the rank of Major. After returning to the Geschwader he watches as his machine is camouflaged as per standing orders.

Keiner älter als 30 Jahre

Deutschlands beste Jagdflieger

Oberstleutnant Werner Mölders.

Sohn eines Reserve-Offiziers aus Gelsenkirchen, der im Weltkrieg fiel, erfolgreichster Jagdflieger der Legion „Condor" mit 14 Abschüssen, Träger des Spanienkreuzes in Gold mit Brillanten, der Medalla de la Campana und Medalla Militar, 1940 Major der Luftwaffe und Kommodore eines Jagdgeschwaders, nach 20 Abschüssen im Westen der erste Jagdflieger, dem der Führer das Ritterkreuz verlieh — und dabei erst 27 Jahre alt: Das sind einige Daten aus dem Leben eines jungen deutschen Fliegeroffiziers, der am 25. Oktober 1940 nach seinem 50. Luftsieg vom Führer bevorzugt zum Oberstleutnant befördert wurde.

Major Adolf Galland.

Der 28jährige Offizier ist Kommodore eines Jagdgeschwaders. Seit 1935 Jagdflieger, nahm er am polnischen Feldzug als Staffelkapitän teil und erhielt zwei Wochen nach Kriegsbeginn schon das Eiserne Kreuz II. Klasse. Mit 50 Abschüssen führte er Mitte Oktober die Reihe der erfolgreichsten Jagdflieger an. Der Führer verlieh ihm zwei Tage nach Major Mölders das Eichenlaub zum Ritterkreuz.

Hauptmann Helmut Wick — 25 Jahre alt.

Im April 1936 trat er als Fahnenjunker bei der Luftwaffe ein, wurde 1938 Leutnant, 1940 Hauptmann. Im September erhielt er das Ritterkreuz für seinen 20. Luftsieg. In den folgenden vier Wochen schoß er weitere 26 Jäger ab und wurde dafür vom Führer mit dem Eichenlaub zum Ritterkreuz ausgezeichnet.

Major Wolfgang Schellmann

Oberleutnant Hans Hahn — 26 Jahre

Major Günther Lützow.

Hauptmann Wilhelm Balthasar — 26 Jahre alt.

Several days later the Berlin Illustrated News published this feature. Five of the officers depicted held or would later hold senior positions in JG 2 "Richthofen": Hauptmann Wick, Major Schellmann, Hauptmann Hahn, Hauptmann Balthasar and Hauptmann Oesau.

The Reichsmarschall inspects the Richthofen Geschwader at Beaumont-le-Roger. From left to right: Oberleutnant Hepe, unidentified, Leutnant Meimberg, Oberfeldwebel Bühligen (who would later rise to the rank of Oberstleutnant and command JG 2 until the end of the war), Göring, Sperrle and Major Wick, who was appointed Kommodore of JG 2 on 20 October 1940.

Above: With the help of his ground crew, Major Wick prepares for another sortie with the Geschwader.

Right: An enemy fighter has been shot down over France. The pilot was buried amid the wreckage of his machine. Flowers have been placed on the grave, while his helmet is hung on a stake opposite the simple cross.

The Kommodore leaves the cockpit of his Messerschmitt after a mission. Note the life vest, dye marker pouch and compressed air bottle for inflating the life vest.

A Bf 109 E of 1./JG 2 parked at the edge of the airfield. "White 11" was the aircraft of Oberleutnant Pflanz, who in 1942 assumed command of the 1. Staffel.

The 1. Staffel prepares to take off on another mission. The first aircraft's engine is already running. Note the Balkenkreuz on "White 15" and the victory bars on the rudder. On the engine cowling is the Staffel's "Bonzo" emblem.

Cockpit readiness for Unteroffizier "Jupp" Bigge of the 8. Staffel. The sunshine is still bright on this day in the late autumn of 1940.

The 8. Staffel's alert Rotte has taken off and is over the Channel.

Major Wick exchanges a few words with his crew chief before takeoff. The smile on the Kommodore's face suggests that the topic was not serious.

After returning from a mission over England his expression is much more serious. The struggle has become difficult, and often the fighters fight for survival rather than victory.

Major Wick welcomes an officer from the air warfare school on a visit to the unit's airfield. Wick's aircraft wears an unusual style of Kommodore marking.

The Bf 109 E-4s of III./JG 2 lined up as if on parade, unusual for a front-line airfield. Note the rear-view mirror atop the windscreen of the first aircraft and the additional armor-glass panel.

A Bf 109 E-4 of 1./JG 2 about to take off.

Major Wick's camouflaged Bf 109 E-4, photographed on the airfield at Beaumont-le-Roger on 27 November 1940. based there at that time were the Geschwaderstab plus I. and II. Gruppe.

The tail of Kommodore Helmut Wick's Bf 109 E-4 with 54 victory bars on its rudder.

Helmut Wick beside the rudder of his machine. The Kommodore is wearing the leather jacket commonly worn by fighter pilots at that time.

Above: On 28 and 29 October 1940 Reichsmarschall Göring visited the Richthofen Geschwader at Beaumont-le-Roger. Here Göring is seen in conversation with Bruno Stolle. In the center is "Jupp" Bigge. Note the cuff title worn by the Reichsmarschall, which reads "Jagdgeschwader Freiherr von Richthofen Nr. 1 1917/1918". This photo was made into a popular postcard in Germany. Above right: 28 November 1940: Major Helmut Wick shoots down his 55th and 56th enemy aircraft. Soon afterward he becomes separated from his unit south of the Isle of Wight and is not seen again. The Luftwaffe loses one of its best fighter pilots and most capable leaders.

Left: This edition of the Berlin Illustrated News, with a photograph taken during Göring's visit to JG 2 on the cover, appeared on 28 November 1940, the day Helmut Wick was killed. It shows, from left to right: Oberfeldwebel Werner Machold, Leutnant Bruno Stolle, Reichsmarschall Hermann Göring and Major Helmut Wick.

The Bf 109 E-4s of the 9. Staffel at the unit's winter quarters in Bernay. A camouflage net has been draped over the propeller of the aircraft in the foreground. A recent snowfall has augmented the camouflage of both aircraft. The Staffel's mosquito emblem is visible on the second aircraft.

Feldwebel Pfeiffer with his dog. Note the three victory bars on the rudder.

The three main phases of the Battle of Britain are over. Heavy losses have forced the German bombers to switch to night raids on targets in England. As the RAF assumes a more offensive posture, the roles of the opposing fighter arms are reversed. Now it is the German fighters that must defend against enemy attacks.

On 16 February 1941 Hauptmann Wilhelm Balthasar becomes the new Kommodore of JG 2 "Richthofen". On 4 September of the previous year he had been seriously wounded while Kommodore of III./JG 3. He was the second fighter pilot, after Werner Mölders, to receive the Knight's Cross. He was awarded the decoration on 14 June 1940 after his 23rd victory.

New missions lie ahead. Here "Red 7" is seen being serviced and refueled.

In January 1941 the fighter units began receiving the new Bf 109 F. Compared to the Bf 109 E, it had an improved DB 601 E engine and a redesigned airframe incorporating a number of aerodynamic improvements, especially in the engine area.

Quiet period at a front-line airfield. Members of the ground crew sun themselves beside the aircraft, while others rest in the shade beneath their wings.

Beaumont-le-Roger at the beginning of 1941. Pilots and ground crew of the 2. Staffel: back row, left to right: Feldwebel Mund, Oberwerkmeister Feldwebel Wels, Staffelkapitän Oberleutnant Bethke, Feldwebel Leipelt; bottom row, left to right: Oberleutnant Griesbach, an unidentified Oberfeldwebel, Fahnenjunker-Feldwebel Erich Rudorffer, Feldwebel Geinitz. In June 1941 Rudorffer assumed command of the 6. Staffel. On 1 May 1941 he received the Knight's Cross after his 19th victory. On 23 January 1945, while serving as Kommandeur of II./JG 54 with the rank of Major, he became the 126th recipient of the Swords after 210 victories. In February 1945 he assumed command of II./JG 7, part of the first Jagdgeschwader to be equipped with the Me 262 jet fighter. He destroyed 12 enemy aircraft while flying the Me 262 to raise his victory total to 222.

A conference of unit commanders with General der Flieger Ernst Udet, Chief of Aircraft Procurement and Supply in the Luftwaffe High Command. Udet is seen here wearing a leather coat. To the left of Udet is Hauptmann Balthasar, while standing behind him, partly concealed by his peaked cap, is Major Galland, Kommodore of JG 26. To the right of Galland are Major Werner Mölders, Kommodore of JG 51, and Hauptmann Rolf Pingel, Kommandeur of I./JG 26.

Kommodore Hauptmann Balthasar in the cockpit of his Bf 109.

In November 1940 orders were issued for the formation of a fighter-bomber Staffel. The 10. Staffel was designated the Jabostaffel and was assigned to attack airfields, shipping and other military targets. On 10 November 1940 Oberleutnant Frank Liesendahl, who had experience in fighter-bomber operations, was named Staffelkapitän.

A Bf 109 E-4/B, a fighter-bomber equipped with a fuselage bomb rack. Two members of the ground crew have hoisted a bomb onto the rack using an hydraulic bomb trolley. A third activates the lock which will hold the bomb in position.

This Bf 109 E-4/B is fueled and armed and ready for the next mission. The pilot is already in the cockpit.

The 10.(J)/JG 2 also operated a fighter-bomber version of the Bf 109 F. here the Staffel's F-4/Bs are seen parked on the unit's airfield. In the foreground is Franz Langhammer's "Blue 12".

The 10. Staffel's dispersal. The first warm spring days have arrived, but the war goes on.

Inspection work on a new Bf 109 F-4/B of the 10. Jagdbomberstaffel. The aircraft in the foreground is that of Oberleutnant Liesendahl. The ship outlines on its rudder indicate the number of vessels sunk or damaged by him.

The 10.(J)/JG 2 is visited by the Jagdführer 3, Generalmajor Max Ibel. Oberleutnant Liesendahl reports while Major Oesau looks on.

Above: Oberleutnant Liesendahl's aircraft. The Staffelkapitän's successes against enemy shipping are recorded on the machine's rudder.

Right: A close-up of the rudder showing the ship silhouettes. On 17 July 1942 Hauptmann Frank Liesendahl failed to return following an attack on a freighter off Brixham and was reported missing in action.

5

Air Defense in the West

The aerial fighting over England in 1940, the Battle of Britain, ended as a defeat for the *Luftwaffe*. While it had been the *Richthofen Geschwader*'s severest test to that point in its history, the air defense of the west would become a crushing test of endurance for the *Geschwader*. Two *Jagdgeschwader*, JG 2 and JG 26, were the only major fighter units left in the west following the German invasion of the Soviet Union. To them would fall the responsibility of defending German industry and population centers. We now know that they could never have achieved this task with the forces available and the indecisive German leadership.

In the beginning, the German fighter arm's main responsibilities in the west were the defense of armaments factories, airfields and other military installations in the occupied territories.

The British soon began launching day and night raids against targets in occupied Europe. Gradually these attacks were extended to include targets inside the Reich. When the United States entered the war there resulted a division of responsibilities, with the Americans attacking by day and the British by night. From the late summer of 1942 the fighting in the skies over Germany grew in intensity, however the German air defenses held.

The German leadership had long neglected the production of fighter aircraft. The development of new types capable of meeting the demands of a defensive war and increased production to counter that of the Americans came too late.

Beginning of June 1941
A reorganization of the units under the command of the *Jafü 3* is carried out. As a result, *JG 2*'s area of operations extends over the entire French Channel and Atlantic Coasts. It becomes necessary to move all elements of the *Geschwader* to new bases.

18 June 1941
The *II. Gruppe* flies to Abbeville-Drucat. Later, in August, the *5. Staffel* moves to Le Touquet as a forward unit.

22 June 1941
The *III. Gruppe* moves to Ligescourt.

End of June-beginning of July 1941
The *Stab*, together with the *II.* and *III. Gruppe*, are stationed at St. Pol, while the *I. Gruppe* is based at Brest.

Their principal task is the defense of German submarines, cruisers and battle cruisers which are based in Brest, from where they operate against convoys sailing to Great Britain and Russia.

The Royal Air Force launches its major bombing campaign at the end of June, attacking industrial centers in northern France and Belgium. Their purpose is to weaken the German defenses in the west and take pressure off the Soviets in the east. In the west the *Luftwaffe* is forced onto the defensive. The focal point of the fighting at this time is in the north in *JG 2*'s area of operations around St. Pol and Abbeville. As the enemy frequently changes targets, units have to be moved often to meet the threat.

23 June 1941
The *9. Staffel* is virtually wiped out while intercepting a major British raid against industrial targets in northern France and Belgium. *Staffelkapitän Oberleutnant* Röders is killed in this action. The *Staffel* has to be reformed.

The British provide their bombers with powerful fighter escorts, which results in heavy German losses in men and machines. But the aerial defense front holds. *JG 2*'s victory total continues to climb steadily.

2 July 1941
Hauptmann Wilhelm Balthasar, *Kommodore* of *JG 2*, is awarded the Knight's Cross with Oak Leaves after his 40th victory. He is the 17th member of the German armed services to receive the decoration.

3 July 1941
Wilhelm Balthasar, *Kommodore* of *JG 2* for just five months, is killed. During combat with British fighters his machine is hit and he attempts to escape by diving. His Messerschmitt loses a wing and crashes to earth. Balthasar is promoted to the rank of *Major* posthumously.

6 July 1941
The British have lost 192 aircraft since the start of their air offensive on 26 June. Of this total, German fighters have accounted for 138.

8 July 1941
The *Wehrmacht* High Command announces the 644th victory by *Jagdgeschwader 2 "Richthofen"*, matching the total reached by the *Richthofen Geschwader* at the end of the First World War. At this time *Leutnant* Schnell scored his 38th, 39th and 40th victories. The *Geschwader*'s situation was extremely difficult. With the start of the campaign against Russia it had become one of just two *Jagdgeschwader* in the west, the other being JG 26. The unit's defensive area extended from Calais to Brest, almost 600 kilometers. The units were continuously in action and losses mounted. As a result, the *Geschwader* usually had just 70 to 90 pilots available at any time, and on some days fewer than 30. The general situation required the *Geschwader* to spread out its *Gruppen* and *Staffeln*. As the British frequently shifted the focus of their attacks, the German fighter units were forced to move often, and this situation remained unchanged until *JG 2* was withdrawn from France in August 1944. In spite of, or perhaps because of, the threatening situation in the west, the pilots and ground crews of *JG 2* gave their all and achieved amazing success. The *III. Gruppe* of the *Richthofen Geschwader* was particularly successful. Commanded by *Hauptmann* "Assi" Hahn, it soon became on of the best *Jagdgruppen* on the Channel front. Its success was reflected in the awarding of high decorations to three of the unit's officers. The *Gruppe*'s fiercest battles were fought over Dunkirk, Calais and St. Omer. *III./JG 2* was also the first to encounter enemy four-engined bombers, Boeing B-17 Fortresses on 6 July and Short Stirlings on 8 July. At that time the *III. Gruppe*'s victory total stood at 141. The *II. Gruppe* was close behind with 125.

10 July 1941
The OKW announces the death of the *Kommodore* of *JG 2 "Richthofen"*, *Major* Wilhelm Balthasar. He is buried beside his father, who had died in the First World War, in Illies near Lille.

On account of the heavy casualties being suffered by the *Gruppe* at this time, the replacement training *Gruppe* forms an operational *Staffel* which is based at Cherbourg.

18 July 1941
In Hitler's "Wolfsschanze" headquarters, *Major* Walter Oesau, *Kommandeur* of III./JG 3, is awarded the Swords after his 80th victory.

20 July 1941
Major Walter Oesau becomes the new *Kommodore* of *JG 2 "Richthofen"*. He declares, "In the spirit of Manfred von Richthofen and following the example set by my predecessors *Major* Wick and *Hauptmann* Balthasar, constant readiness and fulfillment of duty will enable us to achieve further successes!" One of the most outstanding German fighter pilots was now in command of *JG 2*. Oesau had scored eight victories in Spain and was awarded the Knight's Cross on 18 August 1940 while serving as *Kommandeur* of III./JG 53. In February 1941 he had become the 9th member of the German armed services to receive the Oak Leaves after raising his victory total to 40. On 20 July Oesau's total stood at 86 victories.

23 July 1941
On this day Rudi Pflanz shoots down six English aircraft.

24 July 1941
The German battle cruisers Scharnhorst and Gneisenau are anchored in the French port of Brest. The RAF attacks the two warships and loses 23 aircraft. German losses amount to five fighters.

Mid-August 1941
JG 2 "Richthofen" scores its 800th victory.

20 August 1941
Since 22 June the RAF has lost 931 aircraft and 2,800 aircrew in its attacks on targets in France and western Germany.

6 September 1941
In the period from 2 July until this day, three members of *JG 2* receive the Oak Leaves and five more the Knight's Cross.

26 October 1941
Major Oesau becomes the third German fighter pilot to reach 100 victories.

17 November 1941
The *III. Gruppe* moves to the Théville airfield. It assumes responsibility for the air defense of Normandy and also carries out reconnaissance missions.

7 December 1941
The German Reich and Italy declare war on the United States of America. This follows numerous instances of barely-disguised intervention by America on the side of Great Britain.

American President Roosevelt has been determined to go to war with Germany since the outbreak of hostilities in Europe, systematically aiding Germany's enemies. His declarations of neutrality were just a façade.

America's Path to War

14 August 1941
American President Roosevelt and British Prime Minister Churchill announce the signing of the Atlantic Charter.

16 September 1941
American transport vessels deliver war materiel to Great Britain. American destroyers flying the British flag and crewed by Anglo-American crews provide the escort.

7 December 1941
Without a declaration of war, Japan attacks the American Pacific Fleet and shore installations at Pearl Harbor.

December 1941
Germany and Italy declare war on the USA. Immediately after entering the war, the United States begins setting up a new strategic air force in Great Britain. It will begin operations with attacks against targets in occupied western Europe, before launching raids against targets within the Reich. The commander of the 8th Air Force is General Spaatz. Moving the flying units from the United States to England is an extraordinary feat of organization, logistics and airmanship. Preparations have to be made for en route stops in Labrador and Iceland. Meteorological facilities have to be established and bases built and expanded. Thousands of personnel must be shipped to Great Britain. Half a year is to pass, however, before the American air force can join the war against the *Luftwaffe*. At the same time, the Royal Air Force is putting growing numbers of four-engined bombers into service. Germany did not place its industries on a total war footing until several years after the outbreak of war. The mistakes of the past, including those of the *Luftwaffe* command, its executing branches and especially the aviation ministry, now make themselves felt. At this decisive phase of the war the *Luftwaffe* lacks new high-performance aircraft and engines. The performance capabilities of the existing German fighters are still sufficient for the time being, enabling German fighter pilots to record an astonishing number of victories, but they are far from adequate to enable them to meet the demands of the future. The German aviation industry also made mistakes in planning and design, wasting effort on senseless projects which unnecessarily further dissipated the forces of the German armaments industry, which were inadequate in any case.

Mid-December 1941
I./JG 2 successfully intercepts another heavy raid on Brest, diverting the British bombers from their target.

21 and 25 December 1941
The *Stab* and *II./JG 2* move to Brest to bolster the forces defending the warships based there. The *I. Gruppe* transfers to Morlaix with the exception of the *1. Staffel*. This regrouping is made necessary by the concentration of fighter forces in Brest.

January-June 1942
JG 2 begins converting to the new Focke-Wulf 190 A fighter aircraft. This machine introduces a number of improvements, such as an air-cooled BMW 801 radial engine producing 1,700 h.p. This engine addresses one of the shortcomings demonstrated by the Bf 109 over England. Even relatively minor damage to the vulnerable cooling system of the Bf 109 usually resulted in engine seizure, after which the pilot was forced to abandon the aircraft or make a forced landing. The Fw 190 also more heavily armed than the Bf 109, with four cannon and two machine-guns. As well, these weapons were cocked electrically rather than mechanically. The Focke-Wulf fighter's wide-track undercarriage was more robust, giving it superior takeoff and landing characteristics. The undercarriage legs of the Bf 109, which retracted outwards, frequently sheared off during landing and were less robust than those of the Fw 190. The weakness of the Bf 109's undercarriage could cause problems during takeoff and landing, especially for inexperienced pilots. The Fw 190 was also capable of carrying greater loads than the Bf 109 and subsequently became the workhorse of the fighter and fighter-bomber units.

The Bf 109 possessed a superior high altitude performance, however. The *1. Staffel* retained the Messerschmitt fighter for the high-altitude role and was renamed *11./JG 2*.

Beginning of February 1942
The *I. Gruppe* is based at Brest. It leads its own way of life. The enemy rarely appears by day. The RAF carries out several heavy night raids but the warships are not hit. The small size of the airfield at Brest and other tactical considerations result in several flights or even *Staffeln* being transferred temporarily to Morlaix or other distant airfields.

February 1942
The *Stab*, *I.* and *II. Gruppe* move to Calais-Marck, the *III. Gruppe* to Caxyde. "Operation *Donnerkeil*" (Thunderbolt) begins. For the first time in 200 years, hostile warships will sail through the English Channel during time of war. The battle cruisers *Scharnhorst* and *Gneisenau* and the heavy cruiser *Prinz Eugen* have been threatening British supply convoys from Brest, however they are vulnerable to air attack. The vessels will therefore sail through the English Channel to a port in Germany. Hitler also fears an invasion of

Norway and wants the ships closer and immediately available. *JG 2* and *JG 26*, which have about 180 fighter aircraft between them, are responsible for providing air cover for the ships from the Straits of Dover to the Schelde Estuary. Eighteen fighters will be in the air above the convoy at all times. Takeoff, assembly, transit to the operations area, loiter, return flight and refueling and rearming all take time. The available number of fighters is insufficient. Reinforcements come from *JG 1*, and *Oberst* Galland, who as *General der Jagdflieger* is responsible for planning the operation, has more than 251 fighters at his disposal. Even with this number of fighters the *Luftwaffe* is still inferior to the RAF, which has 600 fighters in southern England plus 300 bombers and 20 torpedo bombers. *Oberst* Galland advises the units that the returning fighters must be refueled and reamed in no more than 30 minutes so as to keep the minimum number of fighters in the air at all times. If all goes smoothly and there are no losses, this will be 16 aircraft. "Operation Cerberus", the navy's codename for the Channel dash, begins. English bombers attack the warships as they prepare to leave port but fail to score any hits. At 2000 hours on the evening of 11 February the vessels sail from Brest, one hour late.

12 February 1942

The first of *JG 2*'s fighters arrive over the fast-moving warships at 0900 hours. There is no sign of the enemy. At about 1100 hours a radio transmission from a British fighter aircraft warning ground stations of the presence of the German warships is intercepted. The British Admiralty refuses to believe it, however. The task force, consisting of three major warships, several destroyers and torpedo boats plus numerous minesweepers, approaches the narrowest part of the Channel between Dover and Calais. The first sign of resistance, British torpedo boats, appears. English coastal artillery opens fire on the warships. The *Scharnhorst* returns fire with its 28-cm guns. The first enemy aircraft, Swordfish torpedo bombers, appear shortly after 1300 hours. Eight Bf 109s of *II./JG 2* attack the biplanes and shoot three of them down. The British are now wide awake and commit additional aircraft. Fighting erupts above the task force. Several torpedo bombers break through the fighter screen. Five Bf 109s engage two enemy bombers directly above the *Prinz Eugen*. One of the bombers is shot down in flames into the Channel. The fighters of *II./JG 2* attack the torpedo bombers again and drive them off. Then *Scharnhorst* strikes a mine. The ship is forced to reduce speed and then comes to a halt. *Vizeadmiral* Cyliax, commander of the task force, and *Oberst* Ibel, the fighting control officer, leave the flagship and transfer under fire to a destroyer. Aboard the *Scharnhorst*, damage control parties work feverishly and the ship is soon under way again. Later the Scharnhorst strikes another mine but is able to continue. More Swordfish attack, but the Messerschmitt pilots are alert. The weather worsens, and some of the pilots have difficulty finding their way back to their bases, landing instead at other airfields. *I./JG 2* drives off a group of enemy bombers consisting of one Hampden and six Beauforts. Then a squadron of eight Skuas with an escort of Spitfires approaches the task force. These aircraft, too, are driven off before they can attack the warships. Meanwhile the *II. Gruppe* engages Hampden and Wellington twin-engined bombers. The fighters lose sight of the task force in the sea mist. The fighters are unable to reach their own airfields, therefore the *Gruppenkommandeur* orders them to head for The Hague and Vlissingen. There is only a narrow gap in the minefields northwest of the West Friesian Islands, and a Wellington drops magnetic mines into this gap. A *Schwarm* from *III./JG 2* had sighted the enemy aircraft as it flew in front of the task force at low level, but were unable to shoot it down. Later, at about 2035 hours, the Gneisenau detonates one of the magnetic mines north of Terschelling. Luck stays with the Germans, however, and the ship is quickly repaired. By nightfall the outcome is decided. The Channel dash has succeeded. *Gneisenau* and *Prinz Eugen* anchor in the mouth of the Elbe during the night. *Scharnhorst* and the destroyer *Hermann Schönemann* sail into Wilhelmshaven.

The British losses total 49 aircraft, possibly even more. On this day *JG 2* flies 10 missions and engages in 20 combats without loss.

18 February 1942

The *Jabostaffel* formed at the urging of *Oberleutnant* Liesendahl is now fully operational and is officially designated as *JG 2*'s fighter-bomber unit. Its primary mission is to attack enemy shipping, but other targets include port facilities, airfields and other military installations. Liesendahl, who had gained experience in fighter-bomber operations as *Staffelkapitän* of *6./JG 2*, is named *Staffelkapitän* of *10.(J)/JG 2*. On 4 March 1942 it is declared operational by the fighter commander.

February 1942

Air Marshal Harris is made Commander-in-Chief of RAF Bomber Command. By order of the war cabinet under Winston Churchill he is to wage a bombing campaign against German cities. It is hoped that these attacks against civilian targets will shake the resolve of the German soldier at the front and demoralize the labor force by attacking its homes. In the end they succeed in doing neither. While the British conduct area bombing by night, the Americans conduct daylight raids against armaments factories, railway stations, bridges, airfields and transportation targets. Later in the war the bombers are joined by fighter-bombers which attack anything that moves, including farmers in their fields and even women and children trading for food.

The constant bombing fails to break the morale of the German soldiers and the men and women working in the armaments industry. It in fact achieves just the opposite, strengthening their will to carry on. How could they surrender to an enemy who sought to win by ruthlessly bombing civilians?

Spring 1942

The enemy bombing campaign intensifies. The raids are concentrated in the areas of Rouen, Le Havre, Caen, Cherbourg and Brittany. The lengthening of the defense front and the German tactic of concentrating their fighters forces the fighter arm to become more mobile. The units of *JG 2* are forced to move from airfield to airfield more frequently, most of them in the rear areas.

17 April 1942
Twelve four-engined bombers of the RAF launch a deep-penetration raid against the MAN factory in Augsburg. Consisting of six Lancasters of No. 44 (Rhodesia) Squadron and six of No. 97 (Straits Settlement) Squadron, the attack force flies low to avoid detection by German radar. The Lancaster, which has just entered service, has a heavy defensive armament, and Bomber Command believes that it is capable of attacking targets inside Germany without fighter escort. The bombers are intercepted by fighters of *JG 2*, however, and four of No. 44 Squadron's aircraft are shot down. *Unteroffizier* Pohl of the *5. Staffel* shoots down one of the Lancasters for the *Geschwader*'s 1,000th victory. His victim is aircraft KM-P of No. 44 Squadron, serial R5506. *Hauptmann* "Heino" Greisert, *Kommandeur* of the *II. Gruppe*, scores the *Geschwader*'s 998th victory by shooting down Lancaster KM-V, serial L7565, while *Feldwebel* Ernst Bosseckert of 5./JG 2 registers the *Geschwader*'s 999th kill by downing KM-T, serial L7548. Bosseckert will later be killed in action over Poix on 27 September 1943. *Kommodore Major* Walter Oesau shoots down the *Geschwader*'s 1,001st victim, Lancaster KM-H, serial L7536. *Leutnant* Fritz Edelmann of the *Stabsschwarm* is wounded by return fire. The surviving bombers attack the MAN factory and three more Lancasters are shot down by flak. Only five return to England.

Although the mission is a disaster for the RAF, the commander of No. 44 squadron, Squadron Leader John Nettleton, is awarded the Victoria Cross, Great Britain's highest award for valor. He flew Lancaster KM-B, serial R5508. Nettleton was later killed in a raid on Turin on the night of 12-13 June 1943. Of the *Geschwader*'s 1,00th victory, *Major* Oesau said, "All of us who are familiar with the air war in the west know that this represents a tremendous accomplishment by our pilots and ground crews."

The breakdown of victories to date is as follows:

Stab JG 2	113 victories
I./JG 2	346 victories
II./JG 2	267 victories
III./JG 2	258 victories
Replacement Training *Gruppe JG 2*	16 victories

The defensive air war continues unabated and the fighting in the air in 1942 reaches its climax in May and June.

4 May 1942
Hauptmann Prestele, *Kommandeur* of the *I. Gruppe*, is killed in air combat. He is succeeded by *Oberleutnant* Erich Leie, formerly *Geschwader* adjutant and a wearer of the Knight's Cross. He had previously flown with Helmut Wick in the *Geschwaderstabsschwarm*.

Mid-May 1942
The *1. Staffel* is renamed *11. Staffel* and is equipped with the Bf 109 G for the high-altitude role. It initially moves to St. Pol, later to Poix.

30 May – 4 June 1942
JG 2 "Richthofen" scores 50 victories in just five days, claiming 24 enemy aircraft shot down on 3 June alone. On that day *Oberleutnant* Schnell scores his 58th, 59th, 60th and 61st victories in the space of just ten minutes. *Oberleutnant* Mayer records his 43rd and 44th victories, *Oberleutnant* Rudorffer his 41st and 42nd, and *Oberleutnant* Leie his 48th. The day before *Oberfeldwebel* Wurmheller had scored his 46th and 47th victories, and *Oberleutnant* Pflanz shot down his 44th enemy aircraft during this period.

31 May 1942
More than 1,000 British bombers attack Cologne. The raid causes 1,700 major fires, destroys 3,300 houses, damages 9,500 and kills 474 civilians. The German defenses shoot down 36 enemy bombers.

23 June 1942
The first American heavy bombers, Boeing B-17 Flying Fortresses, arrive in England. In the weeks that follow, 900 American aircraft arrive in England, 882 of them bombers. The first American escort fighters, P-38 Lightnings, also arrive. The Lightning is soon followed by the P-47 Thunderbolt. At first the escort fighters lack the range to escort the bombers to targets inside Germany. The Allies begin the combined bombing offensive while the bulk of Germany's forces are engaged in the struggle against the Soviet Union. The two-front war has become a reality for the *Luftwaffe*. The lack of a roof over Fortress Europe begins to make itself felt.

4 July 1942
On this day six aircraft carry out the first American bombing raid against a target on the European mainland. General Eisenhower, Commander-in-Chief of the American forces in Europe, visits the airfield prior to takeoff and addresses the crews. The attack's targets are airfields in Holland. Results are poor, however, with only two of the six Douglas Bostons reaching the target area. Two are shot down and another seriously damaged.

17 July 1942
The *Kapitän* of the *10. Jabostaffel*, *Hauptmann* Frank Liesendahl, is shot down and killed during a mission against enemy shipping off Brixham. He is awarded the Knight's Cross posthumously. By 9 June the *Staffel* destroyed 20 commercial vessels with a combined tonnage of about 63,000 tons, and the *Staffelkapitän* played a major role in its success. His successor is *Oberleutnant* Schröter, who on 23 July moves with his *Staffel* to St. André.

31 July 1942

Hauptmann Rudolf Pflanz, one of the most successful fighter pilots on the Channel Coast, is shot down an killed by Spitfires near Abbeville. He had been a member of *JG 2* since 1938 and flew in the *Stabsschwarm* with Wick and Oesau. He was awarded the Knight's Cross on 1 August 1941. His victory total was 52.

17 August 1942

The first major raid by the 8th Air Force is a success. Eighteen B-17s led by General Eaker attack Rouen and St. Oterville and return without loss. Waiting for them when they return are the Commander-in-Chief of the 8th Air Force, numerous British and American general staff officers and about 30 journalists. General Eaker is already convinced that deep-penetration raids will only be possible with fighter escort.

18 August 1942

In the period from 13 February to this date, German fighters have shot down 230 single-engine, 18 twin-engine and 4 four-engined enemy aircraft. German losses total 34.

19 August 1942

Units of the Canadian Army, supported by British and American troops, undertake a large-scale landing at Dieppe on the French Channel Coast. The Canadian 2nd Brigade lands in six placed on a front of 25 km, while a large reserve waits at sea in six large transport vessels, three freighters and numerous support ships. In the northern area is the main landing flotilla with 26 transports.

The Allies commit more than 100 bombers over the coastal area to neutralize German coastal defenses and a thousand fighters to secure control of the airspace over the landing zones. More than 300 landing craft deliver infantry, tanks and light artillery to the shore, along with large quantities of arms and ammunition. Defending the coastline is the *302. Infanteriedivision*, which pins down the landing force on the beaches. 2,195 Canadian and British troops are killed or captured. All of the Churchill I and III tanks that land at Dieppe are captured and 127 British aircraft are shot down. The Royal Navy loses four destroyers, 2 torpedo boats, 1 high-speed craft and 7 transports, plus numerous landing craft. Many other vessels, including four cruisers and four destroyers, suffer varying degrees of damage. German losses include 580 personnel and 35 aircraft. The navy loses one submarine chaser.

JG 2 takes part in the defensive effort over Dieppe with its *I.* and *II. Gruppe* and the *9.* and *11. Staffel*. *Oberleutnant* Schröter, *Hauptmann* Liesendahl's successor, and his *Staffel* sink one destroyer and two landing craft and seriously damage another destroyer and four landing craft.

The *Geschwader*'s fighter units claim 59 certain and 7 probable victories. *Oberleutnant* Siegfried Schnell, *Kapitän* of the *9. Staffel*, claims five enemy aircraft to raise his victory total to 70. *JG 2* loses eight pilots on this day.

Oberfeldwebel Josef "Sepp" Wurmheller accomplishes an amazing feat on this day. In spite of a broken leg and a concussion, he shoots down seven enemy aircraft. For his actions he is promoted to *Leutnant* and awarded the Knight's Cross with Oak Leaves.

In the weeks that follow, the Allies restricts themselves to isolated raids on targets in the area between the Seine and the Somme.

6 September 1942

JG 2 reacts to this shift in focus by moving the *III. Gruppe*, less the *8.* and *11. Staffel*, to Poix. The *I. Gruppe* detaches one *Staffel* to Bernay. The *III. Gruppe* intercepts the enemy raids and downs 22 enemy aircraft in a short time, including four B-17s. *Gruppenkommandeur Hauptmann* Hahn scores his final victories before being transferred.

Autumn 1942

German fighter production rises from 500 to 700 machines per month. Production totals rise to 800 fighters in February 1943, 900 in April and 1,000 in June. This is still too little for a two-front war, however.

October 1942

For the first time the 8th Air Force commits the B-24 Liberator heavy bomber. A group of the heavy bombers with strong fighter escort attack Lille. German fighters break through the escort and scatter the formation.

31 October 1942

The *Jabos*, which until now had concentrated their efforts against transport ships, harbors and other military objectives, take off on a special mission against the city of Canterbury. The raid is a reprisal for the RAF's area bombing, which has destroyed priceless cultural sites in Germany. The surprise raid is a success. Strongly escorted by *JG 2* and *JG 26*, the fighter-bombers approach the English coast and arrive over the city undetected. The *Jabos* release their bombs from low level. The British defenses are taken completely by surprise and the Bf 109s are on their way home by the time they react. On the way they strafe targets of opportunity. The escorting fighters shoot down five Spitfires. It is the last major mission of the year.

1 November 1942

Hauptmann Hahn, *Kommandeur* of the *III. Gruppe*, leaves the *Geschwader* and assumes command of *II./JG 54* in Russia. The *Gruppe* has achieved great success under his command. Hahn is succeeded by *Oberleutnant* Mayer.

November 1942
JG 2 moves to southern France to guard against an expected Allied invasion of that country's south coast. There is no invasion and the *Gruppe* returns to the Channel Coast.

27 November 1942
The *8. Staffel* is based at Brest to provide air cover for German submarines entering or leaving the port. Since August it has been intercepting British anti-submarine aircraft operating in the area between St. Nazaire and Lorient, mainly Bristol Beaufighters. To date the *Staffel* has shot down ten of the British twin-engined fighters.

End of 1942
10./JG 2, the *Geschwader*'s fighter-bomber unit, is attached to *Schlachtgeschwader 10* as that unit's *15. Staffel.*

31 December 1942
The *Richthofen Geschwader*'s victory totals on this date are:

Geschwaderstab	124 victories
I. Gruppe	469 victories
II. Gruppe	335 victories
III. Gruppe	418 victories
10. Staffel	2 victories
Replacement Training *Staffel*	15 victories

The *Geschwader* suffered 194 losses in this time. It should be borne in mind that all of these victories came against aircraft of the western allies.

Turn of the Year 1942-43
The Allies have gone over to the offensive on every front. Stalingrad falls in February 1943 and the German *6. Armee* surrenders. The *6. Armee* attacked Stalingrad with a force of about 350,000 men and was subsequently sent additional reserves. Approximately 34,000 men were flown out of the pocket. Of the remaining 236,000 soldiers, 128,000 are killed and about 90,000-100,000 become prisoners of war. Only 6,000 ever return home. The fall of Stalingrad marks a decisive turning point in the war.

In North Africa the end of the Africa Corps is near.

In spite of the constantly growing superiority of the western allies in the air, the will of the German pilots manning the day and night fighters remains unbroken. Despite their courage and determination, they are forced to watch as their cities are turned into soot and ashes and German civilians, including their own families, are wiped out. The Allied side asks itself if and more importantly when the German command will realize that its only chance is to strengthen the fighter arm to finally put a roof over Fortress Europe. For only fighters can effectively combat the bombers and sweep them from the sky. Without their heavy bombers and fighter-bombers, the Allies cannot win the air superiority that is necessary for an invasion of Europe. Many front-line German commanders have already realized this, but unfortunately no one in the high command, especially Hitler. Proof of this is his decision to use the Me 262 jet fighter, the most advanced warplane in the world, as a bomber. Had the aircraft been placed in production soon enough, it might have influenced events during the most decisive phase of the air war.

February 1943
An additional *Staffel* is added to each of *JG 2*'s three *Gruppen*, raising their number from three to four per *Gruppe*. The official incorporation of the *Staffeln* into the *Gruppen* occurs with the reorganization of the *Geschwader* on 1 October 1943.

23 March 1943
JG 2 is once again based mainly on the Channel Coast in northern France. One of the first missions by the reunited *Geschwader* is against British heavy bombers with fighter escort attacking the U-boat base at St. Nazaire. Fifteen bombers are shot down.

Spring 1943
The air defense in the west, in which *JG 2* has played a major role in the preceding years, increasingly becomes part of the air defense of the Reich. The focus of operations, however, continues to be over the occupied territories, especially on the Channel and over France.

28 June 1943
Major Walter Oesau, *Kommodore* of *JG 2 "Richthofen"*, celebrates his thirtieth birthday. It will be the last for this outstanding fighter pilot and commander. In the later afternoon on 28 June, shortly after 1800 hours, the airfield at Beaumont-le-Roger is attacked without warning. *Unteroffizier* Otto Happel, a radio operation with the *Geschwader*, recalls what happened: "The airfield was struck by a carpet of bombs. The *Geschwaderstab* and nearby farmhouses were hit especially hard. I was at work in the command post with *Feldwebel* Orlik, but the first falling bombs quickly put an end to that, for a few meters away members of the ground personnel were bleeding from the frightful effects of the fragmentation bombs." Thirty technicians, radio operators and drivers died in the hail of bombs. They were men who never stood in the spotlight, doing their jobs in anonymity and contributing to the success of the pilots. A number of French civilians were also killed. A new housing complex was built near the airfield and one of the streets was named *Rue Du 28 June 1943* in their honor.

30 June 1943
Oberstleutnant Oesau leaves *JG 2* and becomes *Jagdfliegerführer Bretagne* (Fighter Commander Brittany), formerly *Jafü 4*. He subsequently takes command of *JG 1*, which is active in the Defense of the Reich. On 11 May 1944 he is killed in action over the Eifel Mountains in combat with P-38 Lightnings.

4 July 1943
Major Egon Mayer, *Kommandeur* of the *III. Gruppe*, is selected to succeed *Oberstleutnant* Oesau as *Kommodore* of *JG 2*.

Beginning of July 1943
JG 2 "Richthofen" flies both day and night missions. *Oberleutnant* Haberland's *Staffel* (Fw 190) is retrained for night operations and is subsequently employed in the day and night fighter roles. Then *Oberfeldwebel* Josef Bigge wrote the following in his private memoirs of the war:

"At the beginning of July 1943 an order was received from the General der Jagdflieger that one *Staffel* of the *Geschwader* was to receive addition training for the night fighter role. (In his book *The First and the Last*, Galland wrote: `One of my worst ideas was to use fighter aircraft for both the day and night fighter roles. It placed a heavy strain on men and materiel and proved impractical.')

Our *2. Staffel* was selected for this additional training. On 22 July 1943 the pilots and some of the technical personnel were sent to Tours. There we carried out instrument flights in Arado Ar 96 trainers, including instrument takeoffs and landings. The course ended on 7 August 1943 with the issuing of Class III Instrument Flying certificates.

We returned to our base at St. André on the afternoon of 7 August. After dark we carried out instrument flights in the Fw 190. The command post and our aircraft had been fitted out with the necessary radio and navigation equipment. The aircraft had also been painted in a dark camouflage, but after a few missions this proved unsatisfactory. After experimenting with various colors we selected a pale blue tone for the lower surfaces, and the same shade was used as the base color for the camouflage on the upper surfaces.

My first night scramble came at 2335 hours on 9 August 1943. The mission was controlled from the command post, watched by the fighter commander (*Jafü*). Radio communications and navigation worked perfectly. Although I was in the air for one hour and forty-five minutes, there was no contact with the enemy (landing at 0120 hours).

My next night scramble on 13 August 1943 (takeoff at 0311 hours) brought me both misfortune and extremely good luck. After about twenty minutes in the air my engine began to sputter and finally quit. My altitude was about 4000 meters. I immediately informed the command post of my situation and asked for my position and a heading to fly for our airfield at St. André. Based on my altitude and range, I believed that I could glide to the airfield. As there were no enemy aircraft reported in the area, the airfield lighting was turned on. My heading for the airfield was good, the glide was proceeding smoothly and the airfield lighting gave a reassuring feeling. But when I chanced to scan the instruments a chill ran up my spine, for I realized that my altitude was 350 meters at most. As quickly as I could, I jettisoned the canopy, removed my flying helmet, released the straps and jumped. This did not go all that well, however: the slipstream pressed me against the fuselage and one leg was stuck in the cockpit. After a few kicks I got free, but then my right shin struck the tail. I must have opened the parachute quite automatically; I don't remember any jerk as the parachute opened nor do I recall falling through the branches of a tall tree. In any case, I ended up hanging in my parachute straps about two meters above the ground; the parachute had become caught in the top of the tall tree. I hit the quick release and—thud—mother earth had me again. My first reaction was a short prayer of thanks to almighty God and then a cigarette. My right leg was hurting and I could barely stand, so I fashioned a splint around my shin and calf using branches and my leather belt. I had some bloody scratches on my face from falling through the branches, but that wasn't so bad. I then set about retrieving my parachute from the tree. It took tricks and patience, but I finally succeeded. I knew that I had come down somewhere in Evreux Forest, and I tried to figure out in which direction the nearest village or farm might be. As it was only about four in the morning, I rolled myself up in my parachute and rested for about an hour. When I heard a cock crow I got up and, with my parachute under my arm, began hobbling in the direction from which I had heard the call. After a difficult and what seemed to me a rather long walk, I arrived in the small village of Les Ventes (about 20 km SW of St. André). I must have looked quite beaten up, for when I knocked on the doors of several houses those inside refused to open them. I finally came to a house with a sign on the door that read "*Poste*". I knocked for a long time and finally madame appeared in her nightgown. She was about to close the door when she saw me, but I got my foot in and after a lengthy palaver I was able to communicate to her that I wished to use the telephone. She told me that was possible, but not at this early hour as there was no one at the nearest agency until eight o'clock. So I had to be patient and wait outside on a bench. Help soon came, however, the shape of a French worker from the village, who recognized me as a German airman. He was on his way on his bicycle to St. André, where he worked at the airfield. I scribbled down a note for him to deliver to the airfield commander, saying that I was still alive and would like to be picked up as soon as possible. After about two hours someone from the *Staffel* collected me. They had already given up on me. After making my report to the *Staffelkapitän* and a stiff drink, I was taken to the nearest hospital for a complete examination. They could find no injuries apart from abrasions and bruises. After the examination I was able to return to the *Staffel* with my comrades.

The *Staffelkapitän* gave me the next day off (14 August 1943) to rest. My next night sortie was on 15 August. I took off at 2250 hours. The ground control was so good that I soon spotted the enemy aircraft emerging from the dark sky. It was an Avro Lancaster, a British four-engined bomber. I was able to close in to optimum firing range unseen. I opened fire with all guns and my first burst was on target; it crashed near Courville (about 20 km west of Chartres). I had to dispense with the usual victory pass over the airfield, as a shell had detonated in the barrel of my starboard outer cannon, bursting the barrel and tearing a large hole in the leading edge of the wing. This made the aircraft very unstable, and I had to counteract a tendency to roll. The landing was more difficult than usual, but I managed to get the machine down in one piece. I landed at 2335 hours. The fighter commander, who was at the command post during the mission, congratulated me.

I was scrambled again the next morning at 1027 hours (16 August), however I did not make contact with the enemy. On this occasion I flew 'Black 8', the aircraft of one of my comrades. My original aircraft 'Black 1' had been written off in the action of 13 August, and 'Black 5' was under repair as a result of the premature explosion of a cannon round on 15 August, consequently I was assigned a new machine with the tactical marking 'Black 2'. At 2130 hours I took off on a thirty minute test flight which also served as a radio and navigation flight. The next scramble came at 2250 hours. There was no contact with the enemy and I landed at 0011 hours. (As far as I can recall, the *Staffel* lost three pilots on a day mission on this 16 August 1943.) That night I was again at alert readiness. I was scrambled at 0307 hours (on 17 August). Although I remained in a so-called loitering area for an hour and a half, there was no enemy contact. I landed at 0510 hours. From this period of operations the events of 24 August are worth describing briefly. At 1245 hours we moved from St. André to Brest-North (440 km; landing at 1356 hours). Scramble at 1410, however the mission produced no contact with the enemy. Landed at 1456 at Morlaix, 50 km to the east. Took off from Morlaix at 1630 hours and landed back at St. André at 1745. At 1855 hours we were scrambled against Flying Fortresses leaving Reich territory. After almost an hour in the air I spotted a Flying Fortress near Dreux in the area west of Paris. In spite of heavy return fire, which inflicted several certain hits on my machine, I was able to fire accurate bursts which heavily damaged the four-engined machine. I was unable to continue the pursuit, however, as fuel was running low. I landed at the nearest available airfield, which was St. André. On 6 September 1943 I took off at 1124 hours with my wingman *Unteroffizier* Klein. Our mission was to act as a so-called shadowing pair, remaining above a group of about 120 Boeing Fortress IIs flying out of the Troves area (about 160 km southeast of Paris) in the direction of Chartres. After completing our assignment we attacked the formation and together shot down a Boeing Fortress II near Voves (approx. 30 km south of Chartres). As we landed at 1311 hours our airfield was being heavily bombed by another formation of bombers. We had no choice but to land on the runway. Once down on the runway I was hit." This ends Josef "Jupp" Bigge's account titled *Single-Engined Night Fighting in the Richthofen Geschwader*.

25 July 1943
The 8th Air Force and the RAF launch major raids on Hamburg on this day. The RAF had heavily bombed Kiel and Hamburg the previous night and the city was still burning. The American attack results in further destruction and fresh fires.

26 July 1943
More attacks on Hamburg, Hanover, Kassel and Oschersleben, location of a Focke-Wulf branch plant where Fw 190 fighters are assembled.

28 July 1943
Attacks on Kiel and Warnemünde.

29 and 30 July 1943
More attacks on Kassel, home to the Henschel Flugzeugwerke. During the action on 28 July the German fighter pilots encounter a new problem which will have a decisive effect on the air war: American long-range fighters. Following the attack on 28 July the American bombers rendezvoused with more than 100 P-47 Thunderbolts over Holland which then escorted them back to their bases in England. The enemy fighters are equipped with jettisonable tanks containing 450 liters of fuel, giving them greater range. This represents a decisive turn in the air war against Germany.

September 1943-Beginning of 1944
The problems facing the German fighters come to a head. In addition to the P-38 Lightning the Americans are now using the P-47 Thunderbolt and P-51 Mustang long-range fighters to escort bombers over Germany. Jettisonable tanks and other technical improvements soon make it possible for them to accompany the bombers all the way to targets deep inside Germany.

In spite of this, the German fighter pilots continue to have great success and some, including members of *JG 2*, become true heavy bomber specialists.

Examples of these specialists are *Major* Georg-Peter Eder and *Major* Egon Mayer. They develop a new tactic, attacking the heavily-armed bombers from the front and then diving away.

Eder, who joined *JG 2* in December 1942, shoots down 36 four-engined bombers. In February 1944 he becomes *Staffelkapitän* of the *6. Staffel* in *JG 1 "Oesau"*. *JG 1* had by then assumed this honorary title in memory of its fallen *Kommodore*.

Oberstleutnant Mayer was the first German fighter pilot to reach 100 victories on the Channel front. A member of the *Geschwader* since 1939, he once shot down three B-17s in 19 minutes. He survived the war. It is worth noting that he was one of the few "old hands" who received their training at the beginning of the war who survived the war. The young replacement pilots of 1943-44 received 50-60 hours of flight training at best and were lost in terrific numbers. By late 1943-early 1944 the *Luftwaffe* had lost the initiative. A clear sign of this was the drop in attacks on England, which finally stopped completely.

Construction of an initial batch of 100 Fw 190 A-1 fighters began toward the end of 1940 and the first aircraft were delivered to combat units for frontline evaluation in the late spring of 1941. Several examples were received by JG 2. This A-1 with the WerkNr. 033 was flown by the 8. Staffel.

A Fw 190 taxis out for takeoff. At some point the aircraft was given the name Würger (Shrike), hardly apt given the type's stout, robust appearance. This view illustrates well the principal differences between the Fw 190 and the Bf 109: the Focke-Wulf's BMW 801 C air-cooled radial engine and its wide-track, inwards-retracting undercarriage.

Hauptmann Balthasar led the Geschwader for barely five months before he was killed on 3 July 1941 when his Bf 109 lost a wing during combat. Just one day earlier he had been awarded the Oak Leaves after his 40th victory. Balthasar was promoted to Major posthumously.

Hauptmann Wilhelm Balthasar's coffin during the funeral ceremony.

Hauptmann Balthasar was buried in a military cemetery near Lille next to his father, who had died in the First World War. The mourners included (from left to right): Mayer, Hahn, Pflanz, Hohagen, unidentified, Leie, unidentified, Generalfeldmarschall Sperrle, General Ibel and (right) General of Fighters Oberst Galland.

22 June 1941: State radio announces the start of the Russian campaign. The pilots of II./JG 2 listen to the reports as they are broadcast over loudspeakers. Concern is visible in the faces as they try to grasp what this new war means.

Leutnant Julius Meimberg concerned and reflective about what he has just heard. The two-front war has begun.

Depressed, these three pilots walk to their quarters to be alone with their thoughts.

The new Kommodore, Major Walter Oesau. In 1940-41 he was at the apex of German fighter pilots together with Mölders, Galland and Wick. With eight victories in Spain, when war broke out Oesau was Staffelkapitän of 7./JG 51, and from August to November 1941 he was Kommandeur of III./JG 51. He was the third fighter pilot to record twenty victories and on 5 February 1941 became the fourth to reach 40 victories. He then served as Kommandeur of III./JG 3 in Russia until July 1941, after which he was Kommodore of JG 2 "Richthofen" until June 1943.

Two members of the original Richthofen Geschwader of the First World War. General Ritter von Greim (center), who was named the last Generalfeldmarschall of the Wehrmacht on 26 April 1945, and Generaloberst Udet (right), Chief of Aircraft Procurement and Supply in the OKL. Overburdened by this office, and recognizing the futility of the war, Udet committed suicide on 17 November 1941.

Summer 1941 at St. Pol—Feldwebel Günther Seeger of 3./JG 2 greets Leutnant Rudolf Pflanz, who has just returned from a sortie.

Günther Seeger, who joined 3./JG 2 as an Unteroffizier in February 1940, saw action on the Channel front until December 1942. He then went to the Mediterranean and North Africa with 11./JG 2. In March 1943 he was transferred to 6./JG 53 and later to 7./JG 53, becoming Staffelkapitän in September 1944. He was awarded the Knight's Cross on 26 March 1944 after 46 victories. His final record was 56 victories, all in the west, including 8 heavy bombers, in 504 combat missions.

Rudolf Pflanz joined JG 2 in 1938 and flew in the Geschwaderstab with Wick and Oesau. On 23 July 1941 he shot down 6 British aircraft and in May 1942 became Staffelkapitän of 1./JG 2. He was awarded the Knight's Cross on 1 August 1941 after 20 victories. His final victory total was 52, all in the west. He was shot down and killed in combat with Spitfires near Abbeville on 31 July 1942.

The Commander-in-Chief of Luftflotte 3, Generalfeldmarschall Hugo Sperrle, during an inspection tour in the west. Here the field marshal is seen taking a catnap during a break in the tour. His adjutant, an anti-aircraft Major, discusses the next phase of the tour with a Major wearing a non-standard Luftwaffe uniform.

Generalfeldmarschall Sperrle about to board a Ju 52 for the flight back to Paris, location of Luftflotte 3's headquarters.

The Bf 109s of 2. Staffel fly escort for the high-ranking guest.

Kommodore Major Oesau and three of his leading officers walk past a parked Bf 109 F. It is a special day and they are on their way to have their picture taken.

On this August day three recently decorated unit leaders pose with the Kommodore for the Berlin Illustrated News: from left to right: Hauptmann Egon Mayer, Kommandeur of the III. Gruppe; Hauptmann Rudolf Leie; Major Walter Oesau, Geschwaderkommodore; and Oberleutnant Rudolf Pflanz. Mayer, Leie and Pflanz were all awarded the Knight's Cross on 1 August 1941.

Hauptmann Hans "Assi" Hahn after returning from a combat mission in which he shot down two British aircraft. Here he is seen being greeted by his dog "Wumm".

Bear against dog, or a cautious feeling-out by two teenagers, watched by Hans Hahn and two of his pilots. On the left is Stöckelmann.

Oberleutnant Pflanz, exhausted after a tough engagement against the ever stronger British enemy.

The stress of the recent air battle is still visible in the pilots' faces. Once again several have failed to return. From left: Oberleutnant "Rudi" Pflanz, Oberleutnant Kuhtei, Oberfeldwebel "Sepp" Wurmheller, Stabsfeldwebel Fritz Stritzel and Hauptmann Philipp.

Two aircraft have collided on the airfield. One pilot was seriously injured in the collision. Technical personnel prepare to remove the damaged aircraft from the airfield.

From left: Major Oesau, Oberleutnant Pflanz and Hauptmann Leie during a break between sorties, and there was also something to celebrate.

Oberfeldwebel Josef "Sepp" Wurmheller (left) and Oberfeldwebel Kurt Bühligen were awarded the Knight's Cross on 4 September 1941 after 24 and 21 victories respectively. Wurmheller and Bühligen had more in common than just receiving the Knight's Cross on the same day: both were Oberfeldwebel, both scored their 100th victory on 12 June 1944, and in each case the aircraft shot down was a P-47 Thunderbolt.

The new holder of the Knight's Cross, Oberfeldwebel Wurmheller, in front of his Bf 109 F and ground crew.

This machine probably had engine start problems. The hand crank for the inertia starter is still in place. Here the aircraft is seen being pushed into a well-camouflaged hangar.

Hans "Assi" Hahn was a member of JG 2 "Richthofen" from the start of the war. His first command was the 2. Staffel. On 24 September 1940 Oberleutnant Hahn was awarded the Knight's Cross after 20 victories.

Hahn was Kommandeur of the III. Gruppe from October until November. His name inspired the Gruppe's emblem—a cockerel. Under his command the unit was very successful. He became the 32nd recipient of the Oak Leaves after 42 victories. He scored 68 victories in fighting against the RAF, making him one of the most successful fighter pilots in the west. On 1 November 1942 Hahn was named Kommandeur of II./JG 54 in Russia. He scored his 100th victory on 26 January 1943. On 21 February 1943 his machine suffered engine failure and he was obliged to make a forced landing near Demyansk. Seven years of Russian captivity followed. Hahn's final tally was 108 victories, including 4 heavy bombers. 36 other victory claims were not confirmed.

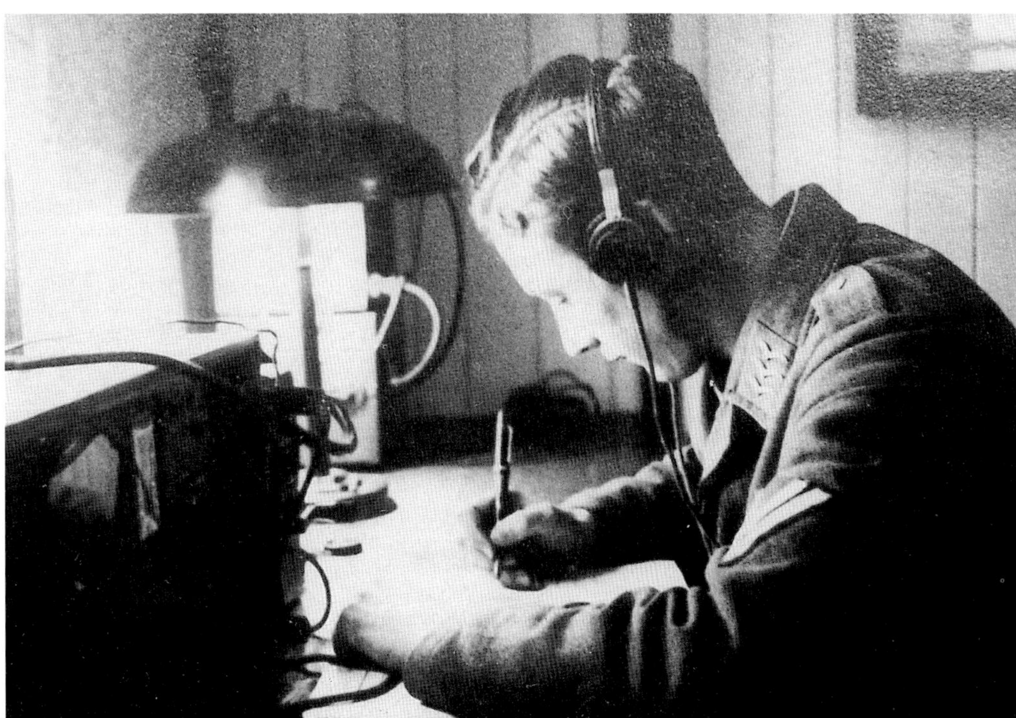

Above left: Stabsfeldwebel Fritz Stritzel was one of the old "Döberitzer". He went from I./JG 2 to the Stabsschwarm and at the end of 1942 returned to the I. Gruppe. He was killed in action over the Channel on 30 May 1944 while serving in the 3. Staffel. Abobe right: Major Oesau with his shepherd dog at the Brest-North airfield. The Kommodore has a troubled look on his face. Right: Radio operator Obergefreiter Otto Happel. He was one of the many members of the Geschwader who received little mention, but without whom the success of the Richthofen Geschwader would not have been possible. Many of the photographs in this book were provided by him. Happel died on 18 April 1994.

A Bf 109 during undercarriage checks. The mechanics who serviced and repaired engines, weapons, radios and other systems faithfully performed their difficult tasks, often working round the clock when the situation required.

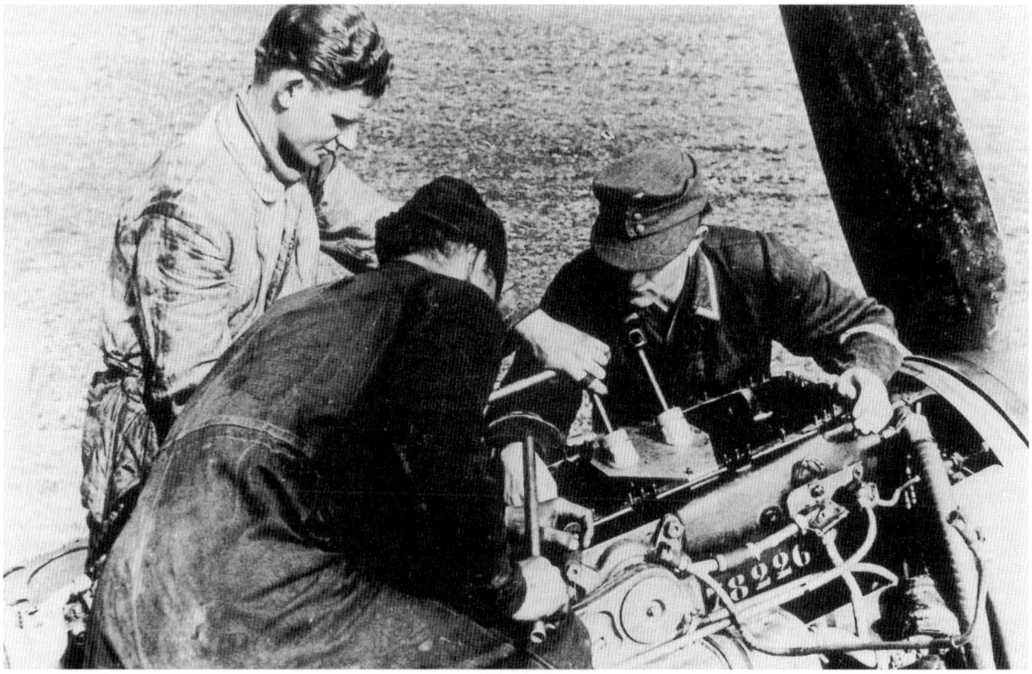

Motor mechanics working on a Daimler Benz aircraft engine. The "Black Men" saw to it that the aircraft were always ready for "their" pilot's next mission.

Between missions the technical personnel had to work quickly but precisely to service and, if necessary, repair their charges. The pilots' success in combat, indeed their very lives, depended on the work of the ground crews.

A big reception for Kommodore Major Walter Oesau after landing. On 26 October 1941 he scored his 100th victory. Closest to the machine is Rudolf Pflanz, himself an expert fighter pilot.

Victor in 100 air combats, including eight in Spain. Oesau was the third fighter pilot, after Werner Mölders and Günther Lützow, to reach this figure. 82 of his victories were against western opponents.

Autumn 1941—Major Oesau's Bf 109 F at St. Pol.

Brest-North airfield. A tarpaulin-covered Bf 109 F sits in the autumn morning sun.

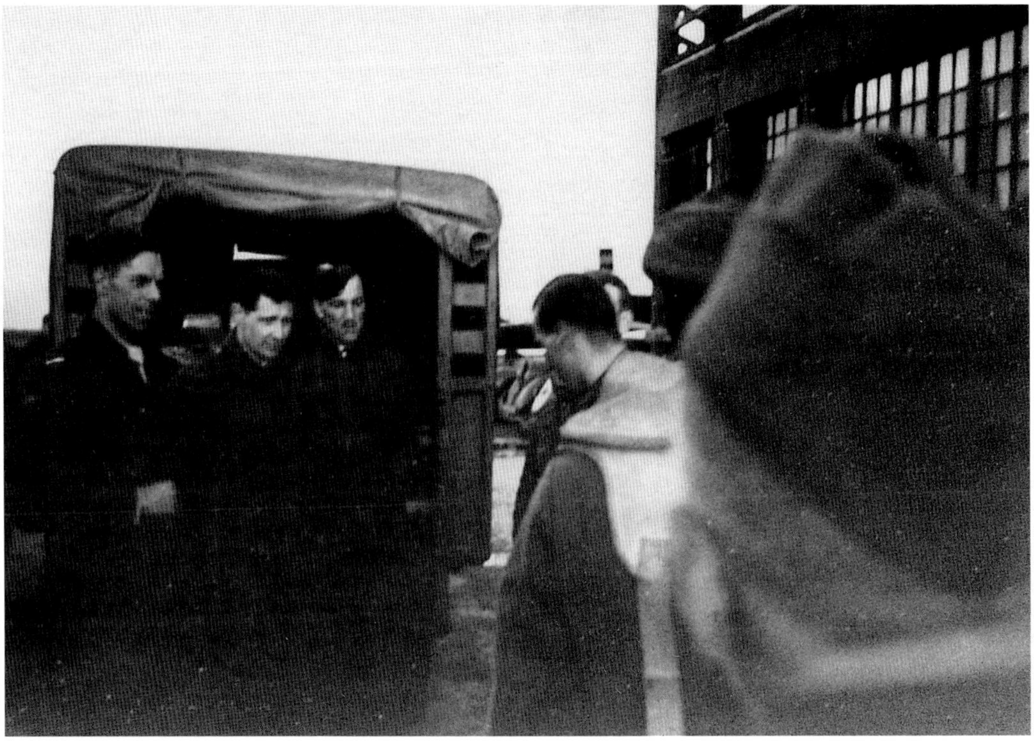

The crew of a British bomber shot down by Oberleutnant Erich Leie is interrogated at Brest-North airfield.

The Bf 109 F of Feldwebel Georg "Schorsch" Hippel of the 8. Staffel after undercarriage failure.

"Operation Cerberus"— three German capital ships dash east through the English Channel. Here the battle-cruiser Scharnhorst is seen steaming through the Channel on the morning of 12 February 1942 within sight of the English coast. Providing air escort are two Bf 110 Zerstörer of II./ZG 76, the "Shark" Gruppe.

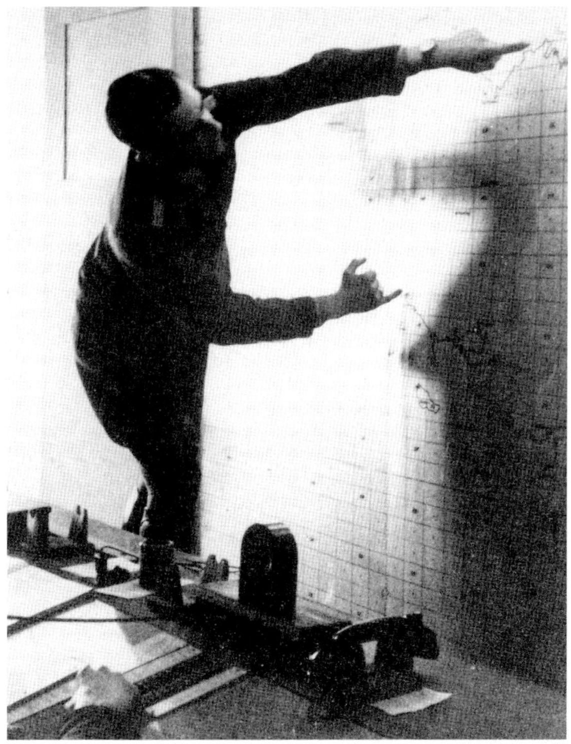

In an operations room set up specially for this operation, a staff officer explains the most critical phase, passage through the narrowest part of the Channel between Dover and Calais.

Still wearing his life vest after completing an air cover mission over the warships, Gruppenkommandeur Major Mayer monitors operations by his pilots.

The aircraft of Unteroffizier Bigge, who flew in the Stabsschwarm with Major Oesau.

"Jupp" Bigge napping on the wing of his Messerschmitt. He also provided many of the photographs that illustrate this book. Bigge also kept a written record of his war experiences, which he made available to the author.

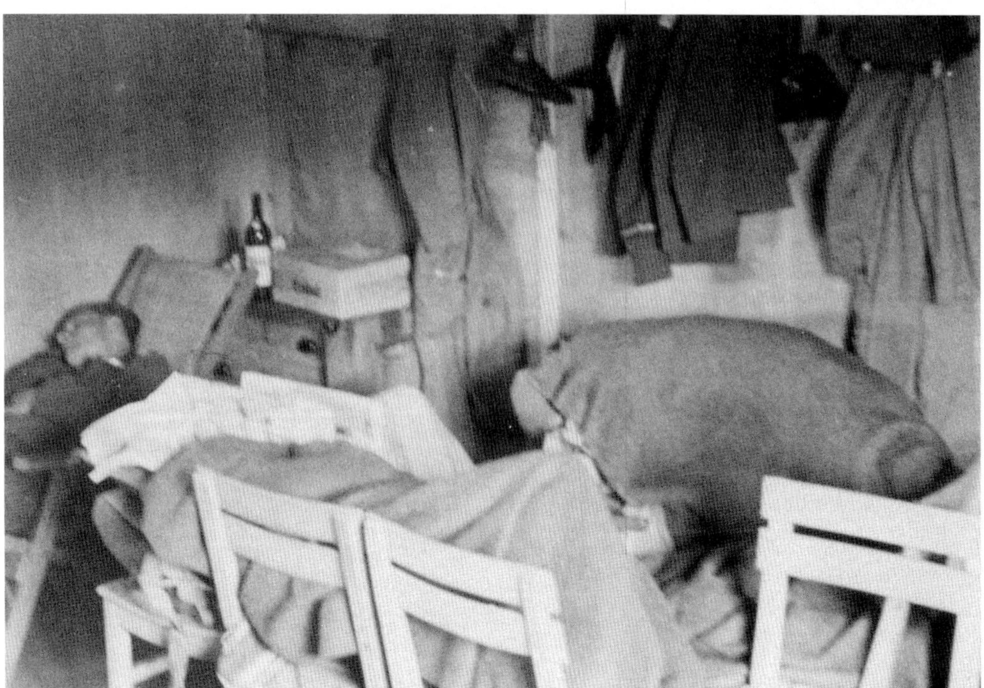

For the fighter pilots the duty day began at dawn. Those not assigned to alert readiness (sitting in the cockpits of their machines), tried to get some sleep in full kit, stretching out on chairs, deck chairs or whatever was available.

A Bf 109 F about to touch down.

The Staffelkapitän of 3./JG 2 has parked his aircraft at the edge of the forest to wait for what is to come. An Unteroffizier of a propaganda unit uses the opportunity to tape an interview.

Back from a mission over the Channel, Egon Mayer uses his hands to recreate an engagement for the Kommodore. Pilots Beitz (left) and Edelmann (center) listen intently to the account.

Signboard signifying the location of the Geschwader command post and the Geschwader's base at Beaumont-le-Roger.

Several pilots doze in the sun. From left: Hauptmann Edelmann, Oberfeldwebel Stritzel and Hauptmann Philipp. Note the unusual tactical insignia on the Bf 109 in the background on the right.

Another unusual tactical marking. A half chevron on the Bf 109 F of Hauptmann Fritz Edelmann, a member of the Stab of JG 2. Also interesting is his "Victory Stick". Beaumont-le-Roger, early summer 1942.

Deliveries of the new Fw 190 to the front-line units began in the spring of 1942.

A pair of Fw 190s overfly the airfield.

The new Focke-Wulf Fw 190 A fighter began reaching the combat units in significant numbers in the spring of 1942. JG 2 also converted its first Staffeln to the new aircraft. The Fw 190 offered a number of improvements over the Bf 109, for example its air-cooled radial engine. Many Bf 109s were lost over England because of relatively minor damage to the cooling system which forced the pilot to abandon his aircraft or make a forced landing. The electrical gun cocking system of the Fw 190 proved less troublesome than the mechanical system of the Bf 109. The Fw 190 was also more heavily armed, with four cannon and two machine-guns. The wider track of the Fw 190's inward-retracting undercarriage made landings and takeoffs safer, and it was more robust than the undercarriage of the Bf 109. Many former Bf 109 pilots still have unpleasant memories of the ground loops to which that machine was prone during landing and takeoff.

Fw 190s at Beaumont-le-Roger.

This view illustrates the wide stance of the Fw 190's undercarriage and its radial engine, which was protected by an armored nose ring.

A Staffel of Fw 190s takes off in flights of three (Ketten). At this time it was important to get as many aircraft into the air as quickly as possible whenever approaching enemy aircraft were reported.

An Allied fighter scores hits on the engine and wing root of a Fw 190. In the second half of 1942 RAF Spitfires began escorting B-17 heavy bombers of the American 8th Air Force. American escort fighters with sufficient range to accompany the bombers to their targets and back did not appear until much later.

Combat Report No. 16 of 24 April 1942, 1,000th Victory by JG 2
Battle alarm! The men run to their machines, climb aboard and fasten their parachute harnesses. There is a brief silence on the field, then the engines roar to life. The first flights take off, and finally the sound of the fighters' engines disappears in the north. Hectic activity in the command post. Soon we know that the Tommies have turned back prematurely. The first aircraft land again.
There, what is going on at the opposite edge of the airfield? British heavy bombers! Three, no six! Flying low, they pass by, slowly, like fat carp. Don't any of our landing fighters see the bombers? There, the nearest machine has seen the bombers. Already on approach to land, it pulls up, retracts its undercarriage and sets out after them. Others follow, several that have already landed take off again. They fall upon the bombers, one of them goes down from low altitude. Black smoke rises high. The second explodes in the air like a shining star, immediately afterwards another pillar of smoke shows the fate of the third. Three black pillars of smoke on the horizon. The fighters return, circle over the airfield waggling their wings. Then the pilots climb from their cockpits, beaming with joy: Hauptmann Greisert, the 998th victory; Feldwebel B., the 999th; Unteroffizier Pohl, the 1,000th.
Last to arrive is Kommodore Oesau. He has shot down a fourth bomber. He positioned himself 10 m above the Liberator and shot up its two port engines.
(Author's note: Feldwebel B. was Fw. Ernst Bosseckert; the enemy aircraft were Lancasters, not Liberators.)

17 April 1942—the 1,000th victory by the "Jagdgeschwader Richthofen", an Avro Lancaster of the RAF. It was brought down by Uffz. Pohl of the 5. Staffel. This victory was mentioned in the Wehrmacht communiqué on 17 April 1942.

Major Walter Oesau scored the Geschwader's 1,001st victory during the same mission.

Major Oesau in front of his aircraft "Green 13".

Two crew members from a British bomber, a Flying Officer observer and a gunner. For them the war is over. They are on their way to interrogation then a POW camp. Both are visibly relieved to have survived being shot down.

Major Oesau (center) with the Kommandeur of the III. Gruppe, Oberleutnant Hans "Assi" Hahn (left), and Hauptmann Karlheinz Greisert, Kommandeur of the II. Gruppe, with officers of the Stab on their way to the command post. Hauptmann Greisert led JG 2 in an acting capacity from 29 November 1940 until 15 February 1942 after the death of Major Wick.

Place-name sign of Beaumont-le-Roger, where JG 2 was based.

Spring 1942 at Beaumont airfield. The Fw 190 A-2s of 6./JG 2. In the foreground is Unteroffizier Günther Gegans' "Yellow 2". In the background are two Bf 109 Fs of the I. Gruppe. Not all Gruppen were equipped with the Fw 190. The Bf 109 F was used as a high-altitude fighter on account of its superior performance at higher altitudes. Also visible is a Junkers Ju 86. This twin-engined machine served in the bombing role before the war and was later used as a transport. The tail of the Bf 109 in the foreground belongs to an aircraft of the Geschwaderstab.

Fw 190 A-3s of the 9. Staffel, whose black eagle emblem is clearly visible on the forward fuselage. Beneath the cockpit is the cockerel emblem of "Assi" Hahn's III. Gruppe. The aircraft are being refueled.

This Fw 58 B has flown high-ranking visitors to Beaumont. This is suggested by the staff car in front of the aircraft, which bears the name "Irene".

The Commander-in-Chief of Luftflotte 3, Generalfeldmarschall Sperrle, with the Jafü 3, Generalmajor Ibel, and the Kommodore of JG 2, Major Oesau. Map in hand, he discusses the tactical aspects of a mission. In the background are two Fw 190s ordered to standby readiness.

Oesau with his machine. The radio compartment access door is open, with two technicians standing in front of it. Visible on the rudder are silhouettes of four-engined bombers.

Major Oesau's motto above the door to his room in the command post at Beaumont-le-Roger. It reads: "Complaining is the bowl movement of the soul."

The dispersals of the Stabsschwarm and I./JG 2 at Beaumont.

Fw 190s parked between blast walls consisting of a log shell filled with earth.

This Fw 190 A-3 sustained heavy damage in the wing root area where the 20-mm MG 151/20 cannon was located. Note the tie-down cable intended to prevent the machine from being blown about by the wind. It was also possible to tow unserviceable aircraft by means of two cables attached to the undercarriage legs.

This BMW 801 engine has been removed from the airframe for repairs.

From the Illustrated Observer: "They dive away, nose down." Kommodore Oesau, a wearer of the Knight's Cross combines a description of combat with some gymnastics.

Walter Oesau the gardener.

These photographs show the various sides of Kommodore Major Oesau.

No hands! Sitting on a motorcycle, Oesau fires at a target as he drives by. In the background is his Bf 109.

In full regalia, Oesau tends a small garden plot.

Official call in "light service uniform".

Rudi Pflanz's Bf 109 F. Standing in front are the pilots of the Stabsschwarm (from left to right): Oberleutnant Erich Leie, Major Walter Oesau, Oberleutnant Rudolf Pflanz and Oberfeldwebel Günther Seeger.

Oberleutnant Erich Leie was one of JG 2's best-known fighter pilots. During the Battle of Britain he flew in Major Wick's Stabsschwarm. When this photograph was taken he was still a member of the Stabsschwarm with Major Oesau. On 4 May 1942 Leie was named Kommandeur of I./JG 2. He was transferred to the Eastern Front in January 1943 and assumed command of I./JG 51 "Mölders". After 118 victories, on 7 March 1945 he collided with a Russian Yak 9. Leie bailed out from a height of 60 meters but sustained fatal injuries.

Standard with the command pennant of a Geschwader in front of the Geschwader command post of JG 2 "Richthofen" in Brest. Beyond are automobiles of the Geschwaderstab. One of them has a command pennant in a protective sheath mounted on the fender. Bf 109 Fs are parked in the background.

Oberleutnant Pflanz explains the cockpit of the Bf 109 to a nurse sitting on the aircraft's cowling. Günther Seeger (left) and Erich Leie (right) watch with amusement.

Major Oesau is congratulated after another successful mission.

Oberleutnant Pflanz watches as fresh victory bars are painted on the rudder of his Bf 109. Although officially forbidden, just about every fighter pilot had the victory markings applied to the rudder of his aircraft.

The Fw 190s of the 6. Staffel are readied for the next mission.

Oberleutnant Bühligen exits the cockpit of his Fw 190 A-3. The powerful BMW radial engine produced 1,700 h.p. The Fw 190 was armed with two MG 17 machine-guns above the engine, two 20-mm MG 151/20 cannon in the wing roots and two 20-mm MG FF cannon in the outer wings.

Engine failure forced the pilot of this aircraft to make a wheels-up landing.

The pilot of the Fw 190 had a poor view forward while taxiing. This was probably a contributing factor in the collision illustrated here.

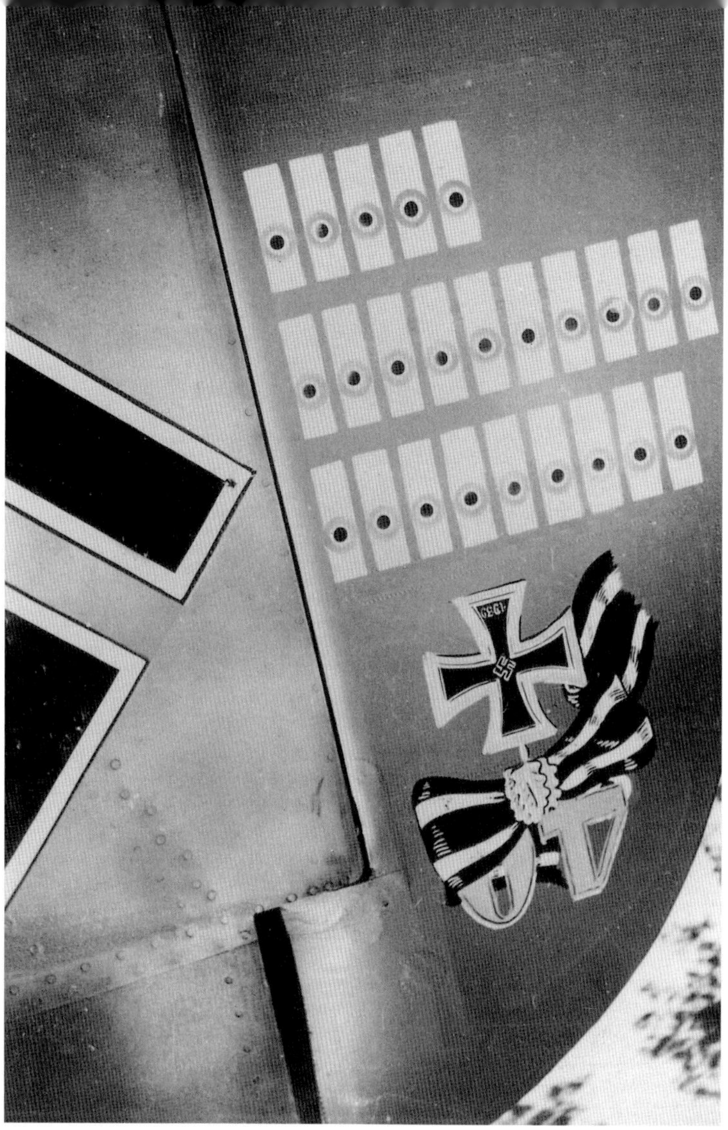

Siegfried Schnell was awarded the Oak Leaves on 9 July 1942 after his 42nd victory. 24 additional victories had been added by the time this photograph was taken.

Major Oesau and Hauptmann Siegfried Schnell, Staffelkapitän of 9./JG 2. The photograph was taken on 18 August 1942, when Schnell shot down five enemy aircraft to raise his victory total to 71. In the background a Bf 109 and a Fw 190.

A Fw 190 parked at the edge of an airfield. The aircraft of this Staffel are being prepared for takeoff in a rather unusual way. Tarpaulins still cover the engine area. An amused Oberleutnant Bühligen looks on. From left to right: Oberleutnant Bühligen and Leutnante Sturm, Eicher, Rhymüller, Hankemann and Thalacher.

Oberleutnant "Rudi" Pflanz in the cockpit of his aircraft following a sortie talking with his crew chief. An unusual perspective.

Combat Report – The Death of Oberleutnant Pflanz

At 1452 hours on 31 July 1942 seven aircraft of the 1. Staffel led by Oberleutnant Pflanz took off to intercept enemy aircraft in the Abbeville area. The formation of enemy bombers, which was attacking an airfield, had a strong fighter escort. The Staffel climbed to altitude over its airfield and subsequently sighted the English bombers at a height of 2500 meters over Abbeville. Oberleutnant Pflanz attacked three Spitfires as they reversed course over the coast, however he was unable to open fire as he was attacked from above by other Spitfires. The Staffel became split up in the ensuing dogfight. North of the mouth of the Somme Oberleutnant Pflanz attacked several more Spitfires. His wingman, Feldwebel Gruber, was attacked from above and shot down but was able to parachute to safety. Believing that his wingman was still with him, Oberleutnant Pflanz attacked a Spitfire and shot it down. At that moment he was himself attacked from above and to the right. His machine immediately caught fire and exploded, and he had no chance to bail out (time approx. 1505 hrs.). He was shot down 12 km south of Berck sur Mer (south of Moncheaux) near the coast. Burial in Abbeville on 4 August 1942.

19 August 1942. Canadian troops attack the port of Dieppe on the coast of France. The German army unit defending that sector of the coast, the 302. Infanteriedivision, inflicts heavy casualties on the attack force.

The Royal Air Force committed about 100 bombers and numerous fighters to support the landings. Here Canadian soldiers are seen being led into captivity.

Combat Report Dieppe – 19 August 1942 / Leie

After moving from its inland bases at Rouen-Boos and Dreux to Triqueville, I./JG 2 saw action against British and Canadian troops which had landed at Dieppe. The British operation was strongly supported by the RAF. There were always 30 to 40 fighters in the combat zone and Blenheims, Whirlwinds and Hurricanes carried out low-level attacks on our coastal fortifications. Because of its lowered operational strength the Geschwader flew Schwarm-strength missions. The first missions achieved little success as the English squadrons coordinated their efforts, providing excellent cover and spotting every attack in time to thwart it. During the third mission, at 1150 hours, I fired at a Spitfire which crashed in flames among the landing craft. While covering my wingman as he attacked a Spitfire, I was attacked from behind and hit in the fuselage and wings. I dove away steeply. When I looked around, I saw a Spitfire above me, climbing away to the right. I decided on a forced landing and turned toward a field, but then I saw the flat helmets of the English who had taken shelter there. I climbed back up again. Twenty kilometers from Abbeville my machine began to smoke heavily and the ammunition exploded. By the time I jettisoned the canopy the aircraft was in flames. I jumped from a height of 800 meters but sustained burns to my face and right arm. Strong thermals over a grain field caused me to swing wildly. At 200 meters it seemed as if the parachute might collapse, and I had to pull myself up on the lines to increase the load on the canopy.

The Kommandeur of I./JG 2, Oberleutnant Erich Leie, visits the 1. Staffel after being wounded. From left to right: Leutnant "Sepp" Wurmheller, Oberleutnant Erich Leie, Hauptmann Jürgen Hepe, Unteroffizier Heinz Dowahn (KIA 21 Nov. 1942). Following the death of Oberleutnant Pflanz on 31 July, Hepe was made Staffelkapitän of 1./JG 2. One of the original "Döberitzer", he saw action in Spain and in 1943-44 was Kommandeur of I./JG 2.

Combat Report – Wurmheller/Dieppe

He lay in his quarters with his broken right foot in a cast. He nevertheless took off and subsequently made a forced landing in a field. He hobbled to a division command post and from there was driven back to his Staffel. He immediately took off again and shot down a Blenheim and two Spitfires. Then he took to the air again and claimed three Spitfires. On his fourth sortie he shot down another Spitfire. He suffered a minor concussion in the forced landing in the morning and flew all day with a slight headache. After his final victory his vision began to blur and he landed immediately.

A downed RAF Hurricane on the beach at Dieppe. JG 2 commited the I. and II. Gruppe to the defense of Dieppe plus the 9. and 10. Jabostaffel. The Geschwader scored 59 confirmed kills and 7 probables for the loss of 8 of its aircraft.

Hauptmann Mayer, Gruppenkommandeur of III./JG 2, greets Kommodore Major Oesau after his return from a sortie.

Major Walter Oesau and Oberfeldwebel Josef Wurmheller in the summer of 1942.

A "Flyer's Monument", Luftwaffe parlance for a nose-stand, by an aircraft of III./JG 2. Here an army officer is seen looking over the aircraft.

This Fw 190 of III./JG 2 was damaged in combat and crash-landed in the southeast of England. Leutnant Jakob Augustin, the aircraft's pilot, was made a prisoner of war.

The Fw 190 A-3 of Oberleutnant Faber, Gruppenadjutant of III./JG 2. On 23 June 1942 he landed in error at RAF Pembrey. In the background is a Bristol Blenheim.

Arnim Faber's Fw 190 A-3 in RAF colors. Bearing the serial MP499, it underwent testing by the British from 3 July 1942 until 29 January 1943, making 29 flights. On 18 September 1943 it was taken out of service and dismantled. The various components were used for firing and other tests.

A Fw 190 A-3, probably of I./JG 2 "Richthofen", on the Channel Coast. At that time the Gruppe was based at a forward airfield near Triqueville.

Hauptmann Kurt Bühligen, Kommandeur of II./JG 2 "Richthofen", in front of his Bf 109 G. Deliveries to the Geschwader of this new variant began in late 1942.

JG 2's replacement training Gruppe at Mont de Marsan south of Bordeaux. Here new pilots were given the "final polish" by experienced fighter pilots. Here the 1. Staffel is seen preparing for takeoff. The atmosphere at Mont de Marsan, near the Bay of Biscay, was much more carefree than at a front-line airfield.

Young fighter pilots of the 1. Staffel of Ergänzungs-Jagdgruppe West (Fighter Replacement Training Group West) prior to takeoff; from left to right: Leutnant Hufnagel (KIA on 7 Nov. 1942 with 8./JG 2), Feldwebel Dessoy, one of the instructors, Leutnant Kleinkorres and Leutnant Eder. Leutnant Greim, son of Generalfeldmarschall Ritter von Greim, also flew with this unit.

Final tips from Oberfeldwebel Bigge. Now an experienced fighter pilot, he passes on his experiences to younger pilots, here Leutnant Rösler (left) and Leutnant Kienzle (right). The engines of the aircraft in the background are already running in preparation for the next flight. White bands have been painted around the outer wings to aid recognition in the air.

A flight of three Fw 190 As during formation practice. Such practice flights could quickly turn into real air combat if enemy aircraft appeared without warning. The photograph was taken by the pilot of the third aircraft.

Pilots forced to ditch or bail out into the sea could rely on the air-sea rescue units for help. The red cross was not always enough to protect these aircraft, however, as the following combat report shows.

Combat Report – No. 34 of 28 August 1942
Shooting Down of He 59 Air-Sea Rescue Aircraft into the Channel by Spitfires
18 August 1942, late morning. Two He 59s attacked by Spitfires. One He 59 crashed, commander dead, two men clung to a broken-off float. The pilot of the second He 59 was killed, the flight engineer seriously wounded. Commander Leutnant W. lifted the pilot from his seat and flew the He 59 back. He then returned to the scene in another He 59 and picked up the two men in the water.
Two Fw 190s provided fighter cover. More than a dozen Spitfires attacked. One Spitfire shot down by Fw 190.

Autumn 1942. Leutnant Julius Meimberg relaxes beside his Bf 109 G-1. Designed for operation at high-altitude, this version of the Bf 109 was equipped with a pressurized cockpit and was powered by a DB 605 motor producing 1,475 h.p.

Fighter pilots pass the time between sorties with a game of croquet.

Hauptmann "Assi" Hahn in his Focke-Wulf shortly before takeoff. The chevron marking identifies the aircraft of a Gruppenkommandeur.

The rudder of Hauptmann "Assi" Hahn's Fw 190 with 61 victory bars.

Hauptmann Hahn's machine is readied for another sortie. On 11 November 1942 he was sent to the Eastern Front to command IV./JG 54.

After the invasion of the Soviet Union, the Luftwaffe was left with just two Jagdgeschwader in France, JG 2 "Richthofen" and JG 26 "Schlageter". It was their task to defend the airspace over France and, to a growing degree, over western Germany and Belgium. One aspect of this defensive role was providing air cover for naval bases on the French coast. These included Brest, where heavy warships were based, and various submarine bases.

The Fw 190 A-4 of Hauptmann Bruno Stolle, Staffelkapitän of 8./JG 2, at Brest. On the tailplane are the pilots life vest and parachute. The fighters provided air cover for submarines returning to port.

Hauptmann Egon Mayer, Gruppenkommandeur of III./JG 2, congratulates Hauptmann Bruno Stolle (left) on being awarded the Knight's Cross. Stolle was awarded the decoration on 17 March 1943 after 29 victories.

U 764, a Type VII C submarine commanded by Kapitänleutnant von Bremen, photographed shortly before entering the port of Brest. The U-boat was attached to the 9th Submarine Flotilla commanded by Korvettenkapitän Lehmann-Willenbrock. The fighters of 8./JG 2 provided air cover for returning submarines.

16 April 1943 – Hauptmann Egon Mayer (this photograph was taken after his promotion to Major) becomes the 63rd member of the German armed services to receive the Oak Leaves.

The Kommodore of JG 2 "Richthofen" during a visit to JG 26 "Schlageter". Major Oesau in conversation with Hauptmann Josef Priller, Kommandeur of III./JG 26. On 11 January 1943 Priller took over the Geschwader as Kommodore and led it until 26 January 1945. "Pips" Priller ended the war as an Oberst, decorated with the Swords (No. 73). Altogether he shot down 101 enemy aircraft, all in the west.

This photograph was taken several months later. The General der Jagdflieger, Generalmajor Adolf Galland, visits JG 2 and JG 26 during an inspection tour. On this occasion he exchanged his personal transport, a He 111, for a Fw 190, as did his staff officers. This was made necessary by the situation in the skies over France in 1943, as well as Galland's desire to keep his hand in.

Until the summer of 1942 the RAF carried the main weight of the air war against Germany. By 1943 the situation was transformed, with the heavy bombers of the American 8th Air Force attacking by day and the RAF by night. This photograph depicts Consolidated B-24 Liberators of the 8th Air Force with fighter escort. American escort fighters initially lacked the range to escort the bombers all the way to their targets, however this changed with the arrival of the P-51 Mustang.

This photograph was taken at the end of June 1943, by which time the air war over Germany was in full swing. Losses mounted on both sides. Seen here is a group of pilots from JG 2: (left to right) Lt. Bialucha, Uffz. Werner Edelmann (KIA 4 Feb. 1944), Oblt. Karl Haberland (KIA 27 Jan. 1944), Uffz. Herbert Treff (KIA 18 March 1945), Uffz. Jürgen von Beuningen (KIA 23 Oct. 1943), Fw. Walter Haase (KIA 29 June 1943), Lt. Johannes Viethoff (KIA 30 Apr. 1944).

Hauptmann Egon Mayer (left), Kommandeur of III./JG 2, in conversation with an Oberst. Mayer's Fw 190 A is in the background.

Jäger am Kanal

Männer des „Jagdgeschwaders Richthofen“

Zum 25. Todestag von Manfred v. Richthofen am 21. April 1918

Hauptmann Egon Mayer.

Unbändiger Draufgänger, 26 Jahre alt, wie Major Graf in Engen am Bodensee geboren. Uebernahm im Frühjahr 41 eine Staffel und schoß in wenigen Monaten 29 Briten ab. Ritterkreuz am 2. 8. 41. In einem Einsatz Abschuß von 3 viermotorigen USA.-Bombern. Immer neue taktische Einfälle. Bei 61 Luftsiegen selber viermal abgeschossen, schwamm einmal über eine Stunde im Kanal.

Hauptmann Erich Hohagen.

Rheinländer, 28 Jahre, in München zu Haus. Flog als Unteroffizier bei Mölders Tiefangriffe und schoß am Kanal 11 Briten ab. Im Osten in wenigen Wochen 20 Luftsiege. Ritterkreuz November 41. Seit vier Monaten wieder am Kanal. Stieß einmal über der englischen Küste durch starkes Jagdgeleit mitten in den britischen Pulk und holte einen Viermotorigen heraus.

Der Kommodore des Geschwaders: Oberstleutnant Walter Oesau.

Dithmarscher, 30 Jahre. Ritterkreuz August 40 nach 20 Abschüssen, Eichenlaub Februar 41 nach dem 40., Schwerter zum Eichenlaub nach dem 80. Luftsieg. Seit Juli 41 Kommodore des ruhmreichen Geschwaders; 100. Luftsieg Oktober 41. Noch heute immer an der Spitze des Geschwaders fliegend.

Hauptmann Bruno Stolle.

Westfale aus Münster, 28 Jahre. Seit Kriegsbeginn im Westen, seit 3 Jahren Staffelführer am Kanal. Bei Begleitschutzflügen 14 Engländer bis Ende 41 abgeschossen. Löst mit Jagdvorstößen weit in den Atlantik hinaus gegen fliegende U-Boot-Jäger eine der schwierigsten Aufgaben der Jagdfliegerei. Glänzender Verbandsführer: 134 Siege bei 6 Verlusten. Ritterkreuz März 43.

Hauptmann Siegfried Schnell.

Brandenburger, 27 Jahre. Feldwebel bei Kriegsbeginn, wegen besonderer Tapferkeit zum Leutnant befördert. Ritterkreuz November 40 nach 20. Abschuß. Juli 41 Erwähnung im Heeresbericht, Eichenlaub als 18. Offizier. Als Staffelkapitän an der Kanalfront 75 Luftsiege. Bei Dieppe fünf Abschüsse an einem Tage. Immer ruhig und voll unerschütterlichem Humor.

Leutnant Hugo Dahmer.

Rheinländer, 25 Jahre. Kommt von der Segelfliegerei. Schoß im Westfeldzug 5, am Kanal 6 Gegner ab. Ging mit Jahresbeginn 41 nach Norwegen und Finnland, erhielt August 41 nach dem 22. Luftsieg als Oberfeldwebel das Ritterkreuz. Januar 43 der 39. Abschuß. Anfang März kurz nacheinander zwei „Fliegende Festungen“ über der Bretagne.

Feldwebel Kappe.

Berliner, 24 Jahre, Vollwaise. Frühjahr 41 zum erstenmal an die Front, nach einem Jahr 20 Luftsiege, ein halbes Jahr später weitere 31. Anfang November 42 Ritterkreuz. Zum Jagdgeschwader Richthofen versetzt, bei einem seiner ersten Kämpfe abgeschossen — kurz darauf holte er eine „Stirling“ und eine „Fortress“ aus dem Himmel.

Feldwebel Karl Gratz.

Aus Wiener-Neustadt, 24 Jahre. Kam Ende 41 an den Südabschnitt der Ostfront, errang Februar 42 seinen ersten Luftsieg — Juni seinen 54.! Ritterkreuz Juli 42. Nach 83 Abschüssen nach dem Westen versetzt, schoß er am Tage des Feindangriffs auf Paris seinen 85. und 86. Gegner ab.

Leutnant Josef Wurmheller.

Südbayer aus Hausham, 25 Jahre, Bergmann, Segelflieger und sportlich geschult. Viele hundert Feindflüge, hauptsächlich gegen England. 67 Luftsiege, fast immer „Doubletten“, manchmal 3 bis 4 Abschüsse am Tage, einmal sogar 5. Am Tage von Dieppe, mit einem Bein in Gips, sieben Gegner abgeschossen. Ritterkreuz September 41, Eichenlaub 42.

PK-Aufn.: Kriegsberichter Brütting (8) Kriegsberichter Boback (1)

From the Berlin Illustrated News. This issue, published on 21 April 1943, marked the 25th anniversary of the death of Manfred von Richthofen and featured biographies of some of JG 2's leading pilots.

Leutnant Wurmheller was awarded the Oak Leaves on 13 November 1942 after 60 victories. On 16 April 1943 he took over the 9 Staffel, initially as acting commander. Because he was a wartime officer, meaning he had been promoted to the officer ranks for bravery in the face of the enemy and had no staff training of any time, he was not confirmed as Staffelkapitän until a year later, in April 1944.

Another victory bar is painted on the rudder of Sepp Wurmheller's Fw 190 A. Vannes, 1943.

A Fw 190 of 9./JG 2. Note the eagle marking on the forward fuselage. Unlike that worn by aircraft of the 2. Staffel, this eagle has an angular beak. The aircraft's tailwheel rests on a rail. This made it easier to push the machine backwards into a space between the trees. The pilot's parachute lies on the folding chair in the foreground.

"Sepp" Wurmheller and Erich Leie share a laugh. Note the concrete walls in front of the buildings on Beaumont airfield, protection against bomb splinters.

The blast walls were constructed for a good reason. On 28 June 1943, which also happened to be Kommodore Oesau's 30th birthday, British heavy bombers attacked the airfield at Beaumont-le-Roger. The Geschwader lost 30 killed. A nearby French village was also hit and many civilians were killed or injured.

One of those killed on this day was Gefreiter Hugo Petri of the medical company.

High-ranking visitors for JG 2 "Richthofen". The Dornier Do 215 visible in the background has just brought Generalfeldmarschall Erhard Milch and Generalmajor Adolf Galland. Kommodore Major Oesau and Hauptmann Mayer, Gruppenkommandeur of III./JG 2, greet the two senior officers.

Presenting the Staffel leaders of the III. Gruppe; from left to right: Leutnant Huppertz, Leutnant Wurmheller, and Hauptmann Stolle. Hauptmann Mayer looks on over the field marshal's shoulder.

Generalfeldmarschall Erhard Milch became Chief of Aircraft Procurement and Supply after Ernst Udet committed suicide. Here he is seen in conversation with Hauptmann Mayer. General of Fighters Galland is probably already thinking about the next unit.

The Kommandeur of III./JG 2, Hauptmann Egon Mayer, was subsequently appointed Geschwaderkommodore of the Jagdgeschwader "Richthofen".

The old and the new Kommodore at the I. Gruppe's dispersal. A Fw 190 of the alert Staffel stands ready in its blast pen.

A farewell gift for the departing Kommodore Major Walter Oesau. In the center of the photo is the Fw 190 A of the Kommandeur of the II. Gruppe, Hauptmann Greisert.

Major Oesau left JG 2 to become Fighter Commander Brittany. This desk job did not satisfy the outstanding fighter pilot and unit commander for long. In October 1943 he became Kommodore of JG 1, which was attached to the Defense of the Reich.

Major Egon Mayer assumed command of the Richthofen Geschwader on 4 July 1943. He had been with the Geschwader since December 1939 and scored his first victory during the fighting in France. On 5 February 1944 he became the first fighter pilot on the Channel Front to reach 100 victories. Mayer had been awarded the Knight's Cross with Oak Leaves on 16 April 1943.

7./JG 2 prepares for takeoff. The Staffel emblem, a thumb squashing a top hat, was probably a reference to the English prime minister's preference for this type of headwear.

Leutnant Rimarski with his mongrel dog at the Epinoy airfield in the summer of 1943. Note the paper band around his left forearm. It probably contained code letters assigned by the fighter control net for decoding position information in radio transmissions. On his left leg are flare cartridges. Rimarski was killed soon after this photograph was taken.

Leutnant Franz Hrdlicka was transferred from JG 77, with which he had served in North Africa, to 1./JG 2 as Staffelkapitän. On 1 April 1944 he received the Knight's Cross after 44 victories. In January 1945 he became Kommandeur of the I. Gruppe. Hrdlicka received the Oak Leaves on 23 March 1945. Two days later he was shot down and killed near Betzenrod in Hesse.

2./JG 2 received special night flying training. Operating from St. André, it flew both day and night missions from July to September 1943. This of course placed a great strain on the pilots.

Happy and filled with élan, they were still filled with optimism; from right: Oberleutnant Haberland (KIA 27 Jan. 1944), Unteroffizier Kreuzer (KIA 11 May 1944), Unteroffizier Edelmann (KIA 4 Feb. 1944), Unteroffizier Pedretti (KIA 8 Nov. 1943), Leutnant Grossfuss, Leutnant Eickhoff, Oberfeldwebel Bigge.

Relaxing with a cigarette after the stresses of day and night missions; from left: Haberland, Edelmann, Pedretti, Elflein (hidden), Bigge and Eickhoff.

The enemy as seen by the pilots of 2./JG 2. A burning city illuminates a British Avro Lancaster bomber. Locating the bombers over open country or in cloudy skies on a moonlit night was often a hopeless undertaking, however. Success was also limited by the short range of the Fw 190.

Above: The Focke-Wulf fighter's element was day fighting. Here a Fw 190 attacks a B-17, part of a raid on Bremen. One of the Flying Fortress' engines is on fire and the bomber is already losing altitude.

Left: Major Egon Mayer (arrow) examines one of his victims, a B-17 Flying Fortress. This type of bomber had 8 or 9 defensive positions and as many as 13 heavy Browning machine-guns.

A P-47 Thunderbolt escort fighter. In 1943 the Americans extended the type's range by introducing long-range tanks and improved engines. This photograph was taken after a raid on Ludwigshafen.

By the end of 1943 the German fighter pilot was increasingly becoming the hunted instead of the hunter. The pilot of this Fw 190 has just abandoned his aircraft. The photograph was taken by the automatic gun camera of an American fighter.

Close-up of the undercarriage leg of a Fw 190 A. In the background is an aircraft of the II. Gruppe.

Gruppenkommandeur Hauptmann Bühligen pins the German Cross in Gold on the flight jacket of Oberfeldwebel Kurt Goltzsch. Vitry en Artois in the summer of 1944.

Oberfeldwebel Goltzsch was one of the veterans of JG 2. He joined the Geschwader as an Unteroffizier. On 5 February 1944, by which time he had been promoted to Oberleutnant, Goltzsch was awarded the Knight's Cross after 43 victories. In November 1943 he forced to crash-land his machine and suffered spinal injuries. He subsequently died in hospital on 26 September 1944.

This Spitfire was shot down by Oberfeldwebel Goltzsch. As it was one of the latest models, the remains were thoroughly examined.

In front of JG 2's command post at Creil; from left to right: Feldwebel Günther Jahn, Leutnant Paul Müngersdorff and Leutnant Eichmann.

Back from a mission; Poix airfield near Amiens.

Cockpit readiness at Epinoy. The crew chief, Feldwebel "Jupp" Sauerbach, with "his" pilot Leutnant Paul Müngersdorff.

An outstanding fighter pilot and unit leader, Major Kurt Bühligen, in his command post at Epinoy in early autumn 1943.

Hauptmann Bühligen, Kommandeur of II./JG 2 "Richthofen" (right), and his Gruppenadjutant Leutnant Müngersdorff in the command post at Epinoy.

"Black 7", the Bf 109 of Leutnant Müngersdorff. Damaged in a taxiing accident, the aircraft is being pushed back to its parking spot.

On 12 August 1943, "Black 7", Müngersdorff's Bf 109 G-6, suffered engine failure as a result of a seized piston and he was forced to make an emergency landing near Aachen. The aircraft sustained 60% damage and was struck off the list of available fighters.

Evreux airfield. A Fw 190 sits in front of the maintenance hangar.

The main gate to Evreux airfield. Damage from a recent bombing raid is still visible.

September 1943. Fires caused by the RAF raid have still not been brought under control.

Flugkapitän Fritz Wendel, a Messerschmitt test pilot, has just arrived to visit II./JG 2. He is greeted by Major Bühligen, wearing the life vest. On 26 April 1939 Wendel had set the absolute speed record for propeller-driven aircraft, achieving 757 km/h in the Me 209.

4./JG 2 at Evreux airfield in September 1943. The new Bf 109 G-6 introduced a heavier armament, with two 13-mm MG 131 machine-guns over the engine with 300 rounds per gun, and a 30-mm MK 108 cannon with 100 rounds mounted between the engine cylinder banks and firing through the propeller hub. The aircraft could also carry two 20-mm MG 151/20 cannon in underwing gondolas with 120 rounds per gun. It was equipped with a Revi C 12 reflector sight.

In September 1943 a propaganda unit visited the 6. Staffel at its airfield in Creil. From left: Uffz. Trieb, Ofhr. Schmidt, Lt. Karch, Ofw. Schreckert, Ofw. Scharper (KIA 31 July 1944), Fw. Javurek, Uffz. Aue (KIA 22 May 1944), and Uffz. Reimer.

The 10.(J)/JG 2 also converted to the Fw 190. This aircraft has been placed in the firing butts to have its weapons aligned.

A Fw 190 A-5/U3 with SC 500 bomb mounted on the ETC beneath its fuselage taxis out for take-off. "Black 4", an aircraft of 10. Jabo/JG 2 "Richthofen", was based at Caen-Carpiquet airfield.

The Fw 190 illustrated here was probably not one of JG 2's machines. It does, however, reveal some interesting details, such as the insertion of bomb fuzes in bombs of different sizes. In the background is a bomb crate for an AB 500 bomb, beside it an hydraulic bomb trolley.

On 6 September 1943 the alarm was sounded for 2./JG 2 at St. André. A force of 120 B-17 Flying Fortresses had been reported in the Chartres area. Oberfeldwebel Bigge and his Fw 190 "Black 2" are ready for takeoff. The overall pale blue color was selected for the combined day and night fighter role. Note the jettisonable fuel tank under the fuselage.

Final checks by Oberfeldwebel Bigge before taking off at 1124 hours. In the ensuing action "Jupp" Bigge was able to shoot down one of the B-17s.

Right: At 1311 hours, as Oberfeldwebel Bigge was landing, his airfield was attacked by American bombers. Below left: Bigge collided with a horse-drawn cart on the runway. It had been abandoned there when the air raid began. His aircraft overturned on the runway at high speed. Below right: Unconscious and seriously injured, Oberfeldwebel Bigge hung suspended in his harness until he could be removed from his wrecked Fw 190. The rack on which the fuel tank was mounted is empty, as the pilot had jettisoned the tank before beginning his attack on the enemy bombers.

Condensation trails mark the progress of American bombers and their fighter escort. This was a regular sight in the skies over France.

The Fw 190s of JG 2 about to taxi out for takeoff. The engine is already running, and one member of the ground crew closes the canopy over the pilot.

In front of II./JG 2's command post in autumn 1943. From left to right: in the window Leutnant Müngersdorff, adjutant; Zahlmeister Heinze; Hauptmann Hesse, commander of the headquarters company; Oberleutnant Andresen, signals officer; Leutnant Dezius; Oberfeldwebel Wessolewski. On the right is "Flitzer", Gruppenkommandeur Major Bühligen's dog.

Staff officer Major Josef Fözö has arrived in Creil for a meeting to be held by the II. Gruppe. Here is greeted in front of the command post by Major Bühligen and officers of the Gruppenstab. Note the Austrian pilots badge worn by Fözö, who served in the Austrian Air Force before that country became part of the Reich.

Left: In II. Gruppe's command post in Creil. While Fähnrich Schmidt waits for his orders, Feldwebel Elbel places the latest intelligence reports before Gruppenkommandeur Bühligen.

Below: The Gruppenstab at work. Adjutant Leutnant Müngersdorff, on the right wearing the life vest, reads a mission order. On the telephone is Unteroffizier Krefft; in the background with the paper in his hands is Feldwebel Elbel.

Major Bühligen with his crew chief, Feldwebel Thieme. Thieme was later killed when a Bf 109 taking off from an airfield with the special codename "Sauwechsel" struck a tree and crashed. On the right is Feldwebel Jahn, Bühligen's wingman. Photograph taken at Creil in the winter of 1943-44.

Major Chouigui in his command post at Creil; on the left is Unteroffizier Elbel and right Feldwebel Jahn.

Eyes right! From left to right: comrade snowman, Leutnant Müngersdorff, Feldwebel Jahn and Unteroffizier Krefft. Photograph taken in front of the command post in Creil.

Creil in the winter of 1943-44. From left to right: Feldwebel Querengässer, Leutnant Kabbe, Staffelkapitän of 8./JG 2, and Leutnant Hamrisch. Querengässer had previously been Oesau's wingman.

Leutnant Kabbe makes ready for takeoff, assisted by Obergefreiter Thieme, crew chief of the Kommandeur of the II. Gruppe, Major Bühligen.

6

The *II. Gruppe* of *JG 2 "Richthofen"* in North Africa

5 November 1942
The 11. Staffel moves to Sicily, where it is attached to JG 53 "Pik As". The Staffel later leaves JG 2.

8 – 12 November 1942
The US Army lands in Morocco and Algeria in the rear of the German Africa Corps. In response the *Wehrmacht* occupies all of France.

Several units of *JG 2* are moved to the south of France to guard the Mediterranean coast against American bombers and help repel a possible invasion.

9 November 1942
The *Stab* and *I. Gruppe* transfer to Marseille-Merignane, two *Staffeln* of the *III. Gruppe* to Bourges and the 10. *Staffel* to Istres. There is no contact with the enemy.

13 November 1942
An advance party is sent to Italy by rail.

November 1942
The *II. Gruppe* also receives transfer orders. It is transferred to San Pietro in Sicily.

17 November 1942
The *II. Gruppe* arrives in San Pietro, where its role is to provide air cover for supply transports to Africa.

26 November 1942
The *II. Gruppe* moves to North Africa.

15 December 1942
The *II. Gruppe* has arrived in North Africa. In spite of the changes conditions, pilots and ground crews soon acclimatize to the new theater of war.

December 1942 – March 1943
Hauptmann Bühligen is one of the pilots who adapts quickly to the changed operational environment. He becomes the *Richthofen Geschwader*'s most successful pilots in Africa. The *II. Gruppe* is the only *Luftwaffe* fighter unit to operate the Focke-Wulf in Africa.

2 February 1943
Oberleutnant Erich Rudorffer, *Staffelkapitän* of 6./JG 2, shoots down eight enemy aircraft over the Tunisian front.

3 February 1943
Kurt Bühligen scores his fiftieth victory. The *II. Gruppe* operates over Bizerte, Tebessa, Souk el Arab and Kairouan.

The 11. Staffel commanded by *Leutnant* Julius Meimberg becomes part of JG 53.

15 February 1943
Oberleutnant Rudorffer shoots down seven enemy aircraft.

17 March 1943
The *II. Gruppe* moves back to Beaumont-le-Roger. There it reequips with the Bf 109 G.

12 May 1943
Army Group Africa, commanded by *Generaloberst* von Arnim, surrenders. Von Arnim had assumed command from *Generalfeldmarschall* Rommel on 9 March 1943.

Extracts from the personal diary of a pilot of II./JG 2 in Tunisia:

17 November 1942: the *Gruppe* arrives in San Pietro.
21 November 1942: two Fw 190s destroyed in a night bombing raid on Bizerte.
21 November 1942: eight Fw 190s attack airfields near Bone and destroy 10 enemy aircraft.
22 November 1942: Fw 190s attack the airfields at Tebessa and Souk el Arab.
27 November 1942: Fw 190s shoot down enemy aircraft.
29 November 1942: Fw 190s shoot down enemy aircraft. *Feldwebel* Ernst Bosseckert injured in takeoff collision with Bf 109 at Bizerte. *Feldwebel* Alois Schnöll wounded, belly landing at Bizerte after air combat.

30 November 1942: one bomber shot down by Fw 190.
1 December 1942: at least 1 Lightning shot down by Fw 190s.
2 December 1942: at least 1 Spitfire shot down by Fw 190s, Teboura.
3 December 1942: numerous enemy aircraft shot down by Fw 190s, mostly Lightnings.
3 December 1942: *Leutnant* Karlheinz Baensch wounded, combat with 15 Spitfires.
3 December 1942: *Leutnant* Alexander Bleymüller wounded.
4 December 1942: several enemy aircraft shot down by Fw 190s.
5 December 1942: several victories by Fw 190s.
7 December 1942: one Spitfire shot down while taking off.
10 December 1942: *Oberfeldwebel* Alfred Kretzschmar killed in crash during transfer flight.
13 December 1942: *Unteroffizier* August Stiefelhagen killed in crash during transfer flight.
17 December 1942: several Spitfires shot down by Fw 190s.
18 December 1942: four-engined bombers, Spitfires and Lightnings shot down.
18 December 1942: Rudorffer 1 Spitfire.
20 December 1942: Rudorffer 1 Spitfire.
2 January 1943: combat with Spitfires.
6 January 1943: at least one Spitfire shot down by Fw 190s.
8 January 1943: Rudorffer 1 Boston, 1 Spitfire.
8 January 1943: *Hauptmann* Adolf Dickfeld injured in takeoff crash at Kairouan.
8 January 1943: *Oberfeldwebel* Karl Pfeiffer killed in combat with 2 Curtiss fighters.
9 January 1943: *Unteroffizier* Heinz Schulze injure din takeoff crash.
11 January 1943: *Unteroffizier* Alfred Sonntag injured, bailed out following takeoff.
17 January 1943: *Unteroffizier* Karch 1 Spitfire.
18 January 1943: Rudorffer 1 Lightning, 1 Spitfire.
21 January 1943: *Unteroffizier* Heinz Gabler missing after combat with Curtiss fighters.
25 January 1943: *Leutnant* Werner Klein injured in landing crash.
1 February 1943: one four-engined bomber rammed by Fw 190.
2 February 1943: several Hurricanes and Curtiss fighters shot down.
2 February 1943: four victories by Bühligen (42-45).
3 February 1943: five victories by Bühligen (46-50), flight of 13 close-support aircraft destroyed.
4 February 1943: Rudorffer 2 Spitfires.
4 February 1943: three victories by Bühligen (51-53), Lightnings?
9 February 1943: Rudorffer shoots down 6 Curtisses and 2 Lightnings.
14 February 1943: Rudorffer 1 Spitfire, probably also victories by Bühligen.
15 February 1943: three victories by Bühligen (61-63).
15 February 1943: Rudorffer shoots down 4 Lightnings, 3 Spitfires.
15 February 1943: *Unteroffizier* Rudolf Weitgruber injured in take off crash.
17 February 1943: *Unteroffizier* Karl Sennewald shot down and killed by Spitfires.
17 February 1943: combat with Spitfires.
21 February 1943: *Oberfeldwebel* Ludwig Jacobs wounded. Shot down by friendly flak, bailed out over own airfield.
23 February 1943: *Oberleutnant* Wolf von Bülow killed in bombing raid on Kairouan.
3 March 1943: combat with Spitfires. *Feldwebel* Richard Übelbacher killed, possibly shot down by friendly fighters.
8 March 1943: *Unteroffizier* Erich Engelbrecht shot down and killed in combat with Spitfires.
8 March 1943: *Unteroffizier* Alfred Sonntag wounded in combat with Spitfires.
11 March 1943: Rudorffer 2 Spitfires.
12 March 1943: Rudorffer 1 four-engined bomber.

II./JG 2 appears to have left North Africa in approximately mid-March 1943.

II./JG 2's top-scoring pilots in Tunisia:

Victories	
Oberleutnant Kurt Bühligen	40
Leutnant Erich Rudorffer	27
Oberleutnant Adolf Dickfeld	approx. 18
Oberfeldwebel Kurt Goltzsch	14
Leutnant Karlheinz Baensch	10
Leutnant Günther Rubell von Bülow	approx. 7

On 5 November 1942 11./JG 2 was transferred to Sicily, where it was attached to JG 53. The *Staffel*, commanded by Julius "Jule" Meimberg, would never return to JG 2, later becoming part of JG 53. Here the *Staffel's* pilots are seen shortly before departing for Sicily; from left to right: Fw. Grüber, Uffz. Zaner, Uffz. Täschner, Ofw. Steege, Olt. Meimberg, Lt. Laube, Lt. Greim, Fw. Steinkühler.

Leutnant Hubert Greim, son of *Generalfeldmarschall* Ritter von Greim. As the title "Ritter von" (indicating that the bearer had been knighted) could not be passed on, it did not form part of Hubert Greim's name. In the summer of 1942 Hubert Greim was a pilot in the *Stabsschwarm* of JG 2 *"Richthofen"*. He later went to 11./JG 2, the high-altitude *Staffel* led by *Leutnant* Julius Meimberg. He saw service in Africa with this *Staffel*, which by then was equipped with the Bf 109 G-4 Trop. During a transfer flight from Mateur to Bizerte, Greim was shot down by anti-aircraft fire. He came down behind English lines and was captured near Ain-Draham.

Tours railway station in France. On 13 November 1942 the *II. Gruppe*'s ground organization began moving to Africa.

17 November 1942. As part of the German move into previously unoccupied France, the *Gruppe*'s Fw 190s arrive at the Merignac airfield. Here is one of the unit's Focke-Wulfs. The white fuselage band was worn by all *Luftwaffe* aircraft operating in the Mediterranean and Africa. On the right is a French Bloch 152 fighter wearing Vichy French markings and national colors.

Hauptmann Adolf Dickfeld puts on his parachute. He arrived in Africa to assume command of II./JG 2. He led the unit from December 1942 until April 1943. On the left is Hauptfeldwebel Wohlert.

This photograph of Adolf Dickfeld was taken when he was still a *Leutnant*. He was an outstanding fighter pilot, receiving the Knight's Cross on 19 March 1942 after 47 victories. By 19 May 1942 he had raised his total to 101 and was awarded the Oak Leaves. Dickfeld was the eighth German fighter pilot to reach 100 victories.

At the beginning of its Mediterranean deployment II./JG 2 flew convoy escort missions from San Pietro in Sicily. The Fw 190s provided fighter cover for transports carrying vital supplies to the Axis armies in North Africa.

17 November 1942: the Fw 190 As of 6./JG 2 have been fitted with external fuel tanks for their flight across the Mediterranean. A Junkers Ju 88 served as a pilot aircraft, guiding the single-seat fighters across the sea via the shortest route.

Bizerte, a desert airfield in Tunisia. The *II. Gruppe* has flown its first sorties over the North African desert. Pilots and ground crews quickly adjusted to their new surroundings.

Mission briefing in the desert. In the center of the photo in tropical uniform is *Leutnant* Erich Rudorffer. In the background is a new Fw 190 A-4.

The topic of this open-air meeting is probably a convoy escort mission. The high-ranking officer on the right wears the Narvik Shield on his left sleeve.

Above: Tindja-South in Tunisia at the end of 1942. *Leutnant* Gehr with his camouflaged Fw 190 A-4.

Left: *Leutnant* Gehr, left, and *Leutnant* Karch of 6./JG 2 *"Richthofen"*.

II./JG 2's forward airfield near Kairouan. The tent houses the *Gruppe*'s command post, while a scissors telescope and a makeshift anti-aircraft weapon, an MG 34 on a tripod mount, are positioned on a nearby sand pile. On the right is one of the Gruppenstab's Fw 190s. The pilot beneath the machine-gun is *Leutnant* Rudorffer.

The highly-decorated "Experten" of II./JG 2 *"Richthofen"* at a table; from left to right: *Leutnant* Bühligen, Stabsarzt Kraus, *Hauptmann* Dickfeld, *Leutnant* Rudorffer. Dickfeld, the *Gruppenkommandeur*, was awarded the Oak Leaves on 19 May 1942 after his 101st victory. Rudorffer shot down 26 enemy aircraft in Tunisia, including 8 on 9 February and 7 on 15 February 1943. By the end of the war he had 220 victories. He was awarded the Swords after his 210th victory.

Soldiers of the security company have placed their Kar 98 K carbines, steel helmets and belts in front of camouflaged Fw 190s during a pause in training. The flying units required defense forces to counter the Long Range Desert Group, a special unit of the British Army which roamed behind German lines attacking airfields and installations.

Generalmajor Adolf Galland during a visit to II./JG 2. Here the General der Jagdflieger is seen inspecting the *Gruppe* in La Mara.

Above: Typical desert scene complete with cactus. Below: *Leutnant* Erich Rudorffer in his Fw 190 A-4. Supply was always the Achilles Heel of the Africa Corps. Almost 60% of its supplies were sent to the bottom of the Mediterranean. At the beginning of 1943 the *Luftwaffe* in North Africa was already suffering under a severe fuel shortage.

When flown by a good pilot, the Curtiss P-40 Kittyhawk was an opponent to be taken seriously. The aircraft, procured in the USA by the RAF, was also an effective close-support aircraft.

Above: This Spitfire was shot down by *Leutnant* Brachmann, who is seen here inspecting the wreckage.

Right: *Oberleutnant* Julius Meimberg, *Kapitän* of the 11. *Staffel*. The unit officially became part of JG 53 in February 1943. On 24 October 1944 Meimberg was awarded the Knight's Cross. He scored a total of 53 victories against western opponents in Europe and North Africa.

Leutnant **Bühligen in his Fw 190 A-4 in Tunisia. He shot down 40 British and American aircraft in Tunisia from December 1942 to March 1943. Bühligen scored his 50th victory on 3 February 1943.**

In mid-March 1943 Kurt Bühligen shot down a Spitfire of the 31st Fighter Group of the American 12th Air Force. The American pilot, here seen second from the right, was probably Lieutenant Merlin Mitchell. As the photo shows, both the captured American and the German fighter pilots at the table were in a somber mood. The end of the Africa Corps was not far off. II./JG 2 would soon be withdrawn from Tunisia and returned to the Channel front in France.

7

Toward the End

Beginning of 1944
On every front the German armies are on the retreat. Allied armies roll through France toward the German frontier. In the east Soviet armies smash Army Group Center and near the German border in East Prussia.

The *Luftwaffe* finds itself in the same situation as 1918: 2,000 enemy fighter aircraft against 365 German.

German aircraft production reaches its high point in 1944. 40,593 aircraft are built, 25,285 of them fighters. By comparison, in 1940 total production was 10,427 machines. Still this is not enough. The Allies, especially the Americans, produce five times as may. In the west the *Luftwaffe* is outnumbered in the air by 11 to 1. As 1944 wears on, it becomes obvious that the war cannot last much longer:

- 25 August 1944: French troops liberate Paris.
- 31 August 1944: France is lost, German troops withdraw.
- 3 September 1944: British forces occupy Brussels.
- 3 December 1944: American forces breach the Westwall near Saarlautern.
- 12 January 1945: the Russians break through the German front on the Vistula.

January 1944
JG 2 "Richthofen" reports its 2,000th victory. From the surviving records it is impossible to determine with certainty how many aircraft are shot down by the *Geschwader* after this date. Based on the fragmentary information from the period 1 January to 8 May 1945 it may be estimated that the unit's final total lies in the area of 2,700 enemy aircraft shot down.

11 January 1944
The American 8th Air Force loses approximately 80 aircraft in daylight attacks on aircraft factories in Brunswick and Oschersleben. The *Luftwaffe* loses 40 fighters, however it is too weak to repeat this success. The *Geschwader* assigned to the Defense of the Reich are receiving too few replacement aircraft and especially pilots.

Beginning of 1944
Improved versions of the P-51 Mustang begin appearing in large numbers. The Mustang is superior to the Bf 109 G and Fw 190 A in a number of respects. The Fw 190 D-9 and Me 262 are equal or superior to the latest Allied fighter aircraft, however they have yet to reach the front-line units.

21 January 1944
American troops land at Anzio and Nettuno in the rear of the German front in Italy.

20 February 1944
II./JG 2 moves to Castiglione and Camino in Italy. From there they attack the beachhead at Nettuno or escort German bombers attacking the Allied fleet assembled offshore.

February 1944
The *Geschwader* is based at the following airfields:

Stab	Cormeilles	Messerschmitt Bf 109 G-6
II. Gruppe	Creil	Messerschmitt Bf 109 G-6
III. Gruppe	Cormeilles	Focke-Wulf Fw 190 A-8

2 March 1944
Oberstleutnant Egon Mayer is shot down and killed by Thunderbolts in the area of Montmedy. At the time of his death his victory total stands at 102, all gained in the west. After 353 combat missions, in which he shot down 25 four-engined bombers, he meets the same fate as many of his comrades. On the same day he is awarded the Swords.

March 1944
Major Kurt "Kuddel" Ubben becomes the new *Kommodore* of *JG 2*. He had previously commanded III./JG 77 in Russia, North Africa and Italy. On 12 March 1942 he was awarded the Oak Leaves after his 69th victory. Ubben scored his 100th victory on 14 January 1943. He will not command the *Geschwader* for long.

21 March 1944
The *Luftwaffe* has exhausted its offensive strength. Nothing demonstrates this more clearly than the fact that on this day Germany initiates an air situation reporting system. Reports are broadcast every hour, day and night, describing the situation in the air. Special bulletins are issued whenever the situation changes. Listeners hear that 500, 800 or 1,000 enemy aircraft are heading for Cologne, Berlin or Schweinfurt and that an attack is expected on this or that city. Only later, when the sirens of the advance and main alarms ring, do the affected citizens know whose turn it is on this day or night.

2 April 1944
The *I. Gruppe* moves back to France.

27 April 1944
Kommodore Major Ubben, not fully recovered from a serious wound, is shot down and killed over France by Thunderbolts. Ubben was able to get out of his blazing machine, but he bailed out too low and his parachute did not have time to fully deploy. At the time of his death he had scored 110 victories, 20 of them in the west. He also accounted for 25 aircraft on the ground, destroyed 15 tanks and sank a torpedo boat.

5 May 1944
The *I. Gruppe* is now based at Cormeilles and resumes operations against the heavy bombers and escort fighters of the American 8th Air Force as they attack targets in the occupied territories and Germany.

May 1944
Major Kurt Bühligen, *Kommandeur* of the *II. Gruppe*, becomes the twelfth and last *Kommodore* of *JG 2 "Richthofen"*. He first joined the *Luftwaffe* in 1936 as a mechanic. Bühligen subsequently trained as a pilot and joined *JG 2* in July 1940. On 4 September 1940 *Unteroffizier* Bühligen scored his first victory over England. He was awarded the Knight's Cross on 4 September 1941 after his 21st victory. In Tunisia he shot down 40 enemy aircraft between December 1942 and March 1943. On 2 March 1944 *Major* Bühligen was awarded the Oak Leaves after his 96th victory. He scored his 100th victory in June of the same year. On 14 August he was awarded the Swords after his 104th victory. By the end of the war, Bühligen had flown more than 700 combat missions over western Europe and North Africa. He destroyed 112 enemy aircraft, including 24 four-engined bombers.

28 May – 10 June 1944
The *II. Gruppe* moves without aircraft to Gütersloh to rest and refit. The planned rest and refit does not proceed according to plan for two reasons: first, there are only 33 aircraft for 59 pilots; second, no sooner does the unit arrive at Gütersloh after a long train ride then the Allies land on the beaches of Normandy. D-Day, the invasion has begun. The *Gruppe* heads back to France at once. On the front-line airfield at Insolinde, code-named "Sauwechsel", it finds a collection of Messerschmitt fighters, some of them in very poor condition. The aircraft are put right, however, in large part due to the improvisational skills of the "Black Men", the mechanics. The *Gruppe* immediately resumes operations against overwhelming numbers of enemy aircraft supporting the invasion. After its return to France II./JG 2 has 63 pilots (authorized strength 120) and just 37 aircraft (authorized strength 140).

1 – 5 June 1944
The American 8th Air Force concentrates its attacks against road and rail installations and airfields in northern France, Belgium and Holland. Located in these areas are the divisions of Germany's mobile reserve, in particular the *2. Panzerlehrdivision* and the *12. SS-Panzerdivision "Hitlerjugend"*. Destruction of the transportation infrastructure will prevent the Germans from moving reserves to the invasion area.

The British and Americans have assembled an unbelievable armada of ships for the invasion. They also have a huge force of combat aircraft, all marked with black and white stripes on the wings and fuselage. One pilot of *JG 2* recalled that they were "like flies on a summer day". The USAAF and RAF had available 13,000 aircraft, including 3,000 bombers. To face 5,000 Allied fighters the *Luftwaffe* could muster just 120 serviceable fighter aircraft. *Generalleutnant* Werner Junck, the general in command of fighters in the invasion area, recalled that the actual number of serviceable, combat-ready fighters was about 80.

6 June 1944
On the day of the invasion there is little aerial combat and only a few German fighter units in northern France. *JG 26* is in the south of France for a rest and refit.

No bombers, no Stukas or torpedo bombers! An interlinking of ill-advised plans, know-it-all attitudes, and especially the dogmatic stubbornness of Adolf Hitler, who refused to believe that this was the actual invasion, resulted in the wasting of precious days. This did not just apply to the *Luftwaffe*, but to the army as well. Hitler only released powerful reserves after it was much too late. On the day of the invasion, the *Luftwaffe* was practically invisible. Unbelievable, but these are the facts. While the Allied air forces flew 15,000 sorties on D-Day, dropping 6,700 tons of bombs, the handful of German fighters were damned to powerlessness. The *Geschwader* kept its few aircraft in the air as much as possible.

7 June 1944

The steady losses were proving difficult to replace.

Operational Strength of *JG 2*

	Stab JG 2 Bf 109 G/Fw 190 A Creil	*I. Gruppe* Fw 190 A Cormeilles	*III. Gruppe* Fw 190 A Cormeilles
Authorized	3	18	17
Actual	2	3	6

In better times the authorized strength of a fighter *Gruppe* was up to 48 aircraft! Even worse than the loss of aircraft, however, was the loss of experienced, well-trained fighter pilots. The training times and resulting level of training of the German fighter pilot sank rapidly. Many new pilots with just 80 to 90 hours failed to survive their first three combat missions.

At the invasion front were *JG 2*, *JG 26* and later *III./JG 54*.

In 1945 W. Heilmann, a pilot in the *III. Gruppe* of the *Grünherz* (Green Heart) *Geschwader*, wrote an article titled "The Front-Line Soldier Speaks": "The obligatory mission order! Attack the invasion fleet in the mouth of the Orne with bombs and guns. Soon the entire German `armada', about 150 machines, was in the air. At a height of 5000 meters the fighters crossed over the coast and headed out to sea before turning back to attack from the direction of England, hopefully deceiving the enemy. While the Bf 109 units providing top cover remained above, the Focke-Wulfs dropped their noses and began the attack. At once ugly black smudges began dotting the sky, but the anti-aircraft fire remained behind the fast-diving fighters like a flock of angry crows frightened away from their food. The flak was replaced by tracer—red, yellow, green—reaching out toward our machines. An aircraft is hit and catches fire—keep diving! The pencils in the blue-gray crater of the Orne quickly grow into respectable objects: transports, guarded by warships, and a teeming mass of landing craft. The naval anti-aircraft fire intensifies into a furious staccato. A final correction, then press the bomb release button. Pull up! This recovery from the dive and the subsequent transition to low-level flight was always the most difficult part of the entire mission for us. As the overstressed airframe creaked and groaned, one pressed his head against the steel armor plate and dropped low in an attempt to fly under the murderous anti-aircraft fire. By the time these suicidal missions over the mouth of the Orne were finally halted, *Jagdgeschwader 2* and *26* and *III./JG 54*, the entire fighter force on the invasion front, had been decimated. We had lost 1,000 machines in scarcely three weeks. Worse than the enormous losses in aircraft were the losses in veteran pilots. The fighter force was reorganized on paper. The *II. Fliegerkorps* became the *II. Jagdkorps* with the *4.* and *5. Jagddivision*. *JG 2*, *JG 26* and *III./JG 54* were rested and brought up to strength. The result: inexperienced students flew behind the few remaining Experten and experienced formation leaders and were hunted down by the Allied fighters like rabbits. The enemy now had about 25 airfields in the invasion area, and his crushing air superiority prevented supplies from being moved by road or rail."

15 June 1944

By this day the greatest massing of ships in history had delivered to France 25 divisions with 427,000 men, 62,000 vehicles of all kinds and 105,000 tons of materiel. Yet in spite of the enemy's crushing numerical superiority, the fighting spirit of the German fighter pilots remained unbroken, and they flew mission after mission. At that time the *I. Gruppe* of *JG 2 "Richthofen"* was commanded by Knight's Cross wearer *Major* Hohagen, while the *III. Gruppe* was led by *Hauptmann* Lemke, also a wearer of the Knight's Cross. The new *Kommodore*, *Oberstleutnant* Bühligen, who had been awarded the Swords, flew with the *Stabsschwarm* at the head of his *Geschwader*.

22 June 1944

Major Josef Wurmheller, the 108th recipient of the Swords, *Kommandeur* of III./JG 2 *"Richthofen"*, is killed in action over the invasion front. He was one of the most successful fighter pilots on the Channel Front. When war broke out Wurmheller was with I./JG 53. In autumn 1940 he was twice shot down over the Channel. In July 1940 he was assigned to *JG 2* on the Channel. On 19 August 1942, over Dieppe, he shot down seven enemy aircraft in spite of a broken leg and a concussion. Wurmheller became *Staffelkapitän* of 9./JG 2 and on 8 June 1944 was appointed *Gruppenkommandeur* of *III. Gruppe*. At the time of his death his victory total stood at 102, of which about 9 were scored in the east. His victory total included at least 13 four-engined bombers.

Some accounts claim that he collided with his wingman in the air. *Leutnant* Christoph Dezius, then a *Leutnant* and *Kapitän* of the 7. *Staffel*, remembers the events of 22 June differently: the *III. Gruppe* was closing in on a formation of American bombers. As *Gruppenkommandeur*, *Major* Wurmheller led the attack. Then Dezius, who with his *Staffel* was flying at the rear of the formation, saw fighters, very high, approaching from the right (4 o'clock). At first he thought they were Bf 109s from another unit, but when they rolled over and dove on the German formation, he recognized the typical features of the P-51 Mustang. He radioed a warning to the *Gruppe*: "Attention, Indians from behind and above!" Wurmheller then put his machine into a steep climb before turning toward the enemy. The enemy fighters were already within firing range, however, and before *Major* Wurmheller could complete the maneuver his aircraft was hit by a burst of fire from a Mustang. Hit in the wings and fuselage, it crashed.

It has since been determined that the enemy fighters were in fact Spitfires from the fighter wing commanded by Johnnie Johnson, the famous RAF fighter pilot.

25 June 1944
On this Sunday morning *Leutnant* Temmler was shot down and bailed out. Then, near Evreux, he was attacked and killed while in his parachute. This cowardly act followed an air battle. Approximately 20 Bf 109s and 20 Fw 190s led by *Leutnant* Müngersdorff were on an intercept mission when they came upon and attacked 20 P-38 Lightnings. While they were engaged with the first group of American fighters, P-51 Mustangs arrived on the scene and joined the battle. Low on fuel, the German fighters were soon forced to break off the engagement. *Leutnant* Dezius together with Beinwerker, Temmler and another pilot were subsequently reported missing. Temmler's body was found still in his parachute harness.

6 July, 1944
The Allies have flown 158,000 sorties since D-Day, losing about 1,284 aircraft to German flak, fighters and other causes. Allied aircraft are constantly in the skies over Normandy, attacking German troop concentrations, positions, supply columns and airfields.

12 July 1944
The *I. Gruppe*, which is down to just five pilots, is transferred to Husum. It will rejoin the *Geschwader* on 13 August with 68 pilots but only 26 serviceable aircraft.

31 July 1944
The Allied beachhead now covers much of the Cotentin Peninsula. On this day the American 1st Army commanded by General Patton and the 3rd Army under General Bradley link up south of Avranches and break through the German lines. The German *91. Luftlandedivision* (15,000 men) is wiped out. The author's father took part in this battle as a *Leutnant* in *Regiment 1057* of the *91. LLD*. The way was now open for the Allies into the heart of France.

6 August 1944
A German counterattack drives ten kilometers into the US Army's attack force. Patton's army is in danger of being cut off. The counterattack, launched during the night, is halted when day comes. 300 German fighters, including the units of *JG 2*, are heavily engaged by superior numbers of enemy aircraft and are unable to carry their mission of providing air cover for the German tanks. The RAF's rocket-firing Typhoon and Tempest fighters knock out 90 panzers in a short time. The last attempt to stop the invasion fails.

23 August 1944
The *III. Gruppe*, which has been reduced to just 7 pilots, must be withdrawn to Königsberg-Neumark to rest and refit. It will not return until 15 October.

25 August 1944
The *Geschwader*'s retreat to Germany has begun. It moves by way of Reims, St. Trond, Asch and Cologne to Wiesbaden-Erbenheim.

4 September 1944
After arriving at Erbenheim, *JG 2* moves to second-line airfields at Nidda, Usingen-Merzhausen and Altenstadt. The various *Gruppen* will be based here for some time.

The *Geschwader* retreats in stages, engaging in fierce defensive battles between moves. It follows the same route it took four years earlier with the then victorious *Wehrmacht*.

September 1944
The *Geschwaderstab* of *JG 2* and the *I. Gruppe* under *Hauptmann* Hrdlicka operate from a second-line airfield near Merzhausen. The *II. Gruppe* under *Hauptmann* Schröder is now based at Eschborn near Frankfurt.

October 1944
JG 2 is now operating as part of the II. Jagdkorps in the Defense of the Reich West. The *Stab* and *II. Gruppe* are based at Nidda, *I. Gruppe* at Merzhausen. The *III. Gruppe* under *Hauptmann* Lemke is based at Königsberg-Neumark.

November 1944
The *Stab* and *II. Gruppe* at Nidda, the *I. Gruppe* at Merzhausen and the *II. Gruppe* now at Altenstedt.

The *II. Gruppe* flies the Bf 109 G-6 and the new K-10, while the other *Gruppen* are equipped with the Fw 190 A-8. Though badly battered, the *Richthofen Geschwader* continues to fly against the enemy air forces attacking Germany by day and night. During the summer of 1944 the *Luftwaffe* lost about 500 aircraft per month. Many of the pilots were able to parachute to safety. In spite of these losses the fighter defense regenerates itself surprisingly quickly.

Beginning of November 1944
To defend the Reich the *Luftwaffe* is able to muster 19 *Jagdgeschwader*, including several units with the Me 262, with approximately 3,500 aircraft.

2 November 1944
Early on this cloudy Thursday two groups of bombers from the American 8th Air Force come in over Holland. The first consists of 325 four-engined bombers, the second 650. The first group's targets are fuel installations in Gelsenkirchen and Castrop Rauxel, while the second heads for the hydrogenation plant at Leuna, about four kilometers from Merseburg. The fighter escort consists of 600 Mustangs of the 8th Air Force and a smaller number of Lightnings of the 9th Air Force. 500 German fighters take off to intercept. Bad weather over the area of Rhein-Main prevents *JG 2* from getting to the enemy. The air battles on this day result in the loss of 134 German fighters—a devastating defeat for the *Luftwaffe*.

21 November 1944

Another enemy incursion is reported heading for central Germany. The weather on this Tuesday is poor, with rain and low cloud. Bombers of the American 8th Air Force are escorted by 650 Mustangs. 400 German fighters wait for the order to take off, but it does not come. It is soon clear that the target is the hydrogenation plant in Leuna. But the corps headquarters hesitates, fearing that the adverse weather will result in heavy losses. Only *Jagdgeschwader 300* and *301* are equipped to fly in bad weather. Both *Geschwader* were originally single-engine night fighter, or "Wilde Sau" (Wild Boar), units. They fly the Fw 190 A-9/R11, which is equipped with the FuG 125 radio beacon receiver. This equipment can also be used to fly beam approaches in bad weather. Losses to escorting fighters are considerable. The other *Geschwader*, including *JG 2*, do not receive the order to take off until the Americans are on their way home. The Mustangs are everywhere. The Thunderbolts of the 366th Fighter Group are now also capable of reaching the Ruhr region, 2 November turns into a disaster. The German fighter arm loses at least 61 aircraft while shooting down just 5 Fortresses and 2 Mustangs.

21 November 1944

III./JG 2, which made contact with the American formation, loses one aircraft and its pilot over the Rhein-Main area.

During these weeks of heavy fighting the losses suffered by the units of the *Reichsverteidigung* reach unbearable levels. Three or four fighters are lost for each enemy aircraft shot down, often with the loss of the pilots as well. On 26 November the German fighter units lose 90 aircraft while shooting down just 20 Liberators. These numbers make it almost impossible to speak of a "Defense of the Reich" any more. Despite the overwhelming numerical superiority of the Americans, the will to fight of the German fighter pilot remains unbroken. They know that their chances of surviving are small, and even if they do get back they are likely to find American fighters waiting over their airfields. Every effort is made to camouflage the German airfields and new fields are cut out of the woods. Fighter aircraft are concealed beneath the trees. Water is sprayed onto the grass after takeoffs and landings to conceal the telltale tire tracks. Cows serve a double purpose: not only does their presence give the impression of a pasture, the fuel shortage means that the animals must also used to tow the aircraft to and from their camouflaged dispersals. German aircraft production in 1944 exceeds the combined total of all previous years, however the omnipresent American fighter-bombers make it impossible for trains to deliver supplies to their destinations. The strategic bombing of hydrogenation plants does the rest, and without fuel nothing can be done. The increasingly poor training of replacement pilots exacerbates the situation further. The sky is full of disciplined, well-trained American pilots. The fierce battles claim most of the young, inexperienced Germans. They watch their comrades go down and are paralyzed by what they see—becoming easy prey for the ever-present Mustangs and Thunderbolts. By this stage of the war the average trainee fighter pilot receives about thirty hours training. In the heat of battle many inexperienced pilots forget to release the safety catch on their control sticks and are thus unable to fire their guns. Under these conditions it is not surprising that most do not survive their third mission. But things have become much tougher even for the battle-hardened "old hares". While many of them have been in continuous action for two or three years, their American counterparts are rotated out after 50 missions.

In spite of all this the German fighter pilots continue to achieve some amazing successes, but the losses continue. On 27 November, for example, 50 German fighters are lost in exchange for just 5 Mustangs. The ratio of forces in November 1944 lies somewhere between 20 and 30 to 1. In spite of this demoralizing situation the German fighter pilots continue to take to the air.

2 December 1944

The 8th Air Force steps up its activities in spite of the bad weather and launches two major raids against Cologne and Bingen. The attacks are supposed to interdict supplies for the final German offensive of the war in the Ardennes. The fighter units report the loss of 65 aircraft. 47 pilots are killed or missing. Elements of *I.* and *III./JG 2* take part in the fighting and report the loss of five pilots killed in combat with large numbers of Thunderbolts.

5 December 1944

American and British heavy bombers, the latter now also operating over Germany by day, attack Berlin. A force of 427 Flying Fortresses approach the capital. In spite of the fuel shortage, the *I. Jagdkorps* puts 300 fighter aircraft into the air. The adverse weather prevents most of them from making contact with the enemy, however. Only *JG 1*, *JG 301* and elements of *JG 26* intercept the enemy. *Staffeln* of *JG 2* make contact with the Americans as they head for home and are heavily engaged. The inferiority of the German replacement pilots is demonstrated once again. At the end of the day the *Luftwaffe* reports the loss of 75 aircraft (the Americans claim 90). Only 5 American bombers are shot down. *II./JG 2* loses one pilot killed and one wounded over the Bonn area. Both Fw 190 A-8s are total losses.

Reports of German pilots being shot at in the parachutes are on the rise.

16 December 1944

It is Saturday. In the early morning hours the *Wehrmacht* launches its offensive in the west. Three armies launch a final counterstrike from the Eifel region into Belgium and Luxembourg. The *Luftwaffe* has massed twelve *Jagdgeschwader*, 40 *Gruppen*, to support the operation. Among them is *JG 2 "Richthofen"*. Bad weather grounds much of the *Luftwaffe* at the start of the offensive.

17 December 1944

On this day there is fierce fighting in the air above the Eifel Mountains. Almost every *Geschwader* of the Reich air defense contributes *Gruppen* or *Staffeln*. The Messerschmitt and Focke-Wulf fighters of *Jagdgeschwader 2*, *3*, *4*, *6*, *11*, *26*, *27*, *53* and *54* meet far superior numbers of P-38 Lightnings and P-47 Thunderbolts. The fighting extends over Belgium, the Moselle area and the Eifel region. The German units lose sixty pilots killed or wounded.

17 December 1944
The *3.* and *4. Staffel* of the *II. Gruppe* encounter American fighters over the border region between Belgium and Germany. A fierce battle erupts. *Oberfähnrich* Kowalski shoots down one enemy fighter but is almost immediately shot down himself. He comes down near Krinkelt and is taken prisoner. *Feldwebel* Fester is hit by flak over the front and bails out near Adenau. *Gefreiter* Fischer is shot down and killed by Thunderbolts near Oberstedem. Four other pilots from the *I. Gruppe* are posted missing on this day: *Leutnant* Elser, *Gefreiter* Eube, *Fähnrich* Selpin and *Leutnant* Snobeck. *Oberfeldwebel* Nowak bails out of his burning machine, as does *Gefreiter* Rebmann. Both return safely to the *Gruppe*. The *I.* and *II. Gruppe* each lose four pilots on this day.

18 December 1944
Between Aachen and Bonn III./JG 2 encounters the American 365th and 368th Fighter Groups. The *II. Gruppe* joins the battle. *Feldwebel* Pfeiffer of the *11. Staffel* is killed and *Obergefreiter* Melda of the *7. Staffel* is reported missing. His Bf 109 K-4 was last seen near Aachen engaging 15 Thunderbolts.

23 December 1944
On this Saturday the Allied air forces are extremely active. Heavy bombers of the American 8th Air Force take off to attack targets in Germany. At the same time approximately 400 light and medium bombers of the 9th Air Force are in action over the Eifel region. The RAF launches a raid on Cologne. Large numbers of enemy fighters sweep ahead of the Fortresses and Liberators to engage the German fighters. Every *Geschwader* in the Defense of the Reich is on alert. *JG 4*, *JG 11* and elements of *JG 27* have already made contact with the enemy. The 9th Air Force's targets are railway installations in Ahrweiler which are helping supply the Ardennes offensive. Sixty B-26 Marauders of the American 386th and 391st Bomber Groups are attacking the rail installations when suddenly a similar number of fighters from *JG 2*, *JG 3* and *JG 11* appear. The German fighters attack the bombers of the 391st Group and shoot down 16 of the Marauders. But as is so often the case, German losses are even higher. *Oberfähnrich* Kusche of the *II. Gruppe* crashes while taking off from Nidda. *Unteroffizier* Kleybrink, and *Feldwebel* Lang of the *I. Gruppe* and *Obergefreiter* Maas and *Unteroffizier* Pfeiler of the *II. Gruppe* are shot down by American escort fighters east of the Rhine. *Oberfähnrich* Aickelin's aircraft sustains heavy battle damage and he heads for Cologne-Wahn airfield. When the heavily damaged Bf 109 G-14 touches down, it flip over. Seriously injured, Aickelin is taken to hospital. *III./JG 2* loses five pilots. *Unteroffizier* Burger of the *12. Staffel* is shot down in one of the first Fw 190 D-9s delivered to the unit. Many years after the war the remains of the aircraft and its pilot are discovered near Meckenheim. *JG 2* loses 11 aircraft on this day. The other nine *Geschwader* suffer 98 pilot casualties, 63 killed and 35 wounded.

End of December 1944
JG 2 has begun reequipping on the new Focke-Wulf Fw 190 D-9, which is powered by a Jumo liquid-cooled engine. The installation of the inline engine results in a lengthened forward fuselage and the type is soon dubbed the "*Langnase*", or Long-Nose. The D-9 is an outstanding fighter aircraft, fully equal to the American fighters in performance and armament. Like so many other advanced German weapons, however, it is a case of too little, too late.

24 December 1944
In the morning the 8th Air Force launches its biggest operation since the invasion: 2,034 four-engined bombers and more than 1,000 escort fighters. The British also send heavy bombers, fighters and fighter-bombers. An astonishing armada of aircraft heads for Germany. When the first American bombers reach Germany, the last are just taking off from their bases in England. Equally astonishing is the fact that the *I.* and *II. Jagdkorps* are able to muster 800 fighters to intercept the incursions. This is in part due to the efforts of the "Black Men", technicians of every kind. In recent days and weeks they have worked day and night, repairing many unserviceable Messerschmitts and Focke-Wulfs. It is an equally unbelievable accomplishment. The objective of the Allied attacks is to halt the German offensive in the Ardennes.

More than half of the Allied bombers, 1,400 in number, escorted by 700 fighters, attack airfields in the Frankfurt—Giessen area. Among them are the bases used by *JG 2*. Units of the American 9th Air Force and the Royal Air Force attack roads, railway stations and other transportation targets in the Trier—Euskirchen area. Another wave bombs *Oberstleutnant* Kurt Bühligen's airfield. The *Geschwader*'s airfields at Ettingshausen, Giessen, Merzhausen, Nidda and Kirch-Göns are heavily damaged.

Unteroffizier Maier of *JG 2* is shot down and killed by Mustangs over his own "Garden Fence", or home airfield. *Unteroffiziere* Kühn and Patzelt are reported missing over the western combat zone. *Unteroffizier* Löbering is killed in a bombing raid on Merzhausen airfield. When the battle ends it is only a few hours until Christmas Eve. It is the sixth Christmas of the war. On this day the *Luftwaffe* loses 85 pilots killed or missing plus 21 wounded, a total of 106 aircrew. 44 British and American bombers have been shot down. Given the number of enemy fighters and the heavy defensive armament carried by the bombers, this is a remarkable achievement. It has become obvious, however, that the German fighter arm is incapable of stopping the bombing or even of inflicting heavy losses on the attackers.

1 January 1945
"Operation Bodenplatte". The *Luftwaffe* launches its last major offensive operation of the war. More than 900 fighters from every unit based in the Reich take part in this last desperate attempt by the German command to regain the initiative in the west. It is intended to be a destructive blow against the Allied air forces on their airfields in France, Holland and Belgium. It does not turn out that way, however.

The attack force suffers losses en route to the target at the hands of German anti-aircraft guns, which had not been fully informed about the operation. Approximately 500 enemy aircraft are destroyed on the ground, however 93 German fighters are shot down, 36 by enemy fighters and 57 by flak. These losses are relatively low compared to those of the Allies, which some sources put at 700 to 800 aircraft, but the flight home becomes a disaster in which about 200 German fighters are shot down by their own anti-aircraft guns.

Seeing large formations of low-flying aircraft approaching from the west, the crews of the anti-aircraft guns assumed them to be hostile. And so the catastrophe began. By the time the anti-aircraft gunners realized their error it was too late.

While the Allies lost hundreds of aircraft, their personnel losses were minimal. The *Luftwaffe*, on the other hand, suffered heavily in both men and machines.

1 January 1945

From the perspective of *JG 2 "Richthofen"*: "It was still night on the north slope of the Taunus Mountains, where the *I. Gruppe* of *JG 2 "Richthofen"* had been based near Merzhausen since late autumn 1944. The pilots of all four *Staffeln* had left their quarters in Altweilnau, Niederlauken and were on their way to the airfield. After a short mission briefing the approximately 30 pilots drove to the airfield. Even the *Staffelkapitäne* had no details about the coming mission, but everyone suspected that the coming day would be difficult. After all, they had lived through the past days and weeks. But 'Operation Bodenplatte' would far exceed even their worst forebodings. *Hauptmann* Hrdlicka, *Kommandeur* of the *III. Gruppe*, opened the mission order he had been given the night before. 'Takeoff at 0800 hours. Assemble over Grid Squares Paula Quelle 4 and 5, wait for the *II.* and *III. Gruppe* to join up. Target: St. Trond airfield in Belgium. Attack will be made together with *Schlachtgeschwader 4*.' *SG 4* was commanded by *Oberst* Alfred Druschel, a wearer of the Swords. The Focke-Wulf Fw 190 Ds with their 1,770-h.p. Jumo engines took off southward and then turned due west. The *Gruppe* flew over Camberg to Koblenz, where the *Geschwader* was to form up. The *II. Gruppe*, ably led by *Hauptmann* Schröder and flying the Bf 109 G-6, had taken off from Nidda. Coming from Weilburg, the *III. Gruppe*, which was also equipped with "Longnoses", arrived over the Westerwald. There the Fw 190 D-9 of *Unteroffizier* Fritz Altpeter of 11./JG 2 began to smoke, and soon flames gushed out from under the engine cowling. Soon afterwards 'Yellow 4' crashed near Dierdorf with its pilot still on board. He was the first of *JG 2*'s pilots to die that day. At about 0900 hours the *Geschwader*'s ninety fighter aircraft reached the area of the front and were greeted by heavy anti-aircraft fire. *Unteroffizier* Dost was shot down and killed, as was *Unteroffizier* Optenhostert. *Unteroffizier* Wilkens and *Feldwebel* Hohenberg were also shot down by flak and were taken prisoner by the Americans. Meanwhile the *Geschwader* had reached its target, the airfield at St. Trond, and began its attack. Parked in long rows there were the Thunderbolts of the 48th and 404th Fighter Groups of the American 9th Air Force. American fighters already in the air had warned the airfield defenses, however, and the German fighters were greeted by fierce anti-aircraft fire. Almost every *Staffel* lost aircraft. The fates of many of the pilots shot down in this attack will never be known. The *II. Gruppe* lost just two pilots killed, but one of them was its *Gruppenkommandeur*. It was an especially painful loss, for *Hauptmann* Georg Schröder was an experienced unit leader, and by this time they were becoming extremely rare. Schröder bailed out successfully and was captured. Pilots suddenly noticed that aircraft that had been flying with them were no longer there, such as 'Blue 1" of *Unteroffizier* Adolf Redlich of the *12. Staffel* or the Messerschmitt flown by *Unteroffizier* Bollwerk of the *5. Staffel*. *Leutnant* Werner Edelhoff of the *Gruppenstab* was shot down. He was taken prisoner near St. Trond. The pilots of the Messerschmitts and Focke-Wulfs destroyed a large number of enemy fighters on the ground, but what did it matter given the masses of American materiel. When the attack was over the fighters turned east. On the way home the *10. Staffel* lost another pilot, its sixth. He was *Leutnant* Christfried Clemens, who was able to crash-land his Fw 190 D-9. Two *Staffeln* of *JG 2*, the *4.* and *10.*, had now suffered fifty percent losses. When 1 January 1945 came to an end, one of the most battle-hardened and successful units of the German fighter arm had suffered a blow from which it would never recover.

The participating units of the *Geschwader* suffered 40% losses. 23 pilots had been killed or were missing, another 10 had been captured and 4 more wounded. It would be two weeks before *JG 2 "Richthofen"* was again able to take part in major action with the Defense of the Reich.

From the start of the Ardennes offensive on 16 December 1944 until the evening of 1 January 1945, *JG 2 "Richthofen"* suffered the loss of 78 pilots.

The numbers compiled after the Second World War are shocking. The German fighter arm lost approximately 230 pilots within the space of five or six hours. Of these 154 were killed, 62 missing and 14 wounded. They included two *Geschwaderkommodore*, *Oberstleutnant* Specht of JG 11 and *Oberstleutnant* Druschel of SG 4, six *Gruppenkommandeure*, including *Hauptmann* Schröder of II./JG 2, and ten *Staffelkapitäne*, for a total of 18 unit leaders. 214 other pilots were lost, bringing the total to 232. For the German fighter arm this was the final blow. It could not recover from such losses.

"Bodenplatte" had cost the *Luftwaffe* 300 fighter aircraft. It had lost 30% of its operational strength on a single day, 1 January 1945. The only units left to defend the Reich were *JG 300* and *JG 301*.

Beginning of January 1945

Generalleutnant Adolf Galland is replaced as General of Fighters. This act by the Supreme Command is a rebuke of the German fighter arm. It is useless and its pilots cowards. Embittered by this action and the blame that had been placed upon them, a number of veteran commanders of *Geschwader*, fighter commanders and division commanders write a memorandum to Göring in which they bluntly lay out the facts concerning the Defense of the Reich.

22 January 1945
In the *Haus der Flieger* in Berlin there is a meeting attended by Göring which goes into the history books as the "Revolt of the Fighter Pilots". It was in fact nothing of the sort. While young, inexperienced fighter pilots are dying in the skies over Germany, and the nation's cities are reduced to rubble and ash with millions of civilians dying horrible deaths by day and night, men like Lützow, Rödel, Steinhoff and Trautloft want to make one last attempt to turn the tide. As we now know, their efforts were in vain. *Oberst* Lützow speaks the truth to Göring's face, telling him that the *Luftwaffe* command, meaning Göring himself, has failed. Göring subsequently banishes Lützow and the dying continues.

February 1945
The *Stab* and *II. Gruppe* of *JG 2* remain at Nidda, under the command of the *II. Jagdkorps*. The *I. Gruppe* is based at Merzhausen and the *III. Gruppe* at Ettingshausen.

25 February 1945
The bombers of the American 8th Air Force, 1,177 Fortresses and Liberators, are sent to knock out the German transportation system and airfields used by the Me 262 jet fighter. The bombers are guarded by 600 escort fighters. *Luftwaffenkommando West* and the *IX. Fliegerkorps* issue a major alarm for all units. Two *Staffeln* of *JG 2* flying Focke-Wulfs take off from Merzhausen to intercept a group of Liberators on their way home after attacking Aschaffenburg. The American escort fighters clash with a number of Fw 190 A-8s of *JG 2* over Gross-Umstadt. Twelve Mustangs and six Lightnings attack the four or five German fighters and immediately shoot down *Unteroffizier* Ewald Kamman of *3. Staffel* and *Oberleutnant* Rossbach of *9. Staffel*. In the early 1960s the wreckage of Kamman's aircraft is discovered by chance along with the remains of its pilot, who was 25 years old when he was killed.

2 March 1945
In the afternoon enemy twin-engined bombers, Martin B-26 Marauders, are reported heading for the *Wehrmacht* depot in Giessen. I./JG 2 is ordered into the air, led by its *Kommandeur Hauptmann* Hrdlicka. In the running battle that follows, *Oberfeldwebel* Butter is shot down by a Lightning and *Oberstleutnant* Hertle by a Thunderbolt. Both pilots parachute to safety. The other pilots are unable to close with the bombers, the American fighter escort is once again too powerful. One bomber is shot down by flak and a straggler is picked off by German fighters. *JG 2* loses three pilots, *Unteroffiziere* Arck and Breijl near Finthen and Erbenheim and *Oberfähnrich* Stempel in the area around Mainz.

The shortage of fuel and the almost constant presence of American and British fighter-bombers have made regular fighter missions virtually impossible. The German fighter pilot has long since become the hunted. Though powerless, they courageously continue to fly.

7 March 1945
An advance detachment of the American 9th Armored Division reaches the still-intact Ludendorff Bridge at Remagen. Attempts by the Germans to blow up the bridge fail. The first American units American cross the old railway bridge built during the First World War. The German defenders attempt to destroy the bridge, first with artillery fire then by air attack. One of the units attacking the bridge is *III./KG 76*, which is equipped with the Arado Ar 234, the world's first jet bomber. Me 262 fighter-bombers also try to knock out the now heavily-defended bridge, but in vain. Stukas of *Schlachtgeschwader 2 "Immelmann"* and bomb-carrying Fw 190 D-9s of *JG 2* attack the bridge but are unable to bring it down. All the while tanks, armored troop carriers and other vehicles of the 9th Armored Division stream across the bridge into the heart of Germany, virtually unhindered. On 17 March the bridge finally collapses from the effects of the demolition attempts, near misses and heavy traffic. Even the first tactical use of V2 rockets, which miss the target, cannot alter the situation.

Spring 1945
According to unconfirmed reports, *III./EJG 2*, under the command of *Oberstleutnant* Heinz Bär, a wearer of the Swords, trains on the Me 262 at Lechfeld. *Hauptmann* Rudolf Engleder, *Staffelkapitän* of *10./EJG 2*, takes part in the conversion training. Other pilots who are trained to fly the world's first production jet fighter are *Oberfeldwebel* Leo Schumacher, *Hauptmann* Erich Hartmann, wearer of the Diamonds and *Kommandeur* of I./JG 52, *Hauptmann* Hermann Staiger and *Oberfähnrich* Erich Kaiser.

16 – 26 March 1945
After crossing the Rhine at Remagen on 7 March, the Americans advance irresistibly to the east. In the face of the enemy advance, *JG 2* abandons its airfields in the area north of Frankfurt. It moves by way of Thuringia and Saxony to Pilsen, Karlsbad and Marienbad, Bohemia.

25 March 1945
The war is nearing its end. Many pilots serving with the *Geschwader*, more than 500, have lost their lives, along with mechanics, technicians and others. One of the last is *Hauptmann* Hrdlicka. He is reported missing after an engagement near Betzenrod in Hesse. The wreckage of his aircraft is discovered in 1951. A second-hand dealer from Giessen digs up what is left of the aircraft. The remains of the pilot are found at a depth of six meters, with the pilot's seat. Personal items, in particular an identity disk, identify the remains as those of Hrdlicka.

March-April 1945
The end is near. The Russians are about to complete the encirclement of Berlin. In the west, British and American forces have pushed deep into Germany. But still the majority of the *Wehrmacht*, in-

cluding the remnants of the *Luftwaffe*, fight on against the overwhelming strength of the enemy with the courage of desperation.

Such men form "Special Unit Beehive". It is based on an airfield near Marienbad together with elements of *JG 2*. It is equipped with the Bücker Bü 181 *Bestmann* and various other training machines that have been modified to carry the panzerfaust anti-tank weapon. The idea is the brainchild of *Oberst* Hajo Hermann, who earlier initiated the "Wilde Sau" or single-engine night fighters, and is responsible for "Rammkommando Elbe", a special unit formed to bring down enemy bombers by ramming. Both operations cost the lives of many pilots but achieved little success. During one of its first missions, "Special Unit Beehive" is intercepted by American fighters while en route to its target and is decimated.

In this desperate situation *Oberst* Hajo Hermann also brings into being the "Special Commando Elbe", better known as the "*Rammjäger*" (Ramming Fighters). *Oberst* Gordon Gollob, Galland's successor as General of Fighters, and *Oberst* Dahl, Inspector of Day Fighters, refuse to sanction the project. The project goes ahead nevertheless, with terrible consequences.

7 April 1945
This day witnesses the first mission by the *Rammjäger*, who are under orders to close to point-blank range to attack with guns and then, if necessary, ram their targets. They lose 77 pilots killed or missing. Only one B-17 is brought down by a head-on ramming attack. Neither the pilot of the German fighter nor the crew of the American bomber survive.

More and more German fighters are being destroyed on the ground by American aircraft. Their airfields are also hit, especially the areas used for takeoff and landing. It is now almost impossible to repair damaged aircraft during the night. The fuel shortage is now so severe that it is almost impossible to mount large-scale operations.

April 1945
American P-51 Mustang fighters attack Marienbad airfield. *Major beim Stab* Donath is fatally wounded while manning an anti-aircraft gun. The attack also kills or wounds four American prisoners of war being held at the airfield.

16 April 1945
Bolstered by pilots from other *Gruppen* and selected members of the technical and general personnel, *III. Gruppe* becomes *"Jagdverband Richthofen"* and is ordered to Jüterbog and from there to Rechlin, Schwerin and Leck.

18 April 1945
The remaining elements of *JG 2* are transferred to Cham.

On or about 20 April 1945
The unit comprising the remaining elements of *JG 2* flies to Berlin Tempelhof. Soviet troops have surrounded the capital. Russian artillery fire gives little time for refueling, and the aircraft take off across the shell-torn airfield. From there they fly over Schwerin to Leck, where they land. From there the unit flies against the Red Army units surrounding Berlin. The airfield is attacked repeatedly by British Spitfires and Tempests.

23 April 1945
Elements of the *II. Gruppe* are wiped out as American troops reach Cham. Personnel from the *Stab* of *II. Gruppe* and elements of *I. Gruppe* are captured. The remaining remnants move to Pocking. From there two aircraft fly one last mission. Afterward all that is left is flight, into the Erding—Holzkirchen—Prien area.

30 April 1945
For the *II. Gruppe* the war ends in Leck, while the rest of the *Geschwader* is on a farm in Föching near Straubing, Bavaria when the end comes. Twelve fighter aircraft are all that is left of *JG 2 "Richthofen"*. *Oberstleutnant* Bühligen disbands the *Geschwader*. As the first Sherman tanks appear at the edge of the airfield, the last aircraft of the once proud *"Jagdgeschwader Richthofen"* go up in flames.

The men begin the bitter journey into captivity.

8 May 1945
The remnants based at Leck surrender to British troops and also become prisoners of war.

Some of the most successful fighter pilots to fly on Germany's western front were members of *JG 2*. All of those listed below scored more than fifty victories while flying the Fw 190 with *JG 2* in 1941-45:

Oberstleutnant Kurt Bühligen
112, including Tunisia, Swords

Oberstleutnant Egon Mayer
102, Swords

Hauptmann Siegfried Lemke
95, Knight's Cross

Hauptmann Josef Wurmheller
93, Swords

Hauptmann Siegfried Schnell
87, Oak Leaves

Major Erich Rudorffer
86, including Tunisia

Oberst Walter Oesau
71, Swords

Major Hans Hahn
68, Oak Leaves

Major Georg Peter Eder
68, Oak Leaves

Oberleutnant Rudolf Pflanz
52, Knight's Cross

Hauptmann Egon Mayer photographed in April 1943. 69 victory bars may be seen on the rudder of his Fw 190 A-4.

Egon Mayer after a difficult mission against the American heavy bombers. His facial expression reflects the stress of the recent air battle.

Major Egon Mayer has scored his 100th victory, 24 of them over heavy bombers. To mark the occasion his comrades presented him with a piglet bearing the number 100. It was probably intended to bring him good luck, however Mayer would soon die in action.

On 2 March 1943 *Major* Egon Mayer was killed in action near Montmedy, shot down by Thunderbolts. At the time of his death Mayer had 102 victories to his credit. He was surely one of the best fighter pilots in the west and an outstanding unit leader. At the time of his death he had the highest number of kills against four-engined bombers and was awarded the Swords posthumously.

Leutnant Hupperts (left), *Leutnant* Wurmheller and four other members of the *Geschwader* make up the guard of honor around Mayer's casket.

Mayer's funeral was attended by high-ranking members of the *Luftwaffe*. In the center is *Major* Erich Hohagen, a *Gruppenkommandeur* in JG 27. In the autumn of 1941 he had been a *Staffelkapitän* in *JG 2 "Richthofen"* and on 5 October 1941 was awarded the Knight's Cross after his 30th victory.

Brüsseler Zeitung

Männer der Luftverteidigung (I)

Der 51. Schwerter-Träger

Oberstleutnant Egon Mayer, Kommodore des Jagdgeschwaders Richthofen, gefallen

bz. Brüssel, 10. März.

Der Führer verlieh am 2. März das Eichenlaub mit Schwertern zum Ritterkreuz des Eisernen Kreuzes an Oberstleutnant Egon Mayer, Kommodore des Jagdgeschwaders Richthofen, als einundfünfzigstem Soldaten der deutschen Wehrmacht. Am gleichen Tage ist Oberstleutnant Mayer gefallen.

Der am 19. August 1917 in Konstanz am Bodensee geborene Oberstleutnant Egon Mayer, ein schwäbischer Bauernsohn und engerer Landsmann des Ritters des Eisernen Kreuzes mit Eichenlaub, Schwertern und Brillanten, Hermann Graf, gehörte zu den alten Kämpfern des Jagdgeschwaders Richthofen. Mit der gleichen Umsicht wie seine Staffel führte er eine Gruppe des berühmten Geschwaders, dessen Kommodore er schliesslich wurde, ein würdiger Nachfolger der Tapferen, die vor ihm Hüter der ruhmvollen Richthofen-Tradition waren: von Bülow, Schellmann, Wick, Balthasar und Oesau. Vor wenigen Wochen meldete der Wehrmachtbericht den 2000. Luftsieg des Jagdgeschwaders Richthofen, an dem auch der Geschwaderkommodore wesentlichen Anteil hatte, durch seine Führung ebensosehr wie durch seine 100 Luftsiege, die dieser schneidige Jagdflieger in rücksichtslosem Draufgehen errang und mit denen er erfolgreichster Jagdflieger im Westen Wir beabsichtigen in zwangsloser

«Der Hexenkessel über'm Rhein!» und viele andere mehr. Aus ihnen geht so klar wie aus keinem noch so langen Bericht die unerhörte Achtung hervor, die die Schlagwort-Amerikaner vor der harten deutschen Luftverteidigung haben.

Wer es erspäht hat, — das Auge eines Heckschützen in einem Viermotbomber oder das eines amerikanischen Jägers im Luftkampf auf Rammnähe, das wird nie genau festzustellen sein. Jedenfalls aber tauchte vor langer Zeit schon im Jargon der Terrorflieger plötzlich der Begriff «Der Mann mit dem weissen Schal» auf. Zuerst nur achtungsvoll vor dem Schneid des Angreifers genannt, bekam Haar, — das ist das äussere Bild dieses jungen Führers des Jagdgeschwaders, das den Namen des grössten Fliegerhelden aus dem ersten Weltkriege trägt. Der Leitsatz Manfred von Richthofen's: «Rangehen bis man das Weisse im Auge des Gegners sieht!», ist neben der Umwertung aller Begriffe des Luftkrieges auf die heutigen Möglichkeiten, auch jetzt noch die Devise aller Flieger des Traditionsgeschwaders geblieben. Eichenlaubträger Oberstleutnant Egon Mayer war es, der beim Auftreten der angeblich «unverletzlichen» viermotorigen Terrorbomber sofort eine neue, erfolgreiche Bekämpfungstaktik entwickelte. Eine Taktik, die nur aus wenig mehr besteht, als eben diesem Richthofen'schen «Rangehen» auch gegen die stärkste Feuerkraft und Abwehr. Rund dreissig viermotorige Terrorbomber fielen dieser Taktik des erfolgreichsten deutschen Jägers im Westen bisher zum Opfer. Ein kühl berechnender Kopf, aber ebenso ein mit sich selbst vergessendem Schneid herangehender Kämpfer, — das ist Eichenlaubträger und Kommodore Oberstleutnant Egon Mayer!

Newspaper article reporting the death of *Oberstleutnant* Egon Mayer.

Above: *Major* Kurt Ubben was named *Kommodore* of the *Richthofen Geschwader* following the death of Egon Mayer. A wearer of the Oak Leaves, Ubben scored his 100th victory on 14 January 1943. He would not serve long as *Kommodore*, falling in action against Thunderbolts on 27 April 1944. Ubben was able to bail out, but he was too low for his parachute to open. Right: 2 March 1944: Kurt Bühligen receives the Oak Leaves on the same day that Egon Mayer is killed. Following the death of Kurt Ubben, Bühligen is named *Kommodore* of the *Richthofen Geschwader*. He will lead the unit until the end of the war.

At the Berghof, Adolf Hitler's summer residence and sometimes headquarters on the Obersalzberg near Berchtesgaden, Bühligen receives the Oak Leaves from the *Führer*. The *Luftwaffe* officers being decorated are (from the left): Barkhorn, Walther, Bühligen, Jabs, Jope, Bätcher.

Leutnant Müngersdorff's Bf 109 G-6. He flew "White 28" in the spring of 1944 as a member of the *II. Gruppe* based at Creil.

The enemy is now everywhere. This B-17, separated from its unit, probably because of battle damage or mechanical trouble. As it tried to regain altitude it was attacked by a fighter and shot down. Several explosions tore the aircraft apart as it went down.

Hauptfeldwebel and senior NCO of 5./JG 2 Wolerz in light summer uniform photographed while making his rounds. June 1944.

At the end of May II./JG 2 transferred to Gütersloh in Germany to rest and refit.

6 June 1944. Soon after its arrival in Gütersloh the *Gruppe* received word of the Allied landings in Normandy. It was immediately rushed back to France. Here personnel receive rations from a "Goulash Cannon" (field kitchen) aboard the train. From left to right: *Oberleutnant* Nikol, *Leutnant* Müngersdorff, *Unteroffizier* Sens, *Oberleutnant* Stein and *Oberfeldwebel* Lorey.

In the weeks leading up to the invasion, the British and Americans intensified their bombing of road and rail bridges and airfields, in an effort to paralyze the German supply system and eliminate the German fighter defenses. The Allies assembled 13,000 aircraft for the invasion, 5,000 of them fighters. The *Luftwaffe* had just 120 fighters in the invasion area.

In the weeks before the invasion the Allied bombers also attacked artillery fire control bunkers and radar stations. These Douglas A-20 Havocs are bombing a position on the coast. While most of the bombs are on target, one has exploded in the water. The fountain of water thrown up by the explosion casts a shadow.

The largest concentration of ships in history heads for the coast of Normandy. The landings begin.

In the early morning hours thousands of British, Canadian and American paratroops landed behind the German defensive positions.

On a French airfield the pilots of the *II. Gruppe* prepare for their next mission. From left to right: Roth, Kühberger, Kowalski, Ille and Kalmanitsch.

Soon afterwards the engines roar as the fighters take off. Here a Messerschmitt is seen flying low over the airfield. The men of the *Richthofen Geschwader* are now almost powerless against the overwhelming strength of the enemy.

A Fw 190 A-4 on its nose. This could even happen to an experienced pilot, however the *Luftwaffe* had few of these left by the summer of 1944. The average training given to a new fighter pilot was about 160 flying hours. Their American equivalents received almost twice as many hours of flight training before they were assigned to a front-line unit.

The pilots of 2./JG 2 gathered in a semicircle around their *Staffelkapitän* as he gives them final instructions before takeoff. In the background is one of the *Staffel*'s Fw 190 A-4s. Note the stylized black eagle. The eagle was also the emblem of the successful *9. Staffel*. The two units used slightly different versions of the emblem: that of the *2. Staffel* had a rounded beak, as seen here, while that of the *9. Staffel* was more angular.

Josef "Sepp" Wurmheller was one of the *Richthofen Geschwader*'s most successful pilots. He led the *9. Staffel* until 8 June 1944, when he became *Gruppenkommandeur* of III./JG 2 following the death of *Hauptmann* Huppertz. This photograph was taken after Wurmheller received the Oak Leaves. In the background is a Fw 190 A-4. Note the servicing flag on the port aileron.

On 22 June 1944 *Major* Wurmheller was killed in aerial combat. He was probably shot down by Spitfires of No. 441 Squadron, Royal Canadian Air Force. This squadron was part of the fighter wing commanded by Johnnie Johnson, the RAF's most successful fighter pilot in Europe with 38 kills. *Major* Wurmheller was awarded the Swords posthumously on 24 October 1944. At the time of his death his victory total stood at 102. This is the last known pilot taken of Wurmheller.

This photograph was taken at the beginning of June 1944. It shows *Oberstleutnant* Kurt Bühligen after returning from the mission in which he scored his 100th victory. As he climbed out of his machine he was greeted by the *Kommodore* of JG 26, *Oberstleutnant* Priller, with a bottle of champagne. Among the group toasting the *Geschwader-kommodore*'s 100th are his crew chief Thieme, *Major* Donath and officers of the *Geschwader*.

The toast was followed by the usual description of the successful combat. Among those listening intently is *Major* Donath (third from right). The *Kommodore*'s machine is in the background.

A snapshot to mark the occasion, with the man of the hour and an appropriately marked sign.

B-24 Liberators of the USAAF on their way to a target in Germany. They are escorted by fighter aircraft flying at a higher altitude.

The cockpit of a Bf 109 G. The large rectangular object behind the control stick is the metal cover over the breech of the engine-mounted cannon.

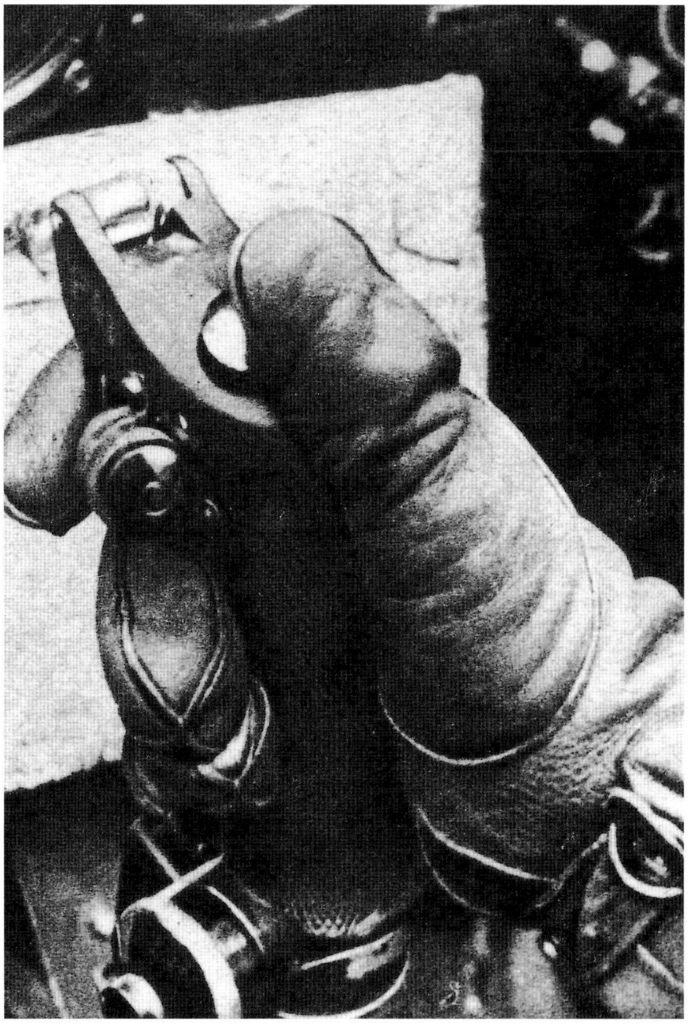

The control stick grip with its various buttons for firing the machine-guns and cannon.

A Bf 109 under fire from an American fighter, photographed by the latter's automatic gun camera. The bright flash indicates that the Messerschmitt has been hit. The light-colored vapor suggests that the cooling system has been damaged. The hunters have become the hunted.

P-51 Mustang flown by Colonel Thomas J.J. Christian of the 375th Fighter Squadron of the 361st Fighter Group. Allied fighters escorted bombers during the invasion. The special markings worn by aircraft taking part in the invasion, black and white stripes, may be seen on the aircraft's fuselage. At the time of the invasion these stripes were applied to the wings and fuselage.

A Focke-Wulf Fw 190 attacks a Flying Fortress, whose port inner motor is already on fire. It was part of a group of bombers that had just attacked the Focke-Wulf factory in Oschersleben, seen at the bottom of the photograph. The American who evaluated this photograph wrote that it appeared as if the smaller bird was defending its nest against a hawk.

The pilot of "Black 1" receives congratulations after a successful mission.

This P-51 B, a somewhat earlier version of the Mustang, was forced down near Herborn.

After pulling up from an attack on a bomber, this Fw 190 flew past the aircraft's nose, where it was captured by an American press photographer.

American soldiers examine the remains of a Fw 190 after it was shot down.

While the hopelessly outnumbered German fighter pilots continued to throw themselves against the enemy bombers, they were unable to protect Germany's cities and their inhabitants. One town after another went up in flames.

After an air raid rescuers desperately search the rubble of houses for survivors.

The search was often in vain. Many of the inhabitants were found dead.

In late 1944 *JG 2 "Richthofen"* began receiving the new Fw 190 D-9 fighter, also called the "Longnose". This aircraft was the equal of the P-51 Mustang, but like so many advanced German weapons it was a case of too late and too few.

Having been serviced for its next flight, this Fw 190 A-8 now serves as a backdrop for a snapshot of the ground crew.

New Years Day morning 1945. "Operation Bodenplatte" is about to begin. On German airfields many hundreds of fighter aircraft stand ready to strike the final blow.

The already weakened *Luftwaffe* does not recover from the losses suffered on this day, however. "Bodenplatte" is a mistake and ends in disaster. *JG 2 "Richthofen"* suffers such losses that it is capable of only limited action for weeks.

The Fw 190 D-9 flown by *Oberfeldwebel* Werner Hohenberg of I./JG 2. On 1 January 1945 he was an element leader in *Gruppenkommandeur Hauptmann* Hrdlicka's command flight. For this mission he was assigned the aircraft of the *Major* beim Stab. The *Gruppe* took off from Merzenhausen to attack the airfield at St. Trond in Belgium. During a second firing pass at American aircraft on the airfield his "Dora" was hit in the tail by flak. By then there were enemy fighters over the airfield. Hohenberg was hit again and he tried to escape by flying low at high speed. As he flew over a town his engine was hit and soon afterwards he was compelled to make a forced landing. His aircraft ended up sliding into an American anti-aircraft position. For him the war was over.

For years after the war the remains of German fighter aircraft senselessly sacrificed in "Operation Bodenplatte" could be found in the forests.

Above: The end is near. In mid-April 1945 American fighter units attacked German air bases from the Main River to the Alps, destroying 644 *Luftwaffe* aircraft on the ground. This photograph was taken by the gun camera of Col. Ben Rimerman's Mustang during an attack on a German airfield. The American photo evaluator's fitting caption: "The *Luftwaffe* coming up—in smoke".

Right: Parked in a revetment cut out of the forest, a heavily camouflaged Bf 109. By this stage of the war the fuel shortage forced the *Luftwaffe* to employ cattle to tow aircraft from their forest hiding places to the runway. The animals also helped camouflage the *Luftwaffe*'s airfields, giving the impression of farm pastures.

American B-17 Flying Fortresses en route to a target in Germany. The aircraft in the background has fallen behind the others and is under attack by a Fw 190 D-9.

Despite the general indications of collapse, the remaining units of *JG 2* continued to fly against the Allies. This Fw 190 D-9 bearing the tactical markings of a Major beim Stab was damaged in combat but managed to make a smooth belly landing. The orthochromatic film used by the Americans makes the yellow stripes of the yellow-white-yellow identity band appear darker, like blue or green.

Major Walter Matoni, *Gruppenkommandeur* of III./JG 2. At the beginning of 1945 the *Gruppe* was based at Nidda airfield. Matoni was awarded the Knight's Cross on 2 January 1945. At that time he held the rank of *Hauptmann* and had 44 victories, including 14 four-engined bombers.

The Inspector of Day Fighters, *Oberst* Hannes Trautloft, during a visit to a unit of *JG 2*, probably the *5. Staffel* at Nidda.

By this stage in the war, camouflaging aircraft on the ground had become of paramount importance. Here a Fw 190 D-9 is seen beneath the trees at the edge of a front-line airfield. The *Luftwaffe* fighter arm continued to fly as much as fuel and aircraft serviceability allowed.

Above: Early on 23 March 1945 *Oberfeldwebel* Besen took off in his Fw 190 D-9 with 10./JG 2 to attack the American bridgehead near Oppenheim on the east side of the Rhine. The *Staffel* flew east across the Rhine and then reversed course to drop their 250-kg bombs on the American positions. Over the Rhine the *Oberfeldwebel*'s aircraft was hi by flak and the engine quit. Realizing that a forced landing was unavoidable, Besen began looking for a suitable place. Gliding earthwards, he spotted a large meadow and turned toward it. Accompanied by loud banging and crashing, his "Longnose" slid across the ground and finally came to a stop. He quickly slid the canopy back and jumped out onto the wing. As he took a deep breath there was a loud explosion from the direction where he had touched down. His bomb had gone off. In his frantic search for a place to land he had forgotten to jettison it. In the photograph above both the "Dora" and the bomb crater may be seen. But the exploding bomb was not the end of his worries. Suddenly projectiles whizzed past his ears, fired from a nearby railway embankment by a member of the Volkssturm, or home guard. On account of his brown leather jacket and his D-9, a type that was not all that common, he had been mistaken for an American. The startled Besen shouted a few less than friendly words—which cannot be repeated here—at the Volkssturm man, who subsequently ceased firing.

Left: On 31 March 1945 *Oberfeldwebel* Besen was seriously injured in a collision with a P-47 Thunderbolt and subsequent parachute descent near Bad Hersfeld. When the war ended he was still in hospital in Bad Hersfeld.

Above: Retreating before the advancing Americans, the surviving remnants of the once proud *JG 2 "Richthofen"* fell back into northern and central Germany and the Marienbad area of Bohemia. When they reached Altenstedt the soldiers of the 6th Armored Division found a number of unserviceable "Doras" which provided backdrops for souvenir photos. The *III. Gruppe*, previously based in Altenstedt, retreated in good time with its Fw 190 D-9s to Quedlinburg.

Left: Another view of the same machine. Note the opened engine cowling panels.

The German Armed Services surrendered on 8 May 1945. As here in Frankfurt, American flying units occupied former *Luftwaffe* airfields. Here a Mustang is parked in front of the remains of a Fw 190 D-9.

A Bf 109 G-10 found by American troops at Frankfurt airfield in April 1945. A souvenir hunter has removed the swastika from the fin.

The war was now over. Many years of tough, costly fighting by the *Wehrmacht* and the pilots of the *Jagdgeschwader "Richthofen"* had come to an end. Many fighter pilots had not survived. Sometimes, as here, all there was to mark the spot where a human life had ended was a large hole produced by the explosion that followed the crash, filled with aircraft wreckage.

Many of the *Richthofen Geschwader*'s dead lie buried in cemeteries in France, particularly in the north of the country, as here at Lisieux. Among them are two *Geschwaderkommodore*, Egon Mayer and Kurt Ubben.

Feldwebel Gustav Sens—killed on the invasion front.

Unteroffizier Hellmut Bollwerk—posted missing on 1 January 1945.

Leutnant Heinz Temmler—killed in his parachute on the invasion front.

Leutnant Christoph Dezius, seen here as a *Feldwebel*. He lost a leg during the war as a result of wounds sustained when he was shot down and forced to abandon his Bf 109 G-6.

8

Jagdgeschwader 71 "Richthofen" in the *Bundesluftwaffe*

In August 1945 the Second World War ended with the surrender of Japan. The end was brought about by the dropping of the first atomic bombs on Hiroshima and Nagasaki. These terrible new weapons ended the war and gave a terrible insight into the nature of future wars. Man was now capable of bringing about the apocalypse himself. Europe soon became divided into two ideological blocks, followed soon afterwards by large areas of the entire world:

On one side was the democratic west, dominated politically and technically by the United States of America, on the other the Communist states of the eastern block and Asia, firmly under the control of the Union of Soviet Socialist Republics.

Faced with a developing threat, especially as the USSR would soon break the American monopoly on nuclear weapons, the western democracies were forced to act. The result was a defensive alliance, the North Atlantic Treaty Organization, or NATO.

The Communists responded by forming the Warsaw Pact, their own counterpart to NATO. The front line of the Cold War ran through a divided Germany in a divided Europe—a new threat.

Germany's former enemies, especially the USA, realized very early what Napoleon had formulated 135 years earlier: "With Germany anything can be achieved in Central Europe, but without it nothing." Germany was beaten and destroyed. Nearly 10,000,000 German soldiers and civilians had lost their lives in the war and the relocations that resulted from it. But because of its central location in the heart of Europe and its astonishing economic recovery in the 1950s, it had become an important factor in the strategic and political considerations of the western allies.

The USA and Great Britain, therefore, pursued plans to integrate West Germany into the western community and to rearm her within the NATO framework. After highly secret talks and negotiations, which had their beginnings in the early 1950s, the new German military, the *Bundeswehr*, was created by Federal Chancellor Konrad Adenauer in Andernach am Rhein in 1956. Its initial strength was 1,500 men. Initially a volunteer force, later supplemented by compulsory military service, the *Bundeswehr* grew. Two years later followed the birth of the new *Richthofen Geschwader*, the second flying unit of the new German air force.

1953
American officers, former enemies, organize a meeting of World War Two pilots in Landshut. General London and Colonel Dasher, both of the USAF, invite German pilots to attend. Some are former members of *JG 2 "Richthofen"*.

15 October 1958
The Royal Air Force hands over Ahlhorn airfield to the new *Bundesluftwaffe*. The first unit at the base is JG 71, a fighter wing without aircraft. The unit's commander is the still young *Major* Erich Hartmann, with 352 victories the most successful fighter pilot of the Second World War. Just a few years earlier he had been released from a Russian prisoner of war camp, among the last German POWs whose freedom was secured by Adenauer's intervention in Moscow. When the war ended Hartmann had been the commander of I./JG 52. He had flown his last mission and scored his final victory on 8 May 1945 over Brünn.

15 January 1959
Generalleutnant Harlinghausen, commanding general of Luftwaffe Group North, inspects the air base group at JG 71's airfield, which is in the process of being renovated and expanded.

19 January 1959
Major Hartmann, the *Geschwader*'s first *Kommodore*, assumes command in Ahlhorn.

26 February 1959
JG 71's first aircraft arrive at Ahlhorn, flown by *Major* Hartmann and *Oberstleutnant* Peters. They are Canadian-built Sabre 6 fighters, developed from the F-86 which was used so successfully in Korea. The unit begins operations, little restricted by manuals, as none exist and must first be written. Much is improvised. The personnel meet and discuss what should be done. *Major* Hartmann meets with *Hauptmann* Harms, operational staff officer, *Major* Kaiser, technical commander, *Hauptmann* Schmieder, *Kapitän* of the *1. Staffel*, *Hauptmann* Drube, *Kapitän* of the *2. Staffel*, medical officer Oberstabsarzt Dr. von Wardenburg, and Captain Willem Jansen of the Royal Netherlands Air Force, tactical advisor assigned by NATO.

13 March 1959
Franz-Josef Strauss, Federal Minister of Defense, arrives at Ahlhorn to inspect the base.

Mid-May 1959
More Sabre 6s arrive at Ahlhorn, enabling the *Geschwader* to reach its authorized strength of 50 aircraft.

25 May 1959
The Inspector of the Air Force, *Generalleutnant* Josef Kammhuber, comes to inspect JG 71.

6 June 1959
On this day JG 71 is officially activated by the Inspector of the Air Force, *Generalleutnant* Josef Kammhuber.

1 June 1960
Effective this date, JG 71 is attached to NATO as "Command Force". Its mission, with the air forces of the other alliance nations, is to defend the airspace over the Federal Republic of Germany.

13 June 1960
Stabsunteroffizier Egon Osenburg is killed in the crash of his Sabre. He is the first member of the *Geschwader* to lose his life.

17-18 August 1960
The air attaches of the NATO partners America, France, Italy, Holland and Denmark meet in Ahlhorn to exchange information concerning operational and organizational matters.

12 January 1961
The start of the new year is overshadowed by the death of *Oberleutnant* Horst Arnoldt, who collides in the air with another Sabre and crashes.

21 April 1961
On this day, the 43rd anniversary of the death of *Rittmeister* Baron von Richthofen, Federal President Heinrich Lübke bestows the honorary title *"Richthofen"* upon the *Geschwader*. This action is the result of an initiative by Defense Minister Strauss. In an official ceremony the Inspector of the Air Force places the first cuff band bearing the proud name on the uniform of *Oberstleutnant* Hartmann. *Oberst* Barkhorn, *Kommodore* of *Jabogeschwader 31* receives a cuff band bearing the name *"Boelcke"* and *Oberstleutnant* Grasemann, *Kommodore* of *Aufklärungsgeschwader 51* one with the name *"Immelmann"*. These three units now bear the names of men who made significant contributions during the formative years of German military aviation.

Oberst Barkhorn flew with Erich Hartmann in JG 52 and, with 301 victories, was second only to him.

26 June – 7 July 1961
At Leeuwarden, Holland JG 71 *"Richthofen"* participates in the fourth NATO gunnery competition. It is the first time that the pilots of the *Geschwader* are able to measure themselves against their colleagues from Norway, Denmark, Holland, Italy and Canada.

9 August 1961
Oberleutnant Hagen Hülfert is killed in a crash after colliding with his wingman. He will not be the last to lose his life while serving his country and defending Europe.

29 May 1962
Major Günther Josten becomes the new *Kommodore* of JG 71 *"Richthofen"*. During the Second World War he commanded *IV./JG 51 "Mölders"*. He ended the war with 178 victories and was decorated with the Oak Leaves. *Oberstleutnant* Hartmann is transferred to Cologne-Wahn.

1 August 1962
On 17 November 1961 the flying group transferred from Ahlhorn to Wittmund, where it was temporarily based with elements of the technical services. It now returns to Ahlhorn.

Look Back 1962
The *Geschwader* suffered the loss of two pilots: *Leutnant* Rohe on 15 May and *Stabsunteroffizier* Luthmer on 13 June.

22 February 1963
JG 71 *"Richthofen"* leaves the command of the 3rd Air Defense Division Münster and is attached to the 4th Air Defense Division in Aurich.

March 1963
The advance party of the technical group of JG 71 *"Richthofen"* under the command of *Major* Simon transfers to Wittmund to take charge of new equipment for the F-104 G Starfighter weapons system.

26 – 30 April 1963
The technical group moves completely to Wittmundhafen. The area was used as a base for an airship wing in 1916. During the Second World War four bomber wings, night fighters and even Me 163 rocket fighters of *Jagdverband 400* were based there. Almost twenty years later the Sabres of the flying group arrive at the historic airfield, which has been turned into one of the most modern NATO airfields. The last of the Canadair Sabre 6s leave Ahlhorn on 30 April.

Beginning of May 1963
The first examples of the F-104 G weapons system arrive, flown by *Oberleutnant* Dieter von Olleschik and *Oberleutnant* Manfred Fischer. JG 71 *"Richthofen"* is the first unit of the *Bundesluftwaffe* to receive the new aircraft. The new air base offers longer runways and improved facilities.

Beginning at the end of April, JG 71 converts from the Sabre 6 to the F-104 G. The type was specially constructed by Lockheed for the *Bundesluftwaffe*. Adapting the type to the specific requirements of the *Luftwaffe* will cause significant problems, of which

Oberst Hartmann had warned some time earlier. He favored the F-106 and on several occasions spoke out against the F-104.

In fact, there are 225 crashes during the F-104 G's service life with the *Luftwaffe* and 106 pilots lose their lives. The reasons for this disaster are many. One was probably the *Luftwaffe*'s requirement for a single aircraft type to be able to carry out the fighter, fighter-bomber and reconnaissance roles.

The USAF flew a specialized variant of the F-104 for each role. Making it into a multi-role machine resulted in an aircraft that was heavier with slightly impaired handling characteristics, which made the F-104 G somewhat difficult to fly. As well, the F-104 G had one engine and one pilot, who had to operate the advanced electronic systems while carrying out his specialized function.

In spite of these problems, most pilots swear by the F-104 G.

17 August 1963
Feldwebel Wendt is killed in a crash at the Brockzetel training area. Five men of the *Luftwaffe*'s 44th Air Defense Battalion, which monitored incoming aircraft, were also killed in the accident.

In addition to normal flight operations and various exercises, there are exchanges with other *Luftwaffe* units and those of the NATO partners.

18 April 1964
The 46th *"Richthofen"* reunion takes place in Wittmund.

While the *1. Staffel* converts to the F-104 G, the *2. Staffel* takes over its responsibilities within NATO.

29 April 1965
The unit standard which Air Chief Marshal Sir Edmund Hudleston, Commander-in-Chief of Air Forces Central Europe, bestowed upon JG 71 and other units of the *Luftwaffe* in Dante Stadium in Munich on 24 April is brought to the *Geschwader* in an official ceremony.

27 September 1965
Air Chief Marshal Sir Edmund Hudleston, Commander-in-Chief of Air Forces Central Europe, inspects JG 71 *"Richthofen"* to assess its operational readiness.

27 January 1966
The Deputy Commander of NATO Forces Europe, Air Marshal Sir Thomas Pike, inspects JG 71 *"Richthofen"*.

18 May 1966
Brigadegeneral Hinkelbein replaces *Brigadegeneral* Hrabak as commanding officer of the 4th Luftwaffe Division and becomes special commissioner for the F-104 weapons system.

10 June 1966
No. 23 Squadron, Royal Air Force based at Leuchars arrives at Wittmund for a squadron exchange. The *1. Jagdstaffel* JG 71 flies from the base in Scotland from 17-20 June.

28 July 1966
Defense Minister Uwe von Hassel visits the *Geschwader*.

4 November 1966
The Inspector of the *Luftwaffe*, *Generalleutnant* Steinhoff, comes to Wittmundhafen to inspect the *Geschwader*.

16 March 1967
While on approach to land, the F-104 Gs of *Major* Frese and *Hauptmann* Rühmann are struck by lightning. Several systems are knocked out and both aircraft lose their nose cones, nevertheless their pilots bring them down safely with the help of *Oberleutnant* Berger.

31 March 1967
Generalleutnant Hoffmann, commanding general of *Luftwaffe* Group North, names *Oberstleutnant* Kallerhoff to succeed *Oberst* Josten as commander of the *Geschwader*.

26-27 April 1967
During tactical evaluation of the *1. Jagdstaffel* of JG 71 by ATAF the unit is awarded a Grade 2. The personnel of the technical group receive a special commendation from the commanding general of the 2nd ATAF.

5-7 June 1967
Air defense exercise. The 32nd Interceptor Squadron of the USAF and JG 71 "R" receive the Hudleston Trophy for the best interceptor team and the Guynemer Trophy for the best team of all air defense sectors in Germany.

21 July 1967
The "Aviation Club" awards the *Geschwader* the "Silver Shield", a special award for outstanding achievements in the various branches of the *Luftwaffe*.

16 February 1968
Major Liedke hands the flying group of JG 71 *"Richthofen"* over to *Major* Frese. Liedke becomes acting *Kommodore*.

13 March 1968
Stabsfeldwebel Harry Giese logs JG 71's 25,000th hour in the F/TF-104 Starfighter.

19 April 1968
To mark the celebrations surrounding the 50th Richthofen reunion the *Geschwader* holds an open house and air show at Wittmundhafen.

21 April 1968
On the fiftieth anniversary of the death of Manfred von Richthofen, the memorial society meets at the base of the new *Richthofen Geschwader*.

Retired *Oberstleutnant* von der Osten, who served with von Richthofen in the First World War, gave a speech that gave some idea of the love and respect still felt by many for von Richthofen, the Knight of the Air, so many years later. The three generations of German fighter pilots spent three days together.

These generations were and continue to be bound by their passion for flying, but also by the example set by Manfred Baron von Richthofen. And they feel bound by this tradition.

19 December 1968
For the first time the *Geschwader* logs 10,000 flying hours in the F-104 in a single year.

End of May 1969
In recognition of his service, *Kommodore Oberst* Kallerhoff is awarded the Federal Republic's Distinguished Service Cross.

9 June 1969
The *Geschwader* holds a parade to mark the tenth anniversary of its creation.

17 July 1969
The commander of the 2nd Allied Tactical Air Force (2nd ATAF), Air Marshal Christopher Foxley Norris, pays a visit to the *Geschwader*.

25 July 1970
Leutnant Walter Lewecke logs the 50,000th flying hour in the F-104 G.

7 September 1970
Aircraft of JG 71 *"Richthofen"* and JG 74 *"Mölders"* take part in the "Black Sky" maneuvers at Neuburg/Donau until 9 September.

24 September 1970
The *1. Jagdstaffel* of JG 71 *"Richthofen"* is named best unit in the 4th Luftwaffe Division by the commanding general of *Luftwaffe* Group North, *Generalleutnant* Mahlke. This was the *General*'s last official act involving JG 71, as *Luftwaffe* Group North is disbanded on 30 September.

25 September 1970
Oberst Pieper is named *Kommodore*, succeeding *Oberst* Kallerhoff. *Oberst* Pieper served with JG 77 in the Second World War and joined the *Bundeswehr* as an *Oberleutnant*. During the war *Oberst* Kallerhoff flew with JG 3 *"Udet"*.

18 April 1971
Three generations of the *Jagdgeschwader "Richthofen"* come together at the 53rd *"Richthofen"* reunion.

13 September 1972
Official opening of the new JG 71 "R" tradition room.

9 October 1972
Oberstleutnant Rentel succeeds *Oberst* Pieper as *Geschwaderkommodore* of *JG 71 "R"*.

16 March 1973
The Inspector of the *Luftwaffe*, *Generalleutnant* Rall, visits the *Geschwader* to assess the progress being made in converting to the new F-4F Phantom weapons system.

May 1973
In the United States the training program begins for crews of the new two-seat F-4F Phantom.

31 August 1973
The *Geschwader* receives the first two F-4F Phantoms. They are used to train technicians on the new weapons system.

End of January 1974
The commander of the 4th *Luftwaffe* Division, *Generalmajor* Coerdt, presents *JG 71 "R"* 71 *"Richthofen"* with the trophy as the division's best unit for the year 1973.

7 March 1974
The first of the *Geschwader*'s own McDonnell-Douglas F-4F Phantoms land at Wittmundhafen. The two aircraft are flown by *Oberstleutnant* Rimmek with his weapons systems operator *Major* Witfer, and *Oberstleutnant* Eggert and *Major* Gade.

The role of the fighter crews has changed constantly to keep pace with technological changes and other factors, especially the political situation. Certain aspects of tactics, however, remain the same or similar. When intercepting an intruder into the airspace of the Federal Republic of Germany, the crew is guided toward the target by ground control until it can lock on with its own radar. In some cases the fighter is assigned a block of airspace in which it is to intercept any approaching object independently. The defense is also capable of deploying patrols to intercept hostile aircraft. In this way, low-flying interceptors are capable of clearing a specific area.

With the introduction of the F-4F weapons system, the multitude of tasks is divided between the pilot and weapons system operator. Unlike the F-104, the Phantom has two engines.

19 September 1974
This is a sad day for many pilots of *JG 71 "R"* 71 *"Richthofen"*. *Hauptmann* Harry Giese of the *1. Jagdstaffel* ferries out the last of the unit's Starfighters.

End of 1974
From this point on the *Geschwader* flies the new F-4F Phantom. The new refers only to the change from the F-104, for the Phantom has already been in service with the US Navy for 14 years. Originally designed to operate from aircraft carriers, the F-4F is a multi-

role version of the aircraft designed to operate in the European theater of operations.

11 March 1975
Generalmajor Barkhorn, Chief of Staff of the 2nd ATAF, visits the *Geschwader* to observe the progress of NATO Exercise WINTEX.

18-20 April 1975
Three generations of fighter pilots are reunited at Wittmundhafen. One of the high points of the 57th reunion is the presentation by *Hauptmann* Kazur of a 1 to 1 scale reproduction of the Fokker Dr I triplane. It and a Bf 109 produced by a working group under *Hauptfeldwebel* Nolde attract the attention of the guests.

15 May 1975
Bundespräsident Walter Scheel, a *Leutnant* and adjutant of III./NJG 1 during the Second World War, visits the *Luftwaffe* for the first time. Accompanied by State Secretary Fingerhut and Inspector of the *Luftwaffe Generalleutnant* Limberg, he arrives at JG 71's base in Wittmundhafen.

1 September 1975
Personnel from the aircraft carrier the USS Nimitz visit *JG 71 "R"*.

30 March 1976
Among the *Geschwader*'s responsibilities is to provide escorts for foreign heads of state flying over Germany territory. On this day it is the aircraft of Egyptian President Anwar Sadat. The escort formation is led by *Major* Menge.

16 May 1976
A Phantom of JG 71 collides with a powered glider. While *Hauptmann* Müller and *Major* Zimprich eject safely, the pilot of the glider is killed in the accident.

20 September 1976
Another change of command: *Oberst* Rentel transfers command to *Oberst* Willing.

15 December 1976
Wittmundhafen airfield is sixty years old. To mark this milestone a memorial bearing the image of an airship is unveiled on the airfield.

9 February 1978
JG 71 "R" provides an honor escort for the outgoing Defense Minister Georg Leber as he flies to Kiel-Holtenau. The 30,000th hour on the F-4F Phantom is logged during this flight.

24 April 1978
The Commander-in-Chief of the Greek Armed Forces, General Davos, visits *JG 71 "R"* accompanied by the Inspector General of the *Luftwaffe*, *Generalleutnant* Wust.

25 August 1978
The technicians of the cross-servicing crew handle the unit's 7,000th aircraft, an RF-4E Phantom of the Aufklärungsgeschwader "Immelmann" from Bremgarten.

17 November 1978
The Naval Airship Veterans Association hold a memorial service at Wittmundhafen for those lost in the First World War.

18 June 1979
While on a training mission, an F-4F crashes into a farmhouse in Lage/Detmold. Five persons in the house and the crew of two are killed.

5 September 1979
The Italian commander-in-chief of the air forces, General Mettimano, visits *JG 71 "R"* with the Inspector of the *Luftwaffe*, *Generalleutnant* Obleser.

2 October 1979
Oberst Willing hands the *Geschwader* over to its new *Kommodore Oberst* Kompich.

28 October—2 November 1979
The 2nd ATAF carries out a tactical evaluation. Of the four marks received by *JG 71 "R"*, three are ones and one is a two. This is the best evaluation ever received by the *Geschwader* in a tactical evaluation. It is also the best evaluation received by any of the sixty units tested in the AAFCE area in 1979.

14 February 1980
The new Defense Minister, Dr. Hans Apel, visits the *Geschwader*. He takes special interest in speaking to military and civilian workers about their tasks.

18 March 1980
Hauptmann Peters and *Hauptmann* Cartensen are on a low-level intercept mission when an engine exploded. The F-4F Phantom sustains heavy damage. The crew nevertheless succeeds in landing their crippled aircraft at Nordholz.

18 December 1980
For the outstanding airmanship and personal courage they displayed in the incident of 18 March, the crew is decorated with the Distinguished Service Cross in Silver on behalf of the Defense Minister.

31 March 1981
Hauptfeldwebel Nolde presents the new tradition room in the domestic offices to *Kommodore* Kompch.

8 January 1982
As it has often done in the past, the *Geschwader* flies to Decimomannu for live firing training.

15 September 1982
In addition to its usual training activities, this year sees the *Geschwader* send a training detachment to Goose Bay, Canada. For technical reasons the eight F-4F Phantoms fly in two waves. On 13 and 14 October they make non-stop flights of 5 and 5 _ hours, refueling five times in the air. In Goose Bay they practice high-speed, low-altitude flying, very important in the event of the real thing. The object of the training is to evade hostile defenses for as long as possible by flying under the enemy's radar. The sparsely settled tundra provides ideal conditions for low flying.

16 September 1983
Major Paulsen becomes the first *Luftwaffe* pilot to reach 2,000 hours on the F-4F Phantom. Altogether he has flown 3,500 hours in a variety of aircraft types.

30 September 1983
After four years in command of *JG 71 "R"*, *Oberst* Kompch is replaced by *Oberst* Egger.

2 April 1984
F-4F Phantoms of the *Geschwader* carry out takeoffs and landings on a new section of the A29 autobahn between Ahlhorn and Sage.

27 April 1984
On this weekend JG 71 *"Richthofen"* can look back on 25 years since its activation. Minister Dr. Manfred Wörner gives the address marking the milestone. The *Geschwader* anniversary ends the next day with an open house.

7 August 1984
Squadron exchange: while No. 338 Squadron of the Royal Norwegian Air Force operates from Wittmundhafen with the *2. Jagdstaffel*, the *1. Jagdstaffel* has flown to Norway to take part in the flying program of a Norwegian unit.

26 February 1985
For its outstanding accomplishments in the field of flight safety in 1983 and 1984, the *Geschwader* is awarded the Inspector of the Luftwaffe's Flight Safety Goblet.

28 June—31 July 1985
The 335th Tactical Fighter Squadron based at Seymour Johnson AFB in North Carolina, USA flies to JG 71's base in Wittmundhafen. Such squadron exchanges involving every NATO air force take place at regular intervals and are intended to improve cooperation in the event of war.

12 March 1986
The *Jagdgeschwader "Richthofen"* becomes the first unit of the *Luftwaffe* to fly 100,000 hours on the F-4F Phantom. The milestone flight is made by the crew of *Oberleutnant* Hilfer and *Hauptmann* Müller.

5 May 1986
In January the DFVLR Science Astronauts Prof. Dr. Furrer and Dr. Messerschmidt flew with the *Geschwader* in preparation for their participation in the D1 Spacelab mission. They promised to take one of the unit's pennants into orbit with them and keep their word.

On this day at a press conference, the pennant, which orbited the earth 112 times, is given back to the *Geschwader*.

12 May 1986
During an air defense sector exercise, *JG 71 "R"* receives the best marks ever achieved.

23 March 1987
Oberst Egger is replaced as *Kommodore* by *Oberstleutnant i.G.* Böcker.

24 March 1987
Tragic accidents are unfortunately a part of military flying in peacetime. During an operational mission two F-4Fs of JG 71 collide and crash near Bremerhaven. *Hauptmann* Wolfgang Riel and *Leutnant* Tore Wrobbel are killed in the accident.

26 May 1987
Two F-4F Phantoms of JG 71's alert section intercept a Soviet Tu-20 bomber. Coming in from the sea, it flew toward the Wittmund-Jever axis, but was intercepted and turned toward British airspace. There it is intercepted again, by fighters of the RAF.

25 June 1987
Wittmundhafen airfield is closed until 1 October for urgently needed construction work. The *Geschwader* operates from the nearby airfield at Upjever, home to *Waffenschule 10*.

30 June 1988
Effective 1 July the *Geschwader* ceases training in its secondary role of fighter-bomber. *JG 71 "R"* is once again a pure fighter unit.

20 October 1988
The crew of *Leutnant* Badia and *Hauptmann* Schönleber complete the *Geschwader*'s 120,000th hour on the F-4F Phantom weapons system.

29 June 1989
Another change of command. *Oberstleutnant* Nowak takes over the *Geschwader* from *Oberst* Böcker.

A military tattoo is held in Wittmundhafen to mark the 40th anniversary of the founding of the Federal Republic of Germany and the 30th birthday of *JG 71 "R"*.

31 October 1989
Major political changes are beginning in Central Europe. Since late summer, citizens of East Germany have been "voting with their feet", fleeing to the Federal Republic by way of Hungary and Aus-

tria. The *Geschwader* makes available to the German Red Cross of Lower Saxony three buildings in the accommodations area with which to house settlers from the other part of Germany.

17 April 1990
For the tenth time a training detachment flies to Goose Bay in Canada. *Hauptmann* Hoffmann and *Oberleutnant* Rasner strike two Canada geese and their aircraft sustains heavy damage. Fortunately they are able to land safely.

21 January 1991
The Gulf Crisis has now reached *JG 71 "R"*. *Oberstleutnant* Lindemann of the *Flak-Batterie 271*, whose 20-mm anti-aircraft guns provide airfield point defense, is flown to Turkey for several days. Its mission, together with personnel from the 4th *Luftwaffe* Division and *Jabogeschwader 43*, is to make preparations for installation of anti-aircraft defenses at Erhac airfield for the fighter-bomber unit. These personnel are among the first air force soldiers of the *Bundeswehr* to experience a real air-raid alarm. There is also a chemical weapons alert, requiring the troops to wear NBC masks for a time.

22 January 1991
The crisis escalates and the *Geschwader* is now affected directly. By order of the *Luftwaffe* command, a transfer of *JG 71 "R"* is considered. The idea is abandoned as the *Luftwaffe* lacks the necessary transport capacity.

This is confirmed by a subsequent transfer of several anti-aircraft missile batteries to Dijarbakir in Turkey. As a purely defensive force, the German *Bundeswehr* lacks the strategic transport capacity needed for such major deployments.

In later missions requiring large-capacity transports, the *Luftwaffe* leases Antonov An-22 aircraft from the Russians.

27 February 1991
Defense Minister Stoltenberg announces that the status of Wittmundhafen will be decided by July. At the same time he announces a reduction in the armed forces to 370,000 men by the end of 1994. As part of these measures 1/3 of the *Luftwaffe*'s flying units will be deactivated. This is a great loss for the affected bases. Located mainly in less developed areas, the 2,500 soldiers and civilian employees represent considerable buying power. As well, many mid-size companies depend on military contracts.

4 March 1991
Five MiG-29 Fulcrums, modern Soviet fighters used by the NVA (East German Air Force), fly from Preschen to Wittmundhafen for technical and flight testing.

25 May 1991
The Federal Ministry of Defense decides to keep the base in Wittmund.

10 October 1991
The *Geschwader* celebrates a triple anniversary—100 years of human flight, 75 years of the Wittmund airfield, and 30 years since the awarding of the honorary title *"Richthofen"*. On this occasion a Bf 109 G-6 restored by members of the *Geschwader* is presented to the public.

11 November 1991
Following protests of the Turkish handling of the Kurdish problem, a planned squadron exchange with Turkey is cancelled following the direct intervention of Federal Chancellor Kohl.

13 December 1991
A Phantom on standby alert accidentally fires two Sidewinder guided missiles. The missiles strike a blast wall and cause no damage. In an interview *Oberst* Nowak stresses the urgency of a replacement for the Phantom. He points our that a single-engined aircraft presents much more of a safety risk than a twin-engined type. The *Kommodore* states that the 158 engine-related crashes in the past 32 years have claimed the lives of 42 pilots and 9 civilians.

26 August 1992
Federal Chancellor Dr. Helmut Kohl lands in Wittmundhafen. Soon afterwards he meets with French President Francois Mitterand. After a brief greeting by the *Kommodore*, the pair board a helicopter of the Federal Border Guard and fly to Borkum, site of the state meeting.

13 December 1992
297 German immigrants arrive in the *Geschwader* barracks from the overflowing acceptance camp.

17 December 1992
It is announced that one *Staffel* of JG 71 *"Richthofen"* has been assigned to the newly-conceived crisis reaction force. No precise orders have yet been issued. Changes in operational and alert readiness are to be expected. A stationary unit becomes a mobile unit with far-reaching changes and consequences.

2 March 1993
Even *JG 71 "R"* does not remain unaffected by the political changes sweeping Europe. During a *Geschwader* exercise, a Russian delegation headed by Colonel Krupin arrives with just six hours notice. The inspection, part of the KSZE Treaties, is part of the mutual disarmament verification process. These measures are designed to build mutual trust, an important component in the new and positive east-west relations.

24 March 1993
General Gerhard John, commanding general of the air fleet, presents *Kommodore Oberst* Nowak with the Flight Safety Goblet in Gold for 38,100 hours of accident-free flying.

26 March 1993
Oberst Nowak hands command of JG 71 *"Richthofen"* over to *Oberstleutnant* Dierk Peter Merklinghaus.

19 April 1993
Two crews and a maintenance crew spend ten days with JG 74 "Mölders" in Neuburg/Donau being briefed on the F-4F KWS. The KWS stands for Combat Capability Enhancement. Instruction of the aircrews focuses on interception missions against low-flying targets, as the new KWS has enhanced capabilities in this area. The ultimate enhancement of combat capabilities, if it is possible to even speak of this with a thirty year old weapons system, will not be achieved until a new radar and the AMRAAM become available.

28 May 1993
The public discussion of and opposition to aircraft noise also begins to affect JG 71 *"Richthofen"*. Politicians prevent the *Geschwader* from moving to nearby Upjever while the runways at Wittmund are repaved. It is forced to go to Hopsten, which is farther away. The additional costs total 250,000 DM.

1 June 1993
The *Luftwaffe* activates *Jagdgeschwader 73* at Preschen Air Base near Cottbus. Formerly JG 3 of the NVA, it is the only unit of the former East German air force to be taken into the *Bundesluftwaffe*. The MiG-29s flown by the *Geschwader* are the most modern fighters in the *Bundesluftwaffe*.

JG 73 subsequently moves to Laage south of Rostock. On 18 September 1997 it is awarded the honorary title "*Steinhoff*". Thus is honored the name of Johannes Steinhoff, who died on 21 February 1994. During the war he was a very successful fighter pilot and commanded JG 77. Decorated with the Oak Leaves and Swords, at the end of the war he joined JV 44. Seriously injured in the crash of an Me 262, he was nevertheless among the first to join the new *Luftwaffe*. *Generalleutnant* Steinhoff became one of the *Luftwaffe*'s most capable commanders, playing a significant part in its expansion.

28 June 1993
Hauptmann Uwe Beyreuther becomes the first member of the former Air Forces of the National People's Army to be transferred to JG 71 *"Richthofen"*.

22 July 1993
The *Geschwader* receives the first example of the KWK version of the F-4F. The aircraft, coded 37+82, is crewed by *Hauptmann* Katz and *Hauptmann* Peinemann.

23 July 1993
Two crews on detachment in Goose Bay fly their Phantoms to Dayton for an air show. The Americans attending the display are very amused to see these "old-timers" and ask the crews how they got the aircraft out of the museum in Dayton.

7 August 1993
A memorial service is held on the 30th anniversary of the crash of a Sabre of JG 71 *"Richthofen"* in which five soldiers of *Flugabwehrbattailon 44* and the pilot lost their lives. The commanding general of the 4th *Luftwaffe* Division and members of the *Geschwader* lay wreaths.

2 September 1994
Opposition to aircraft noise has also surfaced in Goose Bay, Canada. *Oberstleutnant* Merklinghaus discovers that protests against low flying do not happen only in Schorten. This year's training includes exercises in the rapid transfer of elements of the *Geschwader* during time of crisis. Low flying training, which is done at a height of 30 meters, is of vital importance, not just for fighter-bombers, but also for interceptors which must locate and intercept enemy aircraft trying to stay below radar coverage. This means that the F-4F Phantom must also fly intercept missions at that height. This is now possible with the "look down" capability of the KWS. This results in conflicts of interest. On the one hand are the inhabitants, who want their peace and quiet, and on the other the *Luftwaffe* with the mission of defending our nation and participating in actions by the Crisis Reaction Forces.

26 September – 13 October 1993
Six members of JG 71 *"Richthofen"* take part as observers in the exercise "Dynamic Guard 93". Air and sea forces of six NATO countries take part in this major exercise. 300 combat aircraft are deployed over the Aegean and Turkey, suggesting a possible area of operations for the Crisis Reaction Force.

7 March 1994
On this day the "Workhorse of the *Luftwaffe*", the F-4F Phantom, celebrates its 20th year of service with *JG 71 "R"*. The *Geschwader*'s aircraft have completed 143,348 takeoffs and landings and flown 157,385 hours and 35 minutes. While much of this account has dealt with pilots, commanders and generals, this is the proper place to acknowledge the many other areas of the *Geschwader* without which none of this would have been possible: the repair echelon with its aircraft, weapons, electronics and hydraulic technicians, aircraft readiness, the tower and radar crew, the "weather frogs", likewise the drivers and kitchen personnel. Also worthy of mention are the base firefighters, who saved lives in many crashes. This list is of course far from complete, but it shows how many others it takes to keep the men and machines of the *Richthofen Geschwader* flying.

21 June 1994
The Ostfriesen Zeitung publishes a special article comparing the F-4F Phantom with a third-generation jet fighter, the MiG-29 Fulcrum.

Its conclusion: "Until a replacement type is provided for our air defense units, Phantom pilots of the Crisis Reaction Force will face greater risks should they encounter modern fighter aircraft such as the MiG-29 Fulcrum." When one considers that our NATO partner and neighbor Holland has for some years been flying the modern F-16, there is little more to add.

10 March 1995
During a parade to mark the occasion, *Generalmajor* Weber transfers command of the *Geschwader* from *Oberst* Merklinghaus to *Oberstleutnant* Wolfgang Fahl.

29 April 1995
Aircraft of *JG 71 "R"* fly from Goose Bay to Cold Lake to take part in the Maple Flag exercise held there.

1 July 1995
On this day JG 71 *"Richthofen"* officially becomes part of the German Crisis Reaction Force. Possible action beyond the borders of the NATO alliance is part of the unit's mission.

6 July 1995
Ambassador Dr. Hermann Baron von Richthofen visits the *Geschwader*.

17 November 1995
Hairline cracks in the tail sections of the F-4F Phantom result in approximately 50% of the fleet having to be grounded. Flying is reduced indefinitely, although exercises with the Crisis Reaction Force are beginning at this time. The F-4F Phantom has been in service for almost 40 years and is no longer up to the requirements of a modern combat aircraft.

January 1997
Four F-4F Phantoms cross the Atlantic from Wittmundhafen to Holloman Air Base in the USA, refueling in the air several times. They too are to be reequipped with the KWS system. The crews are in the air for ten hours.

1997
The Inspector of the *Luftwaffe*, *Generalleutnant* Bernhard Mende, visits JG 71 *"Richthofen"* to inspect the unit's actual state of training and the readiness of the flying group.

The inspector goes aloft in a Phantom flown by *Hauptmann* Stefan Budrich to get a personal impression of the high state of readiness of the crews of the *Richthofen Geschwader*. At a preceding luncheon, he confirmed the retention of the Wittmundhafen base.

August 1997
Squadron exchange between 2./JG 71 and the 462. Escuadron de Gaza on Gran Canaria. The Spanish squadron flies the Dassault Mirage F 1EE.

17-19 April 1998
Almost 400 former and active members of the *Richthofen Geschwader* get together with members of the von Richthofen family in Wittmund. This is a special occasion that brings them together, for it is the 80th anniversary of the death of *Rittmeister* Manfred Baron von Richthofen, famous the world over as the "Red Baron".

June 1998
The 2. *Staffel* suffers a heavy loss. During the annual deployment to Goose Bay, Canada, the aircraft flown by *Staffelkapitän Oberstleutnant* Schick strikes trees and crashes during a low-level training sortie. Schick survives, however a British exchange pilot, a flight lieutenant, is killed.

21 April 1999
JG 71 *"Richthofen"* celebrates its fortieth birthday.

Dietrich Hrabak, an Oberst in the former Luftwaffe and commander pf JG 52, visits Ursula and Eric Hartmann at their home in Weil im Schönbuch. It was probably during the course of their private discussions that the 33-year-old Hartmann, who was not released from Russian captivity until 1955, decided to join the Bundeswehr, the new German armed forces, to assist in the formation of a new air force.

With 352 victories, Hartmann was the world's successful fighter pilot. Just 22 years of age when the war ended, he had earned Germany's highest decoration, the Knight's Cross with Oak Leaves, Swords and Diamonds.

Erich Hartmann as a Major and commander of the first fighter wing of the Bundesluftwaffe, JG 71. On the right breast of his flight jacket he wears the old style of the Geschwader emblem.

On 15 January 1959 the Geschwader was activated, still without aircraft, at Ahlhorn airfield.

Taken over from the RAF, the airfield still had the feel of earlier days, with its wooden control tower and barracks serving as flight operations and headquarters buildings.

Above: The first aircraft arrived later. The first F-86 Sabres, flown by Major Hartmann and Oberleutnant Peters, landed at JG 71's base at Ahlhorn. Soon there would be more.

Left: On 13 March 1959 the Federal Minister of Defense, Franz-Josef Strauss, visiting the still-new Jagdgeschwader at its base in Ahlhorn. Here he is welcomed by Major Erich Hartmann and several of his officers.

The new Luftwaffe flew the Canadair Sabre 6, a version of the F-86 built under license in Canada. JA-111 was the aircraft of Kommodore Major Hartmann.

Flying again at last! As Erich Hartmann once told the author, he always felt better in the cockpit at the controls of a fast aircraft than behind a desk.

JG 71 was officially activated on 6 June 1959. Here the Luftwaffe Inspector, Generalleutnant Josef Kammhuber, inspects the unit's personnel. During the war Kammhuber had been the Luftwaffe's inspector of night fighters. He is accompanied by the commanding general of Luftwaffe Group North, Generalleutnant Harlinghausen, who during the war commanded a bomber Geschwader and later held senior staff positions, and the Kommodore, Major Hartmann.

Precision flying. The Geschwader number in formation flight.

General Kammhuber in conversation with Major Hartmann and a guest.

Die Jäger von Ahlhorn

Versessen aufs Fliegen, nicht aufs Schießen, sind die jungen Piloten des ersten deutschen Jagdgeschwaders. Ihr Chef ist der erfolgreichste Flieger des zweiten Weltkrieges

Ein Offizier, der einen Namen hat *und über Erfahrung verfügt, das ist nach Ansicht des Bundesverteidigungsministeriums der richtige Mann für das neu aufgestellte Jagdgeschwader. Erich „Bubi" Hartmann übernahm das Kommando auf dem Fliegerhorst Ahlhorn (Oldenburg). Für 352 Luftsiege wurde er im Krieg mit dem Ritterkreuz mit Schwertern und Brillanten ausgezeichnet. Damals war er Hauptmann. Heute ist er Major*

Was Krieg bedeutet, *hat der jetzt 37jährige Hartmann am eigenen Leib erfahren. Als einer der letzten kehrte er aus sowjetischer Kriegsgefangenschaft zurück. Sein einziger Sohn starb, als Hartmann, zu 60 Jahren Zwangsarbeit verurteilt, in Sibirien saß. Unser Bild zeigt ihn mit seiner Frau und seiner Tochter, die heute in Ahlhorn leben*

Wache für die Stunde Null

Heute noch Probe: Alarmstart! *Die Piloten rennen zu ihren Maschinen. In genau geplanten Trainingseinsätzen bereitet sich Hartmanns Mannschaft Tag für Tag auf den Ernstfall vor, von dem alle hoffen, daß er nie eintreten wird. Die Piloten, sämtlich Freiwillige, stellen eine streng gesiebte Auslese dar. Für die Ausbildung jedes einzelnen von ihnen sind etwa 500 000 Mark verwendet worden. Ein Oberstabsarzt überwacht ständig die kleine, hochspezialisierte Pilotengruppe: Beim geringsten Anzeichen von Krankheit wird sofort Flugverbot verhängt. Düsenjägerpiloten sind den größten körperlichen und seelischen Belastungen ausgesetzt. Sie sind alles in einer Person: Piloten, Navigatoren, Funker und Techniker. Für alle, die eine Fliegerkombination tragen, gibt es kaum Rangunterschiede. In der Luft sind alle gleich. Nur das Können zählt. Unter Hartmanns Kommando stehen zur Zeit 42 Düsenflugzeuge, aber erst für 30 Maschinen sind Piloten vorhanden. Das noch fehlende fliegende Personal wird in Kürze zum Jagdgeschwader versetzt werden. Von tausend Bewerbern eignen sich nur 75 als Piloten für Propellermaschinen. Von diesen 75 aber ist nur ein ganz geringer Prozentsatz tauglich, eine Düsenmaschine zu fliegen*

An article published in Der Stern profiling the fighter pilots of JG 71 at Ahlhorn.

Der Pilot allein genügt nicht. *Das rechte Bild zeigt das Bodenpersonal, das ihm erst den Start ermöglicht. Von links nach rechts: ein Mechaniker-Helfer, ein Hydrauliker, ein Elektriker, ein Instrumentenwart, ein Bordelektroniker, ein Fallschirmwart, ein zweiter und ein erster Wart, ein Triebwerkswart, ein Zielgerätewart, ein Waffenwart, ein Nachschubwart, ein Funkwart und ein weiterer Mechaniker-Helfer. Direkt vor den Tragflächen stehen links der Flugroutenchef und rechts der „Wetterfrosch". Links im Hintergrund steht der Tankwagen, davor drei Tankwarte. Rechts neben dem Leitwerk das Hilfsaggregat zum Anlassen der Maschine. Rechts im Hintergrund der Löschwagen mit Feuerwehrleuten. Die Teamleistung entscheidet*

Sie hoffen, daß der Fall nicht eintritt, auf den sie sich vorbereiten

Die Düsenflug-Erfahrung holt sich das junge Geschwader mit der F 86 Sabre VI. Die Piloten sollen jedoch in Kürze den schnelleren Starfighter fliegen

So hat es auch bei ihm angefangen. *Unteroffizier Meisterfeld, 27 Jahre alt, erklärt neugierigen Jungen seine Düsenmaschine, die im NATO-Pakt-Staat Kanada gebaut wurde. Auch Meisterfeld verfiel der magischen Anziehungskraft, die Flugzeuge auf junge Menschen ausüben. Mit zehn Jahren baute er Modelle. Er wollte Pilot werden – und wurde Bergvermessungstechniker. Denn nach 1945 war das Fliegen für jeden Deutschen verboten. 1956 wurde die neue deutsche Luftwaffe in Fürstenfeldbruck bei München aufgestellt. Sechs amerikanische Schulmaschinen standen zur Verfügung. Meisterfeld gab seinen erlernten Beruf auf. Er meldete sich sofort freiwillig. Und sein Traum erfüllte sich*

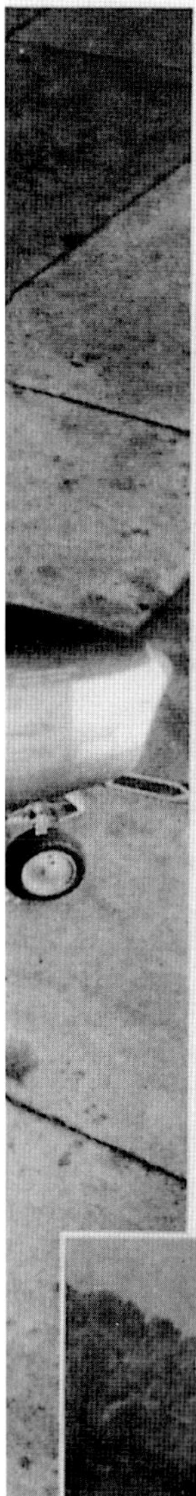

Ruhe und Selbstvertrauen *sieht Leutnant Hagen Hälfert als die wichtigsten Eigenschaften eines guten Düsenpiloten an. Er gehört, wie sein Kommodore und seine Kameraden, zu dem Typ des modernen Soldaten, der überflüssiges Kommißgebaren nicht liebt, dem die Technik näher liegt als das Soldatische seines Berufes: Er kann seine Kräfte auf präzise Leistungen und Selbstdisziplin konzentrieren. Dabei entstammt der 23jährige Offizier einer Familie, deren preußisch-soldatische Tradition bis in das 18. Jahrhundert zurückreicht. Sein Vater war ebenfalls Jagdflieger; sein Onkel wurde als Geleitschutzflieger über Holland abgeschossen und kam nicht zurück*

Ihre Leidenschaft und ihr Beruf *ist die Fliegerei. Lieber Gefahr in Kauf nehmen, lieber ein kürzeres Leben als ein Dasein ohne Erregung: Das ist die Ansicht dieser beiden. Ihre Trainingsflüge in alle Himmelsrichtungen haben sie weltoffen gemacht. Besonders bei den kanadischen Fliegern, in der Türkei und in Spanien haben sie ihre Freunde. England, Frankreich, Italien, Griechenland, die Türkei sind ihre Ziele: Sie sollen alle Flugplätze der europäischen NATO-Partner kennenlernen, denn sie werden später dem Oberkommando der westlichen Verteidigungsgemeinschaft unterstellt. Von jedem Luftstützpunkt Europas aus müssen sie dann operieren können. Über den Ernstfall, für den die Piloten ausgebildet werden, sprechen sie wenig. Sie haben sich an das Risiko ihres Berufs gewöhnt*

Die Tummelplätze *der Touristen sind oft auch Ziel der Übungsflüge des Hartmann-Geschwaders. Gelegentlich läßt sich das Notwendige mit dem Angenehmen verbinden als kleine Entschädigung für die Härte des Dienstes. Unteroffizier Rack hat von dieser Seite des Dienstes nichts gewußt, als er sich entschloß, Pilot zu werden. Er empfindet es dennoch als angenehm, daß die militärische Seite der neuen deutschen Luftwaffe nicht überbetont wird. Denn in erster Linie sind sie alle Flieger*

DER STERN 13

Kommodore Major Hartmann with his pilots after a practice mission. Ground crew are already readying the Sabres for their next sortie.

Feldwebel Buss prepares for a flight. At that time there were still many NCO pilots.

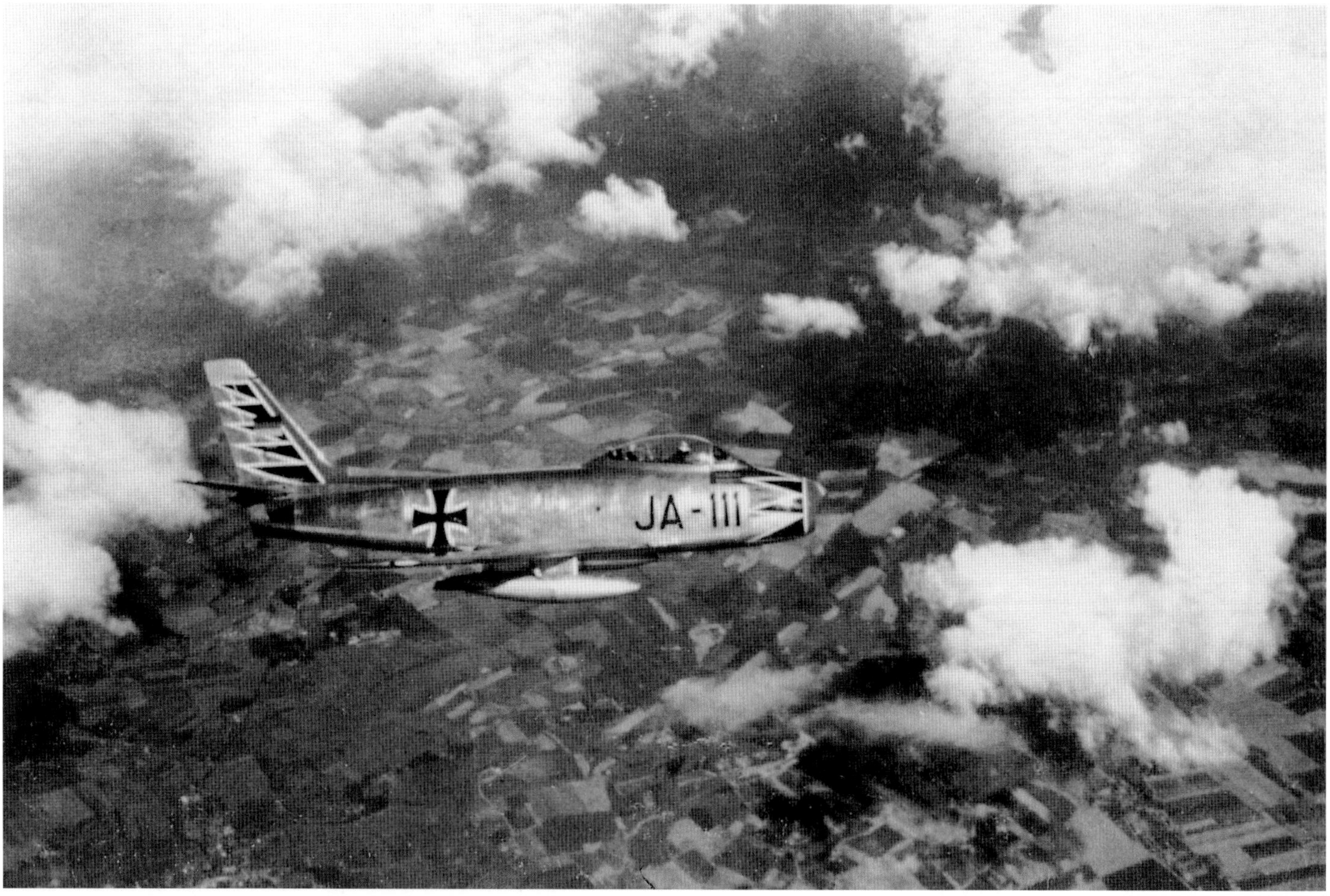

Erich Hartmann's Sabre 6 in flight. The tulip design around the jet's air intake was patterned after the one worn by the Bf 109 G-6s of his 9./JG 52 in Russia. Hartmann's superiors were not exactly overjoyed when he introduced the marking to JG 71. The wily Kommodore claimed that it made it easier to identify pilots who broke the rule against low flying.

On 21 April 1961, the 43rd anniversary of Rittmeister Manfred von Richthofen's death, Bundespräsident Heinrich Lubke bestowed honorary titles on three Geschwader of the new Luftwaffe: Aufklärungsgeschwader 51 "Immelmann", Jagdbombergeschwader 31 "Boelcke" and Jagdgeschwader 71 "Richthofen".

General Kammhuber places the cuff band bearing the honorary title on the sleeve of Kommodore Major Hartmann. Next to him is Major Barkhorn, the world's second highest scoring fighter pilot with 301 victories and Kommodore of Jagdbombergeschwader 31 Boelcke. On the far right is Major Grasemann, Kommodore of Aufklärungsgeschwader 51 "Immelmann".

After the ceremony. Erich Hartmann with Bolko Baron von Richthofen, the Red Baron's youngest brother, and Generalleutnant Josef Kammhuber.

The unit's Sabre 6s lined up on the ramp at Ahlhorn.

The new Geschwader emblem with the "R" for Richthofen on the fuselage of a Sabre 6.

The old and the new Geschwader emblems.

The Geschwader emblem on the fuselage of a Sabre of the 1. Staffel with red-painted nose. The aircraft of the 2. Staffel had yellow noses. The pilot is putting on his back parachute before climbing into the cockpit.

Two pilots of the 1. Staffel wearing all their equipment. The Major checks the fit of the parachute harness.

Gunnery meet for NATO aircraft at Leeuwarden, Holland, held from 15 to 17 November 1961.

Two armorers load the three machine-guns on each side of the Sabre's fuselage. Note the open ammunition boxes.

The aircraft of the participating nations, from the bottom: Canada, Canadair Sabre; Great Britain, Hawker Hunter; Norway, Hawker Hunter; Italy, Hawker Hunter; Germany, Sabre 6. At the far end of the line are the various aircraft used to tow targets.

The German team, from left to right: Feldwebel Uwe Carstensen, Stabsunteroffizier Ferdinand Naruyslo, Feldwebel Joachim Rack, Feldwebel Reinhard Wicke, Oberleutnant Rolf Batz and Oberleutnant Heinz Laube.

The Sabre's nosewheel failed to lock when retracted and collapsed when the aircraft touched down.

Unfortunately, not all accidents were so harmless. Funeral for an airman killed in an accident. The most common causes were midair collisions, landings and takeoffs, and mechanical problems. Bird strikes would also bring down a jet fighter.

Oberst Strümpell (left) and Oberstleutnant Josten (center), who had just assumed command of JG 71 Richthofen, in conversation with the Argentinean military attaché on 21 March 1963. Strümpell commanded I./JG 2 from June to September 1940.

Above: Generalleutnant Johannes Steinhoff and Brigadegeneral Dietrich Hrabak on 19 April 1964 during the Richthofen reunion at Wittmund. Left: Oberstleutnant Günther Josten, the new Kommodore, beside his Sabre. When the war ended he was an Oberleutnant and commander of IV./JG 51. Josten earned the Knight's Cross as an Oberfeldwebel after his 84th victory, the Oak Leaves as an Oberleutnant after 161 victories. When the war ended, Josten had 178 victories to his credit without ever having been shot down himself.

Early May 1963 saw the arrival of the first Lockheed F-104 G Starfighter at JG 71's new base in Wittmundhafen. The Richthofen Geschwader was the first unit of the Bundesluftwaffe to receive the new aircraft. It was capable of Mach 2.2 and carried an armament of one 20-mm rotary cannon and air-to-air missiles.

The new "bird" was sleek, but it could be tricky to fly. In spite of this, for many pilots it was "love at first sight". Every F-104 pilot the author has spoken to was enthusiastic about the aircraft.

There was flying activity at Wittmund long before JG 71 "R" arrived. The flying machines based there during the First World War were far from sleek, though their sheer size made them impressive. They were airships of a naval airship unit.

An F-104 with wing tanks on the ramp in front of a hangar.

The Starfighter was an extremely clean aircraft, especially when it was in its natural element.

Each Starfighter underwent a thorough inspection and overhaul after every 200 hours of flying time.

The Starfighter suffered its share of technical problems. Here an undercarriage leg has collapsed. Regular flying activities took a toll on the equipment.

Much more serious than the material cost was the death of 116 pilots, who lost their lives in 220 flying accidents of all kinds. They gave their lives in the service of their country for peace and freedom.

Mayday over Wittmund. An account of the harrowing experience of two pilots whose aircraft were struck by lightning as they returned to base.

»Mayday« über Wittmund

Durch Blitzschlag »blind« geworden und trotzdem glatt gelandet

Es ist der 16. März 1967, ein rauher Vorfrühlingsvormittag. Über der norddeutschen Tiefebene tobt ein Frühlingssturm. Über den dunklen Wolken aber, in 7 000 Metern Höhe, ziehen zwei Starfighter F-104G ihre eleganten Spuren unter einem strahlend tiefblauen Himmel. Major Dieter Frese und Hauptmann Klausjürgen Rühmann vom Jagdgeschwader 71 „Richthofen" in Wittmund fliegen routinemäßigen Abfangeinsatz. Sie brauchen dabei in ihren schnellen Maschinen nicht zimperlich zu sein, was das rauhe Wetter in der unteren Erdetage betrifft.

Dreiviertelstunden sind sie nebeneinander einhergekurvt, haben sie ein gehöriges Pensum gefechtsmäßiger Abfangübungen absolviert. Der Spritmesser kündigt an, daß es langsam Zeit wird, wieder an den Heimflug zu denken. Major Frese meldet der Bodenkontrollstelle die Landeabsicht der beiden Maschinen, es geht auf 12 Uhr zu. Die Bodenstelle spricht ihnen die üblichen Anweisungen zu, gibt den Anflug zur Landung frei.

Sinkflug, die Piloten haben ihre Maschinen auf die Nasen gestellt. In pfeifender Fahrt ziehen die Starfighter nach unten, 6 000, 3 000, 2 000 Meter. In tausend Metern Höhe fangen die Piloten ihre Maschinen zwischen dem wogenden Gewölk wieder ab, rücken zu engerem Verbandsflug zusammen und setzen das TACAN-Verfahren zum Durchstoß auf ihren unsichtbaren Horst irgendwo dort unten fort. Das alles ist für sie nichts Erregendes mehr, auch der Durchstoß mit ihren Silberpfeilen durch das undurchsichtige Wolkengebräu nicht; denn so alte Jet-Hasen wie der Major und der Hauptmann pflegen ihr minutiöses Handwerk beinahe noch im Schlaf zu beherrschen.

Anflug auf Wittmund. In 3 000 Fuß Höhe legen sich dichte Wolken quer vor ihnen in die Bahn. Durch sie müssen sie hindurch. Sie haben jetzt rund 450 Stundenkilometer drauf, rücken noch ein wenig näher aneinander heran, gewissermaßen auf Tuchfühlung, um sich beim Durchstoßen durch das Gewölk nicht aus der Sicht zu verlieren und dann womöglich im Halbduster zu gefährden. In geschlossener Formation, gleichsam exerziermäßig exakt, stoßen die beiden Maschinen so in die Wolke hinein. Ein paar milchige Dunstfetzen fliehen vorüber, dann wird es dunkel wie in einem Tunnel und dann – dann passiert etwas völlig Unerklärliches. Ein gleißend weißes Licht flammt direkt vor der Kanzel auf, wie der Einschlag einer Rakete. Ein harter Stoß durchfährt das Flugzeug, ein heftiges Zittern durchzuckt den Rumpf und ein elektrischer Schlag staucht die Hände der Piloten. Irgend etwas Schwarzes, Großes, Fauchendes fliegt dicht über die Maschine nach hinten weg – die Verkleidung der Flugzeugspitze. Man wird sie später irgendwo da unten wiederfinden. Es geschieht alles in Sekundenbruchteilen. Zusammenstoß? Explosion? Major Frese ringt einen Augenblick lang geblendet in seiner Kanzel um Atem und Hauptmann Rühmann sieht nur noch grellweiße Kringel vor den Augen und spürt den Puls wie Hammerschläge in den Ohren. Dann wird es für beide einen Moment lang ganz finster und sie müssen die Augen mit Gewalt weit aufreißen, um die Orientierung zu behalten; da spürt jeder von ihnen: die Maschine fliegt noch. Sie sehen den Vogel des anderen noch zügig neben sich – die Wolke ist zerfetzt, durchflogen, die Sicht wieder da... Aber dann reißt es den Major fast aus dem Sitz: Rühmanns Maschine hat keine Nase mehr, sie ist ab, weg – der Starfighter dort drüben sieht aus wie ein Auto, das auf eine Hauswand aufgefahren ist, platt, eingedrückt und der typische Spitzschnabel wie abrasiert. Beide Piloten haben sich blitzschnell wieder gefangen. Frese deutet zu Rühmann hinüber, vorn auf dessen Kanzel. Aber der da drüben tut genau das gleiche und weist mit dem Kopf und mit der linken Hand auf die Maschine des Majors, was ja nichts anderes bedeuten kann, als daß auch bei ihr am Bug nicht mehr alles dran ist. Und ein brenzliger Geruch von Verbranntem – Isoliermasse, Gummi, Öl und wer weiß, was sonst – dringt von vorn ins Cockpit. Vielleicht glimmt und schmort es da vorne, gibt es eine Explosion und die Maschine fliegt auseinander...

Da ist es jetzt doch tröstlich, daß einer am anderen ablesen kann, wie es steht. Es brennt nichts, wir haben nur keine Nasen mehr und stattdessen ist jetzt da vorne diese monströse Wirrnis von abgerissenen Kabeln, Rohren, aufgerissenen Gehäusen. Aber wir fliegen, wir fliegen beide noch.

Sie denken beide das gleiche. Später, als alles hinter ihnen liegt, werden sie sich das einander bestätigen.

Und dann merken beide, daß die Instrumente verrückt spielen oder nicht mehr richtig anzeigen, der Fahrtmesser nicht, der Höhenmesser nicht, der Variometer nicht – die ganze Elektronik scheint zum Teufel zu sein. Aber auch der Funksprech gibt keinen Laut mehr her. Der Major schaltet über den Notsender auf Notruf – „Mayday, Mayday, Mayday" – und weiß nicht, ob der Sender überhaupt noch arbeitet, ob die dort drunten den Notruf überhaupt hören. Und die Maschinen fliegen, als ob nichts passiert wäre, ziehen wie herrenlose Renner dahin, schnittig, zischend – oder wie Renner, deren Reiter sich hinter abgerissenen Zügeln an die Sättel klammern. Die Piloten wissen jetzt, daß es nur ein Blitzschlag gewesen sein kann, der ihren Maschinen die Nasen abrasiert und sie gleichsam blind und taub, regelrecht zu Krüppeln geschlagen hat. Und sie wissen auch, was das nun für sie bedeutet. Ohne die zerstörten Instrumente haben sie keine Aussicht mehr, die Maschinen aus eigener Kraft heil zu landen. Runde acht Tonnen – wenn da die notwendige Landegeschwindigkeit auch nur für Augenblicke um ein Weniges unterschritten wird, fällt der elegante Koloß in der nächsten Sekunde senkrecht durch wie ein Klavier, wie acht Tonnen aus dem Nichts.

Aber noch fliegen sie, beide, als ob nichts geschehen wäre. Nur herunter werden sie die Maschinen nicht mehr bringen, wenn ihnen nicht einer zu Hilfe kommt und sie herunterlotst. „Mayday, Mayday, Mayday"... und der Major und der Hauptmann denken nur: Hoffentlich hören sie es dort unten, sonst müssen wir aussteigen.

Der Blick auf den Spritmesser zeigt, daß es nun eilt. Zehn Minuten können sie sich vielleicht noch in der Luft halten, eine Viertelstunde vielleicht. Bis dahin... Aber sie steigen nicht aus. Sie fegen in geschlossener Formation über den Flugplatz Wittmund

und wackeln mit den Stummelflügeln, um den Kontrollturm auf ihre Notlage aufmerksam zu machen, falls der Notruf dort nicht angekommen sein sollte, und er ist nur einmal während des Überfliegens flüchtig durchgekomemn, als das Notradio Freses augenscheinlich noch für einen Moment funktionierte. Der Blitz hatte auch den Generator 2 und das Funkgerät zerstört. Das wissen aber die beiden Piloten noch nicht, und überdies ist es jetzt ohnehin gleichgültig. Sie kurven erneut auf den Kontrollturm ein und wackeln und spähen aus wie die Luchse, ob sich nichts rührt dort drunten oder hier oben bei ihnen. Daß die Funkgeräte ausgefallen sind, ist ihnen jetzt längst klar. Die von der Bodenstation hätten sich ja sonst schon lange gemeldet... und der Spritzeiger sinkt und sinkt...

Im Kontrollturm sitzt an diesem Vormittagl der Feldwebel Dieter Kunze von der FlBttrStff/JG 71 „R" als Wachleiter. Es ist kurz vor zwölf Uhr, da heulen die beiden stumpfnasigen Maschinen im Tiefflug über den Platz heran, überfallartig. Sie haben sich dem Feldwebel mit keinem Ton zur Landung angemeldet und kommen nun, knapp hundert Meter über dem Boden, wie die wilde Jagd daher. Russen? MiG-21 Fishbed's, diese stumpfnasigen Kisten der Sowjets? Haben sie sich verflogen? Aber da sieht er sie wackeln, hört er das flüchtige Mayday und da erkennt er sie schon, zwei Maschinen vom eigenen Geschwader ohne Radarnasen. Sie haben vermutlich einen Zusammenstoß in der Luft gehabt, wie sonst kämen sie jetzt so daher? Und sie befinden sich in höchster Not. Kunze begreift sofort. Er gibt den Notruf an alle – „Mayday, Mayday, an alle – Luftnotlage über Wittmund". Er setzt die Alarmrotte auf höchste Bereitschaftsstufe und bittet gleichzeitig in Jever um Unterstützung durch ein anderes Flugzeug. Dort befindet sich gerade der Oberleutnant Hans-Joachim Berger vom Jagdbombergeschwader 32 in Lechfeld auf seinem Starfighter im Landeanflug auf Upjever. Er ruft Kunze und teilt ihm mit: „Ich komme." Sprit? – „Noch für 15 Flugminuten, das muß reichen." Seit seiner Meldung beim Kontrollturm sind keine vier Minuten vergangen, als er hinter den beiden angeschlagenen Maschinen auftaucht, sie überholt, wackelt und ihnen auf diese Weise zu erkennen gibt, daß er ihnen helfen wird. Unten auf dem Flugfeld sind Feuerwehr, Arzt, Rettungshubschrauber und Gefechtsstand längst alarmiert und bereits zwei F-104 von der Alarmrotte in höchster Alarmbereitschaft auf der Rollbahn. Aber sie brauchen nicht mehr einzugreifen. Oberleutnant Berger winkt dem nächstfliegenden Hauptmann Rühmann zu, sich neben ihn zu setzen. So verständigen sie sich von Phase zu Phase durch Handzeichen. Rühmann läßt kein Auge von der Flügelkante des Nachbarn. An ihr allein kann er seinen eigenen Landeanflug kontrollieren. Bergers Maschine fliegt wie ein Schrittmacher exakt und maßgenau neben dem Starfighter des Hauptmanns die Landung an, gute 400 km Fahrt, Fahrwerk raus – die angeschlagene, gleichsam blinde F-104 des Hauptmanns setzt parademäßig sauber auf der Piste auf, während Berger wieder durchstartet und nun auch die zweite Maschine mit Major Frese sicher zu Erde bringt. Dann fliegt er – beim zweiten Durchstarten – nach Upjever, wo sein Landeziel ist. Den beiden Offizieren der blitzgeschädigten Starfighter strecken sich alle Hände auf Wittmund mit Glückwünschen zum Fliegergeburtstag entgegen. Fliegerkameradschaft, – man kann ruhig darüber sprechen.

So sah unser Zeichner
H. Arlart die Situation in der
Mittagsstunde des 16. März 1967

After descending through the storm clouds Major Dieter Freese and his wingman Hauptmann Klausjürgen Rühmann realized the full extent of the damage to their aircraft. The nose cones of both aircraft were gone, and the tangled remains of their radars hung free. With their flat noses, the damaged aircraft bore a certain similarity to the MiG 21.

Thanks to the "lightning quick" reaction of *Oberleutnant* Berger, both Starfighters were recovered safely. The two lucky officers, *Hauptmann* Rühmann and *Major* Freese, in front of one of the heavily damaged aircraft.

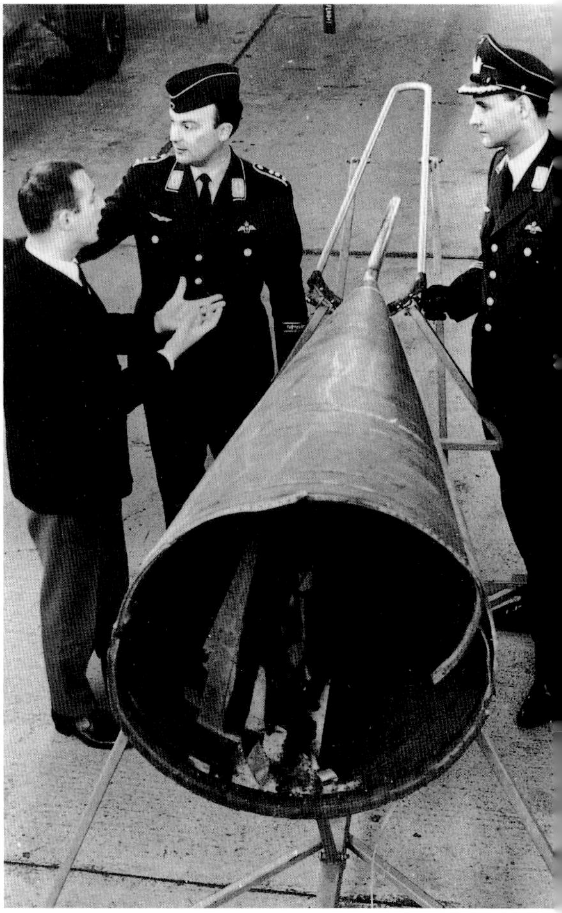

One of the nose cones blown off by the lightning strike, found somewhere by the repair echelon. The two lucky pilots still seem unable to believe what happened.

Major Freese's heavily damaged F-104 G.

The Inspector of the *Luftwaffe*, *Generalleutnant* Steinhoff, honors the four personnel who contributed to the happy outcome (from left to right): *Major* Freese, *Hauptmann* Rühmann, *Oberleutnant* Berger and *Feldwebel* Dieter Kunze.

A Dassault Mirage III of a French squadron next to an F-104 G of JG 71 *"Richthofen"* at Wittmundhafen.

The alert pair scrambles in close formation. The scramble was an oft-practiced procedure, as much would depend on speed and precision if things turned serious.

In addition to its 20-mm cannon, the F-104 G Starfighter was capable of carrying up to 2180 kg of ordnance. The cannon was an M 61 Vulcan, a six-barrel rapid-firing weapon built by General Electric and based on the Gatling Gun of the American Civil War. The AIM 9 Sidewinder air-to-air missile could be carried on the wingtips or on a catamaran-style rack beneath the fuselage.

Photographed during a training sortie, an F-104 G with long-range tanks and Sidewinders on both wingtips.

This F-104 G has been fitted with wingtip tanks for extended range.

A Starfighter taxis from the ramp to the runway.

The new *Kommodore* of *JG 71 "R"*, *Oberstleutnant* Ulrich Pieper, with Bruno Stolle, former *Staffelkapitän* of 8./JG 2 *"Richthofen"*, photographed at the Richthofen reunion at Wittmund on 21 April 1972.

Retired *Generalleutnant* Adolf Galland speaks during the dedication of a memorial stone in the barracks area in Wittmund on 13 April 1973. Galland gave his moving speech to three generations of members of the *Richthofen Geschwader*.

The memorial stone flanked by two pilots of JG 71 *"Richthofen"*. The memorial honors the dead of three generations of pilots.

The *Geschwader* has converted to the F-4F Phantom built by McDonnell Douglas. Here an aircraft of the *1. Staffel* taxis past the tower toward the runway.

Two turbojet engines give the aircraft a maximum speed of over Mach 2. In addition to one 20-mm Vulcan cannon, the F-4F can carry four AIM 9L Sidewinder or four AIM 120 AMRAAM air-to-air missiles. The crew consists of a pilot and weapons systems operator. Here an F-4F is seen on takeoff from Wittmundhafen.

The *Geschwader*'s mission is to keep the airspace over Europe free of intruders from the Warsaw Pact. It shares this responsibility with the air forces of the other NATO countries. Intercept training is a permanent part of the *Richthofen Geschwader*'s program.

In loose formation, three Phantoms are guided toward a target by ground control.

Annual gathering of the Fighter Pilots Association in Giesenheim in 1977, at which many former "Richthofener" were present. From right to left: Trautloft with back to reader, behind Trautloft Wolfgang Falck (adjutant to the *Kommodore* of *JG 2* in 1938), Gerd von Massow, Hans-Joachim Jabs, Wehnelt, *Oberst* Rentel (*Kommodore* of JG 71 *"Richthofen"* until 20 September 1976), the author. On that occasion I showed the manuscript of my book "Die deutsche Nachtjagd" to the two former Kommodore of NJG 1, Falck and Jabs.

Richthofen reunion 1979. A happy group, from left to right: Bühligen, Ille, Happel and Müngersdorff.

It must have been a high-ranking person to deserve an escort of two JG 71 Phantoms.

Two F-4Fs on the taxiway as they head for the runway. They are each armed with four AIM 9L Sidewinders beneath the wings. The first Phantom has a long-range tank under its fuselage.

Wittmund 1984 – wreath-laying ceremony at the memorial stone in honor of the dead. In the first row Kurt Bühligen, van der Osten (who flew with *Rittmeister* Manfred von Richthofen), and Hennig Strümpell. In the next row are Adolf Galland and Dietrich Hrabak.

This F-4F was specially painted to mark the 25th anniversary of JG 71 *"Richthofen"*. Here it is seen on approach to land.

Wittmundhafen, 22 April 1984. Gathered in front of the red triplane are (from left to right): unidentified, Hohagen, Bühligen, Kabbe, Eder, Wegener, Hartmann and Müngersdorff.

Barely one year later the former and active "Richthofener" gather to bid farewell to Kurt Bühligen, former *Kommodore* of *JG 2 "Richthofen"*.

Scramble! Speed is of the essence. Note that the "Remove before Flight" flags are still in place, indicating that this is a staged photograph.

Its two General Electric J79 engines roaring, an F-4F Phantom begins its takeoff roll. The author watched an afterburner takeoff from a distance of about 30 meters. The earth seemed to shake and the engines produced a tremendous roar at full power—an indescribable moment.

A live mission. Two aircraft of the alert pair have scrambled to intercept an unidentified intruder into German airspace. The two "Tigers" (radio call sign) reach their target quickly.

The reported intruder is approaching the Jever-Wittmund axis from over the sea. It turns out to be a Tupolev Tu-95 "Bear", a Soviet long-range bomber. The aircraft has a crew of eight consisting of 2 pilots, 1 navigator, 1 radar operator and 3 gunners for the twin-cannon turrets in the tail and above and below the fuselage. By moving in close to the intruder, the pilots of the *Richthofen Geschwader* make it clear that its presence is not desired, forcing it back out over the Baltic.

The already obsolescent F-4F Phantom has been updated by adding improved radar and weapons systems (KWS). This aircraft has not yet received all the updates. Note the cannon housing beneath the nose and the black radome.

This aircraft has undergone the complete conversion process at Holloman Air Base in the USA. One of the most obvious differences is the gray-painted radome.

A long line of Phantoms has been parked on a taxiway for a recruiting film.

The combat capability enhancement program altered the external appearance of the Phantom. Gone was the gray and green camouflage, replaced by a scheme of light blue-gray.

Refueling and servicing by a Stabsunteroffizier of the maintenance crew.

An armorer, an *Unteroffizier*, helps mount a Sidewinder rocket on the weapons rack beneath the wing. Precise work by these men and their many colleagues in the *Geschwader* help JG 71 *"Richthofen"* maintain a high level of readiness.

An F-4F Phantom breaks from the formation in preparation for landing.

The face of a Phantom. The aircraft is sitting on the runway. Note the tire marks left by numerous landings.

Oberleutnant Erich Hartmann as *Kapitän* of the "Karaya" Staffel in Russia. At the age of 22 he was the world's most successful fighter pilot with 352 victories.

Major Hartmann as first *Kommodore* of JG 71 *"Richthofen"*.

Erich Hartmann died on 10 September 1993. At the grave of Erich "Bubi" Hartmann are *Generalleutnant* Kuebart, Inspector of the *Luftwaffe*, and retired *General* Günther Rall (right).

Flying remained a passion of Erich Hartmann's until the end. He had probably inherited this from his mother, who had her license in the 1920s, very unusual for a woman in those days.

27 October 1997—the author visits JG 71 in Wittmundhafen.

The headquarters building. In front, flanked by a Sabre and an F-104, the gravestone of von Richthofen.

12 March 1975. The gravestone of *Rittmeister* Manfred Baron von Richthofen is moved to the current base of the *Richthofen Geschwader* in Wittmundhafen. The stone, which once stood on von Richthofen's grave in the Invalidenfriedhof in Berlin, was a gift to the *Geschwader* from the von Richthofen family.

Creation of the *Staffel* name Seven Eleven from the *Geschwader* number 71 and the 1 of the *1. Staffel*. Here the emblems of the *1. Staffel* of JG 71, Seven Eleven 711, and of 2./JG 71 *"Richthofen"*.

Briefing by the *1. Staffel*. At the table on the left of the photograph is the *Staffelkapitän Major* Christian Badia. The task for the coming mission is explained to the pilots: rendezvous with an AWACS airborne warning and control aircraft and protect it from attack. The attack force will be simulated by another unit.

Notes on flying time, rendezvous coordinates and other information.

Equipment of the flight crews of the *1. Staffel*.

Putting on the flight suit and other equipment, an oft-repeated exercise done with speed and precision.

Waiting in front of the *1. Staffel*'s building is a minibus which will take the crews to the aircraft. *Staffelkapitän Major* Badia and his weapons systems operator *Hauptmann* Frisch on their way to the bus.

On arrival at the hardened aircraft shelter, the crew conducts a visual inspection of the exterior of their F-4F Phantom. Here *Hauptmann* Frisch is seen climbing into the aircraft while *Major* Badia makes final checks.

The jet engines have been started. The cockpit systems are checked thoroughly. Safety check is under way.

The F-4F has left its bombproof shelter. It then stops at "Last Chance", where the pilot and weapons system operator carry out final pre-takeoff checks before taxiing to the runway.

Watched by the tower controller, two F-4F Phantoms take off.

Front view of an F-4F. Note the landing flaps and extended leading edge slats.

An F-4F after a sortie. The weapons system operator has left the cockpit and is climbing down the ladder. This impressive picture cannot hide the fact that it has been more than forty years since the first flight of the F-4 Phantom.

A MiG-29 Fulcrum formerly operated by the National Peoples Army in service with JG 73 of the *Bundesluftwaffe*. Although it suffers from a number of shortcomings, particularly in the area of electronics, the MiG-29 represents a more modern weapons system than the F-4F Phantom.

The flight simulator. Maintaining a high level of proficiency in aerial combat and emergency procedures cannot be achieved through real flights as the danger is too great. Pilots can, however, be trained to handle such situations through use of the flight simulator, which is a full-scale representation of the Phantom's cockpit complete with electronics and all controls.

An experienced training officer monitors the pilot and weapons system operator from the control position. He can input various practice situations, such as the firing of air-to-air missiles by hostile aircraft, or the loss of an engine after a bird strike.

A British exchange pilot serving with JG 71 *"Richthofen"* in the cockpit of the simulator during training.

This North American F-100 Super Sabre is also part of the training program of the fighter pilots of JG 71 *"Richthofen"*. It is used to tow Darts (seen in the following photo), targets employed in air-to-air firing practice. On 11 July 1994 an F-100 owned by Tracor Flight Services, which provided target towing services for a number of *Luftwaffe* units, crashed into the North Sea. The aircraft's pilot, Colonel (Rtd.) Charles William Bradley, lost his life in the incident.

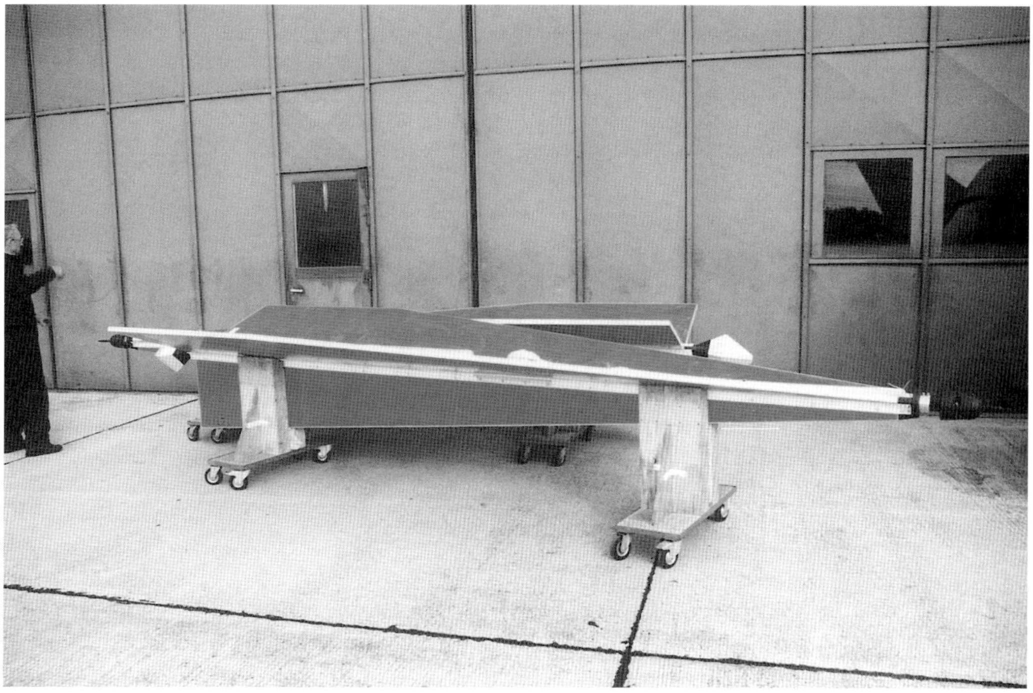

So-called "Darts", towed targets used for air-to-air firing training.

After about 150 hours the Phantom undergoes a thorough inspection in the maintenance hangar, an important procedure given the high g-forces the aircraft is exposed to and the age of the design.

Above: The aircraft's power plants, electronic systems, armament and airframe are carefully scrutinized and repairs are made where necessary. The repair echelons bear a heavy burden of responsibility. While the aircraft have become more advanced, they can still achieve little without the efforts of the mechanics and technicians.

Left: The last Do 28 Skyservants were retired on 23 June 1993 after almost twenty years of service. The one illustrated here is not a secret weapon, rather the product of inventive armorers who fitted it with a rotary cannon.

Another important airfield fixture is the fire-fighting service. Through constant practice, the firefighters are ready at any time to respond to a real emergency.

A special crash team replaces a blown tire. This is a relatively harmless operation.

In one photograph—more than fifty years of German fighter history and three generations of fighter aircraft as flown by the *Richthofen Geschwader*.

The replica of the famous triplane in the *Geschwader*'s tradition room. It represents the first generation of eighty years ago. The sight of the red triplane automatically brings to mind the man who is inextricably linked with the aircraft, the Red Baron, *Rittmeister* Manfred Baron von Richthofen.

The flight suit given to *Oberst* Hartmann on his departure, surrounded by photographs of the unforgettable Erich "Bubi" Hartmann.

Other exhibits in the *Geschwader*'s display provide an interesting insight into the eighty-year tradition of JG 71 *"Richthofen"*.

And they continue to fly for peace in freedom. Hopefully it will not be long before the unit is equipped with more modern aircraft.

Epilogue

In memory of the millions of brave and dutiful soldiers of both world wars:

Many persons and institutions, especially the media and some television broadcasting companies, take pleasure in labeling soldiers in general murderers and the German soldiers of the Second World War in particular as criminals. Even the most democratic army Germany has ever had, the Bundeswehr, is increasingly coming *under fire.*

In response to this conscious renunciation of objectivity two quotations:

"These soldiers did their duty, and one could scarcely demand that they be able to differentiate between their 'moral duty' and its 'immoral basis'."

Dr. Kurt Zentner

"The soldiers are those who shoot at other men they do not know or hate, ordered by men who know and hate each other but who never fire at each other themselves."

Unknown

Appendix

The Geschwaderkommodore of the "Jagdgeschwader Richthofen" from 1934 to 1945

Clockwise from Above left: Oberst Ritter von Greim, Major Kurt-Bertram von Doering, Major Dipl.-Ing. Johann Raithel, and Oberst Gerd von Massow

Clockwise from Above left: Oberst Harry von Bülow-Bothkamp, Major Wolfgang Schellmann, Major Helmut Wick, and Hauptmann Karlheinz Greisert

Hauptmann Wilhelm Balthasar

Oberstleutnant Walter Oesau

Oberstleutnant Egon Mayer

Major **Kurt Ubben**

Oberstleutnant **Kurt Bühligen**

The following compilations were taken from available archives and lists:

Unit Leaders of the *Geschwader*

Geschwaderkommodore

1/4/1936 - 8/6/1936	Major Dipl.-Ing. Raithel, Johann
9/6/1936 - 31/3/1940	Oberst von Massow, Gerd
1/4/1940 - 2/9/1940	Oberst von Bülow-Bothkamp, Harry
3/9/1940 - 19/10/1940	Major Schellman, Wolfgang
20/10/1940 - 28/11/1940	Major Wick, Helmut
29/11/1940 - 15/2/1941	Hauptmann Greisert, Karlheinz (acting)
16/2/1941 - 3/7/1941	Hauptmann Balthasar, Wilhelm
4/7/1941 - June 1943	Oberstleutnant Oesau, Walter
1/4/1943 - 2/3/1944	Oberstleutnant Mayer, Egon
March 1944 - 27/4/1944	Major Übben, Kurt
May 1944 - war's end	Oberstleutnant Bühligen, Kurt

Gruppenkommandeure

Gruppe commanders at the time of the unit's formation at Berlin-Döberitz. The two *Gruppen* had not yet been separated:

April 1934 - 1/4/1935	Major Ritter von Greim
1/4/1935 - 1/4/1936	Major von Doering

I. Gruppe (JG 132)

1/4/1936 - 17/10/1939	Major Viek
17/10/1939 - 22/6/1940	Hauptmann Roth
22/6/1940 - 7/9/1940	Hauptmann Strümpell
7/9/1940 - 20/10/1940	Hauptmann Wick
20/10/1940 - 20/11/1941	Hauptmann Krahl
20/11/1941 - 4/5/1942	Hauptmann Prestele, Ignaz
4/5/1942 - January 1943	Oberleutnant Leie
January 1943 - May 1943	Hauptmann Bolz
May 1943 - 28/9/1944	Hauptmann Hohagen
Sept. 1944 - Dec. 1944	Hauptmann Matoni
Dec. 1944 - Dec. 1944	Hauptmann Karch (acting)
Jan. 1945 - 25/3/1945	Hauptmann Hrdlicka

II. Gruppe (II./JG 132)

1/4/1935 - 1/4/1936	Major Dipl.-Ing. Raithel
1/4/1936 - 1938	Major von Schoenebeck
	Major May
	Major Laumann, Arthur
	Major Huth

In 1938 the *Gruppe* became I./ZG 76.

A new *II. Gruppe* formed at Zerbst in mid-November 1939 from elements of I./JG 2 and I./JG 2. Establishment complete on 13 Dec. 1939.

1939 - 2/9/1940	Hauptmann Schellmann
2/9/1940 - 1/5/1942	Hauptmann Greisert
1/5/1942 - Dec. 1942	Hauptmann Bolz i.V. Rudorffer
Dec. 1942 - April 1943	Hauptmann Dickfeld
May 1943 - May 1944	Hauptmann Bühligen
May 1944 - 1/1/1945	Hauptmann Schröder, Georg
Jan. 1945 - Febr. 1945	Hauptmann Matoni
Febr. 1945 - war's end	Hauptmann Karch

III. Gruppe

Established at Magdeburg 15 March – 10 April 1940 from elements of I. and II./JG 51 and I./JG 20.

March 1940 - 23/9/1940	Major Dr. Mix, Erich
24/9/1940 - 28/10/1940	Oberleutnant Bertram
29/10/1940 - 1/11/1942	Oberleutnant Hahn, Assi
1/11/1942 - 30/6/1943	Oberleutnant Mayer, Egon
1/7/1943 - March 1944	Hauptmann Stolle, Bruno
March 1944 - 8/6/1944	Hauptmann Huppertz
8/6/1944 - 22/6/1944	Hauptmann Wurmheller
July 1944 - war's end	Hauptmann Lemke, Siegfried

Commanders of JG 1 *"Richthofen"* (First World War)

24/6/1917 - 21/4/1918	Rittmeister Manfred Frhr. von Richthofen
22/4/1918 - 17/6/1918	Hauptmann Willy Reinhard
18/6/1919 - war's end	Oberleutnant Hermann Göring

Commanders of JG 71 *"Richthofen"* (*Bundesluftwaffe*)

9/1/1959 - 29/5/1962	Oberstleutnant Erich Hartmann
30/5/1962 - 1/4/1967	Oberst Günther Josten
2/4/1967 - 25/9/1970	Oberst Horst D. Kallerhoff
26/9/1970 - 9/10/1972	Oberst Ulrich Pieper
10/10/1972 - 19/9/1976	Oberst Hans-Jürgen Rentel
20/9/1976 - 2/10/1979	Oberst Erwin Willing
3/10/1979 - 30/9/1983	Oberst Lothar Kompch
1/10/1983 - 31/3/1987	Oberst Klaus Eggert
1/4/1987 - 30/6/1989	Oberst Dirk Böcker
1/7/1989 - 31/3/1993	Oberst Heinz-Gerd Nowak
1/4/1993 - 31/3/1995	Oberst Dierk P. Merklinghaus
1/4/1995 - ?	Oberst Wolfgang Fahl

Recipients of the Knight's Cross and its Higher Grades in *Jagdgeschwader* 2 *"Richthofen"*

Balthasar, Wilhelm
Bertram, Otto
Bühligen, Kurt
v. Bülow-Bothkamp, Harry
Dahmer, Harry
Dickfeld, Adolf
Eder, Georg-Peter
Goltzsch, Kurt
Gratz, Karl
Hahn, Hans
Hannig, Horst
Hohagen, Erich
Hrdlicka, Franz
Huppertz, Herbert
Karch, Fritz
Knappe, Kurt
Krahl, Karl-Heinz
Leie, Erich
Lemke, Siegfried
Liesendahl, Frank
Machold, Werner
Mader, Anton
Matoni, Walter
Mayer, Egon
Meimberg, Julius
Nippa, Erhard
Oesau, Walter
Pflanz, Rudolf
Rudorffer, Erich
Schellmann, Wolfgang
Schnell, Siegfried
Schröter, Fritz
Schumann, Heinz
Seeger, Günther
Stolle, Bruno
Ubben, Kurt
Wick, Helmut
v. Winterfeldt, Alexander
Wurmheller, Josef

Recipients of the Knight's Cross and its Higher Grades in *Jagdgeschwader* 2 *"Richthofen"* Listed by Date

1. Hauptmann Balthasar	RK 14.6.1940
	EL (17) 2.7.1941
2. Hauptmann Oesau	RK 20.8.1940
	EL (9) 6.2.1941
	S (3) 15.7.1941
3. Oberstleutnant v. Bülow-Bothkamp	RK 20.8.1940
4. Oberleutnant Wick	RK 20.8.100
	EL (4) 6.10.1940
5. Oberfeldwebel Machold	RK 5.9.1940
6. Oberleutnant Hahn	RK 24.9.1940
	EL (32) 14.9.1941
7. Major Schellmann	RK 18.9.1940
8. Hauptmann Bertram	RK 28.10.1940
9. Leutnant Schnell	RK 9.11.1940
	EL (18) 9.7.1941
10. Hauptmann Krahl	RK 13.11.1940
11. Leutnant Rudorffer	RK 1.5.1941
	EL (447) 11.4.1944
	S (126) 25.1.1945
12. Major v. Winterfeldt	RK 5.7.1941
13. Oberfeldwebel Dahmer	RK 1.8.1941
14. Leutnant Mayer	RK 1.8.1941
	EL (232) 16.4.1943
	S (51) 2.3.1944
15. Oberleutnant Leie	RK 1.8.1941
16 Oberleutnant Pflanz	RK 1.8.1941
17. Leutnant Huppertz	RK 30.8.1941
	EL (512) 24.6.1944
18. Oberfeldwebel Bühligen	RK 4.9.1941
	EL (413) 2.3.1944
	S (88) 14.8.1944
19. Oberfeldwebel Wurmheller	RK 4.9.1941
	EL (146) 13.12.1942
	S (108) 24.10.1944 postum
20. Oberleutnant Ubben	RK 4.9.1941
	EL (80) 12.3.1942
21. Oberstleutnant Hohagen	RK 5.10.1941
22. Leutnant Dickfeld	RK 19.3.1942
	EL (94) 19.5.1942
23. Leutnant Hannig	RK 9.5.1942
	EL (364) 3.1.1944
24. Unteroffizier Gratz	RK 1.7.1942
25. Major Mader	RK 23.7.1942
26. Hauptmann Liesendahl	RK 4.9.1942 postum
27. Oberleutnant Schröter	RK 24.9.1942
28. Unteroffizier Knappe	RK 3.11.1942
29. Oberleutnant Stolle	RK 17.3.1943
30. Hauptmann Schumann	RK 18.3.1944
31. Oberleutnant Goltzsch	RK 5.2.1944
32. Oberleutnant Nippa	RK 26.3.1944
33. Leutnant Seeger	RK 26.3.1944
34. Leutnant Lemke	RK 14.6.1944
35. Oberleutnant Eder	RK 24.6.1944
	EL (663) 25.11.1944
36. Oberleutnant Hrdlicka	RK 9.8.1944
	EL (802?) 23.3.1945
37. Hauptmann Meimberg	RK 24.10.1944
38. Hauptmann Matoni	RK 2.1.1945
39. Hauptmann Karch	RK 17.4.1945

Acknowledgments

I wish to thank all those persons and institutions who assisted me and thus contributed to the success of this book. I also wish to thank my family for their patience and consideration during my work on the project.

My sincerest thanks to my wife Ute, without whose capable support I would not have been able to complete this project. It was she who edited and proof-read the manuscript.

A special thank you goes to my daughter Gesa, my son Helge and Frau Else Brühl, who gave up many hours of their free time to assist my wife in her responsible task.

I received valuable assistance, whether in the form of photographs, information or advice, from the following persons:

Paul Müngersdorff, Col. Thomas C. Fosnacht, U.S. Army, John Weal, and Ostfw. Falk Hallensleben of *JG 71 "R"*.

Photographs and information were also provided by:

JG 71 *"Richthofen"*, U.S. Air Force, Royal Air Force, Michael Payne, Wolfgang Falck, Lothar Kappe, Jean-Yves Lorant, Otto Happel (†), Christof Dezius, Kees Mool, Josef Bigge, Theo Hartmann, Michael Balss, Heribert Suntrop, Julius Meimberg, James Crow and Erich Rudorffer.

Thank you!

Bibliography

Der rote Kampfflieger, Manfred von Richthofen
Wie die Luftwaffe wirklich entstand, Schliephake
Die deutsche Flugzeuge 1939-1945, Kens/Nowarra
Die rote Baron und seine tollkühnen Männer, K.H. Spaethe
Die Ersten und die Letzten, Adolf Galland
Der Jagdflieger, Erich Hartmann
Ritterkreuzträger der Luftwaffe (Vol. 1 Fighter Pilots), Ernst Obermaier
Markierungen und Tarnanstriche der Luftwaffe im II. Weltkrieg (I – IV), Karl Ries
Dora Kurfürst und rote 13 (I – IV), Karl Ries
Tragödie der deutschen Luftwaffe, David Irving
Angriffshöhe 4000, Cajus Bekker
Das Jagdgeschwader 71 "Richthofen", Arge Tradition Reiner von Rahden
Luftschlacht über Deutschland, Alfred Price
The Augsburg Raid, Jack Currie
Start im Morgengrauen, Werner Girbig
Die Luftwaffe 1939-1945 Schriftenreihe Führung und Truppe, Mehner/Teuber
Stukageschwader 2 IMMELMANN, Holger Nauroth
Die Deutsche Luftwaffe vom Nordkap bis Tobruk, Holger Nauroth
Personal war remembrances by Josef Bigge
Der 50. Jahrestag der Gründung des JG "Richthofen" Nr. 132, G.G. Voss
JG Nr. 2 "Richthofen", Rudolf Rothenfelder
Copies of original documents of JG 132 and *Jagdgeschwader 2*

Notes on personal recollections from almost 30 years, discussions with pilots, commanders and members of the ground services of *JG 2* at numerous reunions of the Fighter Pilots Association in Giesenheim until 1980. In the past two years I had numerous meetings with contemporary witnesses and experts from Germany and elsewhere on the theme "*Jagdgeschwader Richthofen*", obtaining important information, documents and other material.

Jagdgeschwader 3 "Udet" in World War II
Stab and I./JG 3 in Action with the Messerschmitt Bf 109
Jochen Prien & Gerhard Stemmer

Jochen Prien presents JG 3 in its complete history from formation to the end of WWII. This volume begins with a brief account of the Stab from the time of its formation in 1938 until it reequipped on the Fw 190 in the summer of 1944, then follows the operational history of I Gruppe, beginning with the first unit to bear the designation I/JG 3, which was formed in autumn 1938, fought in the French campaign, the Battle of Britain, and Operation Barbarossa, and then in January 1942 was redesignated as II/JG 1 and left the Geschwader to join Jagdgeschwader 1, then being formed. A description of the operational history of the new I/JG 3 "Udet" which was formed at the beginning of 1942 and saw its first action during the German summer Russian offensive of 1942, then served a tough and costly tour of duty in the Defense of the Reich and over the Western Front before seeing several weeks of desperate defensive action in the east of the Reich.

Size: 8 1/2" x 11" ■ 350+ b/w photographs, line drawings ■ 464 pp.
ISBN: 0-7643-1681-8 ■ hard cover ■ $69.95

Jagdgeschwader 3 "Udet" in World War II
II./JG 3 in Action with the Messerschmitt Bf 109
Jochen Prien & Gerhard Stemmer

The unit history of the "Udet" Geschwader's second Gruppe, II./JG 3, beginning with its formation in early 1940 and the subsequent service of the newly formed Gruppe in the Campaign in the West from 1940-1941. Next the Gruppe's 1941 tour of duty in Russia is dealt with, followed by a short spell in the Mediterranean theatre of war, where II./JG 3 was involved in the fighting over Malta in the spring of 1942. In June 1942, the Gruppe was again shifted to the east where it took part in the advance on Stalingrad where it suffered serious losses. 1943 saw the Gruppe still in Russia until it was recalled to the Reich to see further service in the defence of Germany. After its return to the Reich and a short period of rest and re-equiping, II./JG 3 was again called upon for service in the Reichsverteidigung, abruptly ending when it became part of the first jet fighter Geschwader of the Luftwaffe, JG 7.

Size: 8 1/2" x 11" ■ over 350 black & white photos, drawings ■ 408 pp.
ISBN: 0-7643-1774-1 ■ hard cover ■ $69.95